Danger, Will Robinson:

The Full Mumy

A Memoir

By

Bill Mumy

Next Chapter Entertainment LLC

Los Angeles

DANGER WILL ROBINSON: THE FULL MUMY

Copyright © 2022 by Bill Mumy

Manufactured in the United States of America

10 9 8 7 6 5 4 3 2 1

ISBN 978-1-7356215-4-8

First Hardcover Edition: November 2022

Publishers / Editors: Mary McLaren
Tom McLaren

Cover photo by Eileen Mumy
Lost in Space® inset © Legend Pictures, LLC
Licensed by Synthesis Entertainment

Cover & Interior Design by Mary McLaren

Next Chapter Entertainment LLC
Los Angeles, California

To Eileen... For everything.

Contents

In Bishop, California – named for my father.

PROLOGUE

Connectivity is defined as the state of being connective or connected. I seem to be in a very rare position of having been affiliated with a plethora of projects and people that bridge pop culture and film, from the Golden Age of Television to the present.

I am in my sixties as of this writing, and as weird as it sounds, I have worked professionally in television across eight decades.

Albert Einstein famously said, "the distinction between past, present, and future is only a stubbornly persistent illusion." In other words, time… is an illusion.

This memoir was not written in a linear way. My personal thoughts frequently time travel. I honestly often recall with more clarity events that happened over fifty years ago better than I can recall what I ate for dinner last week. So, instead of constructing this project in chronological order, I've allowed it to flow freely, dance back and forth between the decades to form a more cohesive understanding of the chaos that is me.

I often say, "Time is a bizarre river." I'm no Albert Einstein. But, Will Robinson was damn smart.

Onward.

PART 1

SELF-PORTRAIT TAKEN IN MY HOTEL ROOM, SAN SEBASTIAN, SPAIN.
THE DAY MY HAIR GOT CUT OFF FOR *PAPILLON.*

1. WELCOME TO THE JUNGLE

"What the hell am I doing here?!" I thought to myself as I boarded the funky chartered Spantax Airlines plane alongside a couple of hung-over stuntmen and a handful of crew and production assistants. But there were no cell phones or computers in 1973, no way to instantly connect with my agents who were more than five thousand miles away and eight hours behind in time. At nineteen years old, I was past the point of calling my parents for advice, so I reluctantly stepped up the ramp and into the airplane, although I knew that contractually I should have been travelling to New York first class on a TWA flight sitting next to Dustin Hoffman, Steve McQueen, and Ali McGraw who I had been spending the past several weeks with here in San Sebastian, Spain filming the first scenes of the expensive, troubled feature film, *Papillon*.

And it truly was a troubled production right from the very start. When I met with the executive producer, Ted Richmond, and the director, Franklin J. Schaffner, who was best known for his impressive work helming George C. Scott in the epic war film *Patton* and for directing the original *Planet of the Apes* movie, I hadn't been in front of a movie camera for over two years.

After wrapping up starring in Stanley Kramer's *Bless the Beasts & Children*, released to mixed reviews and a not-so-great box office in 1971, I decided to take a hiatus from acting and devote all my energy to my band, an acoustic trio, Redwood. We spent almost a year recording what we believed would be our debut album at the prestigious Record Plant studio in West Hollywood and we were gigging constantly to ever-growing crowds and positive reviews. But by March of 1973, things had stalled for Redwood and when the offer came to me to spend a few months working on a major motion picture opposite two mega-stars, I accepted the gig. However, in the initial meet and greet with Schaffner, I was offered the part and told the start date of the film, but was informed there was, no script to be given yet. Dalton Trumbo was adapting to screenplay the true novel by Henri Charrière, the only man to ever have escaped from the French penal colony known as Devil's Island, and Trumbo was quite ill at the time. I was assured the role they were casting me in was a strong co-starring one whose scenes were mostly all with Hoffman and McQueen. I was a fan of both of those actors work and I'd read Trumbo's *Johnny Got His Gun*. This was going to be a big movie, and I'd been in acting limbo long enough. I was only seventeen when I put my on-camera career on pause. Now, at nineteen, I thought signing on for this project was the right thing to do. Redwood would survive a couple of months without working and I needed to establish myself as an adult actor having starred in television and feature films from the age of five. I certainly would find myself in a new casting category now, and this credit could only be a bonus.

I'd flown first-class from Los Angeles to Madrid, Spain, as the Screen Actors Guild rules contractually guaranteed, alongside actor Don Gordon. Don was a pleasant man who was often cast in supporting roles in Steve McQueen's projects. Don and I knew that we'd be acting together throughout most of our scenes, and we struck up a good connection on the long flight. I'd been to Europe a few times before in my life, France twice and England once, but I wasn't prepared for what I found when we landed and de-boarded the plane in Madrid. Everywhere I looked there were military police and soldiers with rifles and stern frightening faces like stone.

This was not Paris or London. Spain was still under the dictatorship of fascist, Francisco Franco, who had ruled it with an iron hand since the Spanish Civil War ended in 1939. This was a creepy place. Franco's government had received military support from Nazi Germany and the Kingdom of Italy. He was very much anti-communist in his politics, which in the 1950s resulted in the United States aligning themselves with Franco's Spain. But when I got there, in 1973, the man in charge had another two years to live and the vibes were not cool. Still, when travelling with a group of actors and crew members from a Hollywood production, you feel somewhat "taken care of." We proceeded through the necessary customs and were taken to our hotel, in the coastal city of San Sebastian, a Basque town, where political unrest was running high at the time.

Being somewhat jetlagged from the long flight, I checked in and carried my bags up the beautiful ornate stairway that led to my room on the second floor. I quickly crashed out early in my hotel room, only to be awakened in the middle of the night by the sound of drawers opening and closing. Raising my head to check it out, I found myself staring through the darkness at a uniformed man, with a flashlight in his hand rummaging through my luggage, camera case, guitar case, and the dresser drawers. I was terrified. "What's going on?!" I muttered nervously. He replied with a short statement delivered in a staccato monotone in Spanish, which I did not comprehend, before he turned and calmly exited my hotel room.

The next day was even more traumatic. It began with a haircut that I was prepared for, but was still disturbing to me. I had very long hair at the time that hung inches below my shoulders. In a matter of minutes, it was gone, and I had a prisoner's almost-shaved head, apropos for the film of course, but nonetheless, for this nineteen-year-old musician resuming his acting career, it would take me awhile to acclimate to the change. That evening I attended a formal dinner in the dining room of our hotel that included myself, Don Gordon, Dustin Hoffman, Steve McQueen, several production assistants, and the director, Franklin J. Schaffner. We were told that Dalton Trumbo was writing the screenplay in sequence, and we were given a partial script. Filming would begin the next day out at sea. I don't remember many details of the dinner, but what happened after the meal is firmly tattooed in my memory.

A small group of paparazzi photographers had gathered outside on the steps of the hotel after learning that movie stars Dustin Hoffman and Steve McQueen were there. This was a handful of people, nothing like the overtly obtrusive insanity we've come to accept as normal behavior from the paparazzi of today; but as our group exited, they began taking photographs of Hoffman and McQueen. It quickly turned ugly and violent, and I was stunned to watch Steve McQueen go after one of the paparazzi, grab his camera, smash it to the ground and then beat the guy up. Seriously beat him up. Knocked him down and kicked him several times. I'd never seen anyone do anything like that. It couldn't have lasted more than a minute at the most, but... it was memorable. And there were no repercussions of any kind. McQueen made his way back to where he was staying, and no one ever mentioned it again.

"Whoa," I exhaled aloud as I slowly walked up the stairs to my room.

The first scenes filmed for *Papillon* were the initial scenes in the movie, where hundreds of prisoners, including me, Don Gordon, Hoffman, and McQueen, are marched through the village where thousands of extras were cast. It was a series of huge shots that required military precision and it was exactly the kind of thing that Franklin Schaffner was excellent at. However, up until an hour or two before the cameras rolled, I had never discussed the physicality of my character, Lariot, with the director. Lariot was written as frail with a bad leg. I had worked on several different types of limps, but of course, I wanted the director to make the final decision. This shot would be the template for how I moved throughout production and I approached "Mr. Schaffner," as I called him, to observe my options and to make a choice. He could have cared less. Wasn't interested in the slightest. "Just limp any way you want to. It doesn't matter." And with that, he went off to deal with other more important issues. It was a wake-up call that I didn't fully hear at the time.

One of the prop department men, a round-faced, sunburned, funny guy with a walrus mustache named Kent, who I had worked with on other productions in the past, quickly made a small bent bar of metal and strapped it behind my right leg. The result would be a thoroughly consistent limp from Lariot.

The opening shots were technically difficult, but they were done very proficiently, and they were completed on schedule. Schaffner certainly knew how to wrangle thousands of extras efficiently. But he didn't seem to have any interest in communicating with me.

The next several days of production were really tough. We filmed at sea outside San Sebastian on the huge prison ship. There were no trailers or dressing rooms for anyone to go relax in while waiting for the camera to be ready. The sea was rough, and everyone was puking their guts out all the time, myself included. My father had owned two boats when I was a kid, a 25-footer he named *The Billinda* and a 36-foot Richardson cabin cruiser named *Char-Mur* after my father, Charles and my mother, Muriel. I'd always enjoyed being out on the ocean very much. I was a certified scuba diver by the time I was thirteen and I'd been a proficient body surfer for years. But there was little to enjoy about this. The ship was dirty and smelly. It was crowded with extras and crew members that were in constant vomit mode. We were in heavy wool wardrobe that clung to our sweaty bodies and weighed us down. The four of us, Dustin, Steve, Don, and myself were clustered together for days. That was when the lines were drawn, and the camps were made clear.

Having already witnessed Steve McQueen's violence firsthand, I gravitated towards Dustin. He was not a tough guy. He was very funny and I soon learned that he was a fine musician, a piano player. We had both attended Santa Monica College, and he was familiar with and complimentary regarding my past work. *The Graduate* was (and remains to this day) my favorite film. Dustin and I got along easily when we were around each other. He had a habit of blowing bubbles off of his tongue. He was really good at it. It's not hard to form them, but to get them to fly and stay in bubble form is a lot tougher than you might think. I have home movies of him doing it. Don Gordon was 100% in Camp McQueen. Steve had him added to the cast and they had a long-standing relationship. Now, the four of us got along fine, but there was a very interesting dynamic between the two main stars. *Papillon* was an independent film, produced by Ted Richmond on his own, and not originally a major studio project. Richmond was paying his stars an (at the time) outrageous amount of money; I believe McQueen got $2 million and Dustin received $1.5 million. No studio wanted to set that kind of salary precedent, so Ted went about getting the financing on his own. It was a risk that eventually paid off well, but during production it caused some delays and unpleasant time outs.

The four of us were standing on deck and talking about the genesis of the film, the subject turned to how Dustin had prepared for the role. His character, Louis Dega, was a convicted counterfeiter, so Dustin explained that initially he studied French currency from the time, becoming familiar with the papers, inks, etc. He went on to tell us that he'd immersed himself in French culture, the music, fashion, and cuisine. Continuing, he said that he felt working as a counterfeiter, engraving and dealing with such tiny details, would have ruined his eyesight, so he'd created thick glasses for the character to wear, but, because he himself needed to have decent vision, he was wearing corrective contact lenses to balance out the thick lenses of the glasses. He had truly done his extra credit homework.

I'll never forget Steve McQueen's reaction to Dustin's tale of preparation. He tilted his head and stared at Dustin with an enigmatic expression for several seconds before he said, "I read most of the book."

Bam! Let's just acknowledge there were two very dynamic actors starring in this movie and their methods of preparation could not have been more different. Somehow, we survived our scenes at sea.

Steve McQueen was intense to say the least. But there was nothing haughty about him. He hung out with the crew and never pulled any "star" attitude about anything regarding the work. He did his own stunts and seemed to me to be fearless. But, in my opinion, beneath his tough guy exterior, he was insecure and most likely a little paranoid. There's a scene in *Papillon* where both my character, Lariot, and Don Gordon's character, Julot, return from the dead as ghostly visions to haunt a nearly dead Papillon, Steve McQueen.

LARIOT APPEARS AS A GHOST IN PAPILLON'S DREAM.

The day we filmed that bit, I was privy to something I'm pretty sure very few people ever saw: the contents of Steve McQueen's briefcase. I was standing next to Steve as he opened it. We were outside. It was a brownish sorrel in color and just an average-sized briefcase. I had no desire to be intrusive or nosey, I simply happened to be right there when the contents were exposed to my view. Inside, there were a couple of knives, one very large. There was a pistol. Not too big. I don't know much about guns, so I don't know what caliber weapon it was exactly. But what caught my eye more than anything else I saw, beyond the papers and the pill bottles and gloves, was a pair of brass knuckles. It was a chilling sight. I knew that McQueen had been on the "Manson Family Hit List" back in 1969, a lot of big celebrities had discovered they were potential victims of those heinous murderers, and it freaked the entire Hollywood community out for a long time. I could honestly understand why a star of Steve's status might carry a gun. The knives were creepy, but the brass knuckles? They required premeditation. Brass knuckles were something you put on before you consciously set about hurting someone really, really bad. It was hard to understand why he or anyone would carry them around. After that, I must admit, he made me a little nervous.

But I wished I'd been sitting next to him on the airplane he and Dustin were on instead of the chartered flight that was taking me from Spain to Jamaica, a flight that was in trouble from almost the minute it left the ground. Absolutely no one on the plane's crew spoke a word of English but within seconds after we'd left the ground, their instructions were clear. We all had to get up out of our seats and rush to the front of the plane near the cockpit because the tail end of the aircraft was too heavy, it was carrying camera equipment and lights and the weight needed to be distributed differently in order to balance the plane. I remember looking at Stephen, one of the stuntmen, and thinking, "this is totally wrong!" But I was nineteen. You don't sense mortality acutely at that age and besides, I was in a plane full of stuntmen. They're a different breed of human. They challenge death all the time for a paycheck. And when they're not working, they get mighty buzzed. This chartered Spantax airplane was full of buzzed stuntmen and the kid who used to star in *Lost in Space*. The plane eventually balanced itself properly, we went back to our seats and the sun disappeared. Soon stuntmen were snoring as we soared in the darkness on our way to Jamaica to continue making this movie. I think I even dozed off for a while. Until we were all rudely awakened by a little thing called lightning. The plane lurched and the electrical systems shorted off and on. We'd been struck by lightning out in the pitch blackness of God only knows where. The plane was being bounced around like jeans in a dryer. It was awful. Stephen, Eddie, Kent, everyone… everyone's eyes were wide as saucers as we truly anticipated dying. An emergency landing in the Azores was now our only hope.

It's impossible to be a prima donna in the hours pre-dawn at a tiny airport off Portugal in the Azores. I know this to be a fact, because if it were not true, I would have thrown a fit right then and there and demanded another plane. But, as it was, all I could do was sit and wait for our disastrous Spantax plane to be repaired and then board it once again. The flight from the Azores to Montego Bay, Jamaica was uneventful, and we lived to tell the tale.

Once again, however, things went wrong for the production of *Papillon*. Upon arrival in Jamaica, we were informed that there was a problem getting some of the equipment released from customs and that filming would be delayed. I'm not certain exactly what the truth was, perhaps Ted Richmond had temporarily run out of funding and needed a few weeks to find some more money. Whatever the case was, I found myself in a not-so-fabulous hotel on the beach with time on my hands. But, instead of enjoying the island, I was told not to go out in the sunlight. They needed the cast to be pale and look as if we'd been locked inside the funk of a prison ship, not to look like we'd been swimming and sunning in paradise. So, for a couple of weeks, I stayed inside and played my Martin D-41 guitar that I'd brought with me and drank banana daiquiris and Red Stripe beers.

Dustin and McQueen arrived and were staying in rented homes, but they both came by my hotel frequently. Dustin was accompanied by his wife at the time, a very nice lady I enjoyed being around named Anne. Dustin played piano and I played guitar and we entertained by playing "Let it Be" and "The Long and Winding Road" and a few other Beatles tunes and various covers. Paul McCartney came to Jamaica while we were filming, and Dustin and McQueen got to hang out with him for a memorable night. Paul supposedly started writing "Drink To Me (Picasso's Last Words)" in front of them that night. I would have liked to have been invited. But while the stars were visiting with the former

Beatle, I was spending most my evenings with the stuntmen and a few crew members. I contributed $10 of my per diem cash towards a huge bag of Jamaican ganja, and now was supplementing my downtime buzz with excellent marijuana, as well as fresh banana daiquiris.

One night while we continued to wait to restart filming, Dustin and a couple of the guys and I went to the Montego Bay Holiday Inn for dinner and an evening of reggae music. Anne was not there. We gathered at a round table in the banquet room close to the stage and enjoyed some really great local music. After an hour or so, two girls approached our table. They were tourists from the States in their twenties, cute and they had recognized both Dustin and me. "Aren't you Dustin Hoffman?!" "I loved you in *Bless the Beasts & Children*!" Dustin invited them to join our table and they eagerly did. The following is a nearly perfect verbatim of what happened next.

> Dustin: "You know, you remind me of a girl I went to junior high school with."
>
> Girl: "Really?! Cool!"
>
> Dustin: "Yeah. Her name was Judy Potash."
>
> Girl: "Okay."
>
> Dustin: "And you know what I remember most about Judy Potash?"
>
> Girl: "No. What?"
>
> Dustin: "Judy Potash was a terrific farter. She could fart any time you asked her to. She could just let one rip anytime."

And with that having been said, Dustin Hoffman made a face like he was straining and squirmed in his chair and let out the longest and loudest fart I had ever heard in my life. Then he smiled at the two girls who looked aghast and quickly excused themselves from our table.

No one in our little group knew how to react. No one said a word. We all just stared at Dustin incredulously. A moment passed and then, with a grin he reached down and extracted a pink rubber whoopee cushion from underneath his butt and held it up for our approval. Dustin Hoffman had actually brought a whoopee cushion to the Montego Bay Holiday Inn in hopes of using it to entertain us and himself. It was pretty amazing, and I gave him major props for it. He then rose from the table, walked out onto the dance floor by himself while the band played reggae and danced alone just like Shermy from *A Charlie Brown Christmas*.

The waiting game continued.

At this time, Steve McQueen was in a relationship with Ali McGraw, and he wanted her around all the time. Ali was very sweet, bright, and unassuming. She wore very short blue jean cut-offs and white T-shirts a lot. The thing about Ali was, she loved music. I always had my guitar around and she would hang out and listen to me play Neil Young, James Taylor, and Cat Stevens songs. She enjoyed that a lot. I liked Ali. She was easy to talk to and of course she was a very pretty lady. One evening as the sun was setting in Montego Bay and we could finally go outside, Steve approached me. He handed me a Red Stripe beer without saying a word and motioned with his head for me to walk with him down towards the water. We walked in silence for a moment and then he said, "You're spending a lot of time with Ali." I agreed. "Yeah, she really likes the music. She's a great gal." Again, we walked in silence for a few steps until he turned and looked me with his piercing blue eyes and said in a somewhat threatening tone, "Don't fuck with my woman."

The statement staggered me. My mind flashed to his brass knuckles and recalled the way he'd slugged and kicked the paparazzi back in San Sebastian, which now seemed like years ago, although it had only been a few weeks past. I stuttered in my response, "No, no no no no! I have a girlfriend! She's twenty-six, tall, blonde, and gorgeous and I haven't flirted with Ali or anything like that at all, Steve! She just digs the music!" He nodded and walked back to the hotel. I lingered on the beach and finished the Red Stripe waiting until he and Ali had left for the night.

As quickly as production had been halted, it resumed. New Dalton Trumbo pages were disseminated to us, and I was not happy about them. Going into this film, I knew I had a supporting role. I understood that I wasn't a star of the movie. But I had always been cast as a lead or a co-star in everything I had worked on since the age of six. The new pages we were going to begin shooting included my character only in the background. There was little dialogue or interaction between me and anyone else. I felt, justifiably, that my role was becoming not much more than a bit part and I wasn't pleased about it. I called my agent in Beverly Hills and told him what was going down. He suggested I speak to Franklin Schaffner about it. So, I did. I asked to speak with him and privately explained my concerns about the new pages and what I had been originally cast to do. He looked at me like he had better things to do and said, "Do whatever you want." And that was all the time he devoted to my concern. I could have called the production office and told them to book me on the next flight to Los Angeles, but I didn't. I called Paul Gordon, my partner in my band, Redwood. I told him what had happened and we talked for a long time, a couple of hours as I recall. His advice was to ride it out. I'd already cut all my hair off. I might as well do the best acting job I could to salvage what little onscreen time I'd end up with in this sure-to-be-big movie. So, I decided to stick it out.

We traveled to the Jamaican jungle where it was over 100 degrees with 100% humidity. Wearing those heavy wool prison outfits was like living inside a sauna. We took salt pills and lost weight. We traveled in buses that got stuck in the mud. It was a very uncomfortable shoot. But we all continued. We all suffered equally. Production moved to Kingston, where we were seriously warned not to leave our hotels. Ever. The violent crime in the city was at an all-time high and we heard of several murders while we were there.

My character, Lariot, was doomed to die. I was to be in somewhat of a delusional daydream and gaze longingly out at the ocean and limp off into the water, start swimming to freedom, only to have my head blown off by the sharp-shooting prison guards.

The prop men and special effects team prepped me for the scene. It was a dangerous process that involved explosives on my head. A cast metal plate, the size of a small mousetrap, was attached to my skull. A clear thin tube ran from my wrist, up my arm underneath my shirt, behind my neck and into the metal plate that had a spring attachment connected to it. There was a small explosive charge in the plate that was remotely and wirelessly controlled off camera by the pyrotechnician. It's called a "squib," and it hurts when detonated. In my right palm was a rubber bulb filled with fake blood that I was to pump once the squib had been detonated. Since it was my big death scene, I asked my pal Steve McQueen if he'd film it for me on my Kodak Super-8 camera. He agreed. The shot was set up and Franklin Schaffner called "Action!" I limped slowly towards the ocean, then as I got closer my pace increased until I was almost running into the water. I start swimming and after a few yards, I feel and hear the squib on my skull detonate. It went off without a hitch. I floated face down in the ocean and pumped the fake blood with my submerged hand and it looked like the real deal. The funny part was, with my ears under the water and being far from the camera, I didn't hear them yell "Cut!" I just continued to float and pump out the viscous fluid. I was a scuba diver at the time and could hold my breath for quite a while. I continued to silently float. Well, Dustin Hoffman got concerned that something had actually gone wrong, that maybe I'd been seriously hurt, and he waded out into the ocean to help me. But before he could get to me, I'd come up for air and the scene was printed and in the can.

A few days later, I was wrapped on the movie and booked on a flight home that had a stopover in New Orleans. I was glad to be finished with the film and anxious to get home. I called no one to alert them to the details of my return flights and I almost didn't make it back. On the plane to New Orleans, the turbulence was so bad, and the altitude drops so severe, that the oxygen masks were dropped down. Again, I feared for my life on that plane. Again, I survived.

I never saw or spoke with Dustin Hoffman or Steve McQueen again. I went to the cast and crew screening of the movie at the old Samuel Goldwyn Studio in Hollywood and that is the one and only time I have seen *Papillon*.

ME, STEVE McQUEEN, AND DUSTIN HOFFMAN.
FIRST DAY OUT AT SEA.

BORN FOR SHOWBIZ.

2. The Beginning

*I*t's "Moo Me" not, "mummy." And with that…

I came into this world on the first day of February 1954, the only child of Charles and Muriel Mumy. I was born in a hospital in San Gabriel, California, about an hour's drive from the family home in a suburb of Los Angeles called Beverlywood. I was a small baby, four pounds twelve ounces, nineteen inches long. I suppose that's why it only took my mother an hour to push me out.

They named me Charles William Mumy Jr., but right from day one they called me Billy.

We all went home to our nice house in Beverlywood, which was exactly a mile from the prestigious Beverly Hills border, and life was good. Real good.

My father was a native Californian born in 1904. He accomplished more in his lifetime than almost anyone I can imagine.

He came from a relatively poor family in Riverside County. His father, Harvey, was a policeman. As a young boy, my dad and his family actually traveled by covered wagon to Utah to settle a piece of land. I guess things didn't turn out the way Harvey wanted, because it wasn't long before the Mumys returned to sunny Riverside, California.

At the age of eighteen, my dad moved to Bishop, California to work for the power company. By the time he was in his mid-thirties, he was a married millionaire who owned and operated two cattle ranches, one in Bishop and one in Nevada. He also owned the Buick dealership in Bishop, the town's nicest restaurant-tavern, the Golden State, and his own airplane. He used it to fly back and forth from one ranch to another. For fun he played fiddle in a country swing band, and he was president of the Rotary International club and master of the local Masonic Lodge in Bishop.

To this day, I don't think I've ever met anyone who knew my father and had a bad word to say about him.

Charlie Mumy, the country gentleman, was certainly loved in the small cowboy community of Bishop. He had a beautiful house, and a beautiful wife. They adopted a beautiful little girl, Linda. And for quite a while, I suppose my father's world was about as good as it gets.

But after seventeen years of marriage, for reasons he wouldn't talk to me about, when their daughter was four years old, my father got divorced. He sold his ranch in Nevada. He sold his plane. He sold the Golden State. He sold the Buick dealership. He handed the responsibility of his ranch in Bishop to his foreman, rodeo champion Lester Cline, and he left his daughter and Bishop behind. And at a party one night in Las Vegas at the Frontier Hotel, he met Muriel Gould.

My mother was born in Detroit, Michigan in 1912. Her father, Harry Gould, was a prominent Jewish businessman who, like my father, owned a Buick dealership. Harry's was in Pontiac, Michigan. In 1922, Harry Gould decided he'd had enough of the severe Michigan winters, so he packed up his young wife Alma and their two daughters, ten-year-old Muriel and four-year-old Vail, and they moved out west to golden Hollywood.

Harry sold Packard cars on Hollywood Boulevard right next to the Roosevelt Hotel. He was a good-looking, easygoing man. And he was an excellent salesman. He became friends with Edmund Goulding, one of MGM Studios' top movie directors of the day. Goulding took a liking to Harry, and he convinced him he was selling the wrong product. He ought to be repping talent. That was the ticket in this town. So, within a very short time, Harry stopped selling cars and started selling actors, writers, and directors.

Over the years, his business as a Hollywood agent grew more and more successful. His most famous client was Boris Karloff.

When he agreed to be represented as an actor by Harry, Karloff was driving a truck back and forth between Los Angeles and San Francisco to pay the rent. It was my grandfather who got him the audition for *Frankenstein*, and the two of them had a long, successful run together. Karloff once gave Harry and his family two Scottish terriers as a Christmas gift. I know that one was named "Spooks."

Daughter Muriel had been doing modeling work, mostly for *True Story* magazine, the kind of dramatic, stolid poses that accompanied short story titles like "My Husband Loves my Sister but I Won't Let Him Go!" Harry was able to land a recurring part for her in the Universal Pictures series *The Collegians*. From there, she worked in more films, mostly bit parts and background stuff.

Muriel once filmed a scene with Greta Garbo, and the experience left her so nervous that she decided her destiny was not in front of the motion picture camera.

But she enjoyed being a part of the industry, and so in 1941, after a five-year marriage had fallen apart and America was on the brink of entering World War II, Muriel entered the gates of 20th Century Fox Studios in West Los Angeles to work as a writer's secretary, a job she kept for the next ten years.

ME AND JIGGS,
THE COWBOY AND
HIS WAGON.

MY MOM AND ME,
OUTSIDE OUR HOUSE
ON LOCKFORD STREET.

MEET THE MUMYS: CHARLES, MURIEL AND BILLY
OFF TO BEVERLY HILLS PRESBYTERIAN CHURCH.

A TOTEM POLE OF MUMY MALES
ME, DAD AND JIGGS.

Harry passed away before I was born, but I've always felt a kind of closeness to him. I like to think that he has witnessed my success in show business, an arena that he made comfortable for my mother.

Charles and Muriel married in 1951. They settled on Lockford Street in Beverlywood, a wonderful small cul-de-sac that was home to a dozen kids all within a few years of my age. Dad kept the ranch in Bishop, and we'd all go there for several weeks every summer, but that wasn't enough to keep him satisfied. He missed the Golden State, so he bought a restaurant-bar in Hollywood called The Rocket Room. With a space-age logo above him, my father played host as folks munched food and drank cocktails.

It was the 1950s, and the American Dream was ours.

<<>>

"Out of the night, when the full moon is bright, comes the horseman known as Zorro..." Man, I was so into it! I had the cape, the hat, the mask, the sword, I had it all and I loved playing the adventurer! What four-year-old in 1958 didn't want to be Zorro? Or Superman? Or Davy Crockett? Or the Lone Ranger? It didn't matter, they were interchangeable, and they were who I pretended to be. But on this one day in particular, I'm sure it was Zorro.

My mother was with my grandmother out shopping. My grandmother by the way, the only grandparent I ever knew, shared a bedroom with me until I was four years old. Her snoring kept me up for years. It was truly amazing the tone and volume that she could produce. I called her "Lala." She earned the nickname by singing. When I was an infant and a toddler, she used to sit me in her lap and sing the *Davy Crockett* theme song to me. Only she didn't know the words so she just sang "La la la la la la..." Hence, she was LaLa until the day she died. I loved her very much. But I really hated her snoring. When Harry died, Lala moved in with Aunt Vail and Uncle Fred and their two boys Rick and Mark who lived a few miles away.

"ALL I EVER WANTED TO BE."

But after a few years, she came to live with us. My dad never seemed to mind.

Lala drove a 1941 Chevrolet coupe. It was dark blue. She kept it for twenty-five years. It was in mint condition. Lala was kind of anal retentive about her material possessions. She was always polishing and cleaning her stuff, she used to take a toothbrush and shine that Chevy three times a week. When you drove with Lala, she wouldn't let you roll down the window. I don't think she ever rolled down the windows in her car, it smelled like a musty sarcophagus inside. But it was hers, and she liked it that way. Whenever Lala and I would get into arguments, she'd just shrug me off and say, "You should know what I forgot" - which I think is a pretty cool line.

Anyway, on the day in question, my dad was at The Rocket Room, mom and Lala were out, and I was home with our wirehaired terrier Jiggs, and our housekeeper, Essie. Bless her soul, Essie Smith was a part of our family from the mid-1950s until the mid-1970s. I can close my eyes and smell her. A sweet, oily scent. Essie was a very dark-skinned African American, who wore glasses and weighed about thirty pounds more than she should have. Everyone in my family loved Essie, and she loved us.

So, Essie was busy somewhere in our three-bedroom single-story house. Dad had just added on another bedroom and a bar. We needed them both because of Lala's snoring. Anyway, I was busy being Zorro in the new bedroom. I was standing on the bed getting ready to leap on my enemy, the comandante, who was, in reality, my large inflatable Bozo Bop. He and I had many, many battles before I finally punctured him.

"...Zorro, the Fox so cunning and free..." and I was airborne! I bounced off the bedspring through the air onto Bozo and came crashing down right on top of my toy Winchester rifle.

>KRAK<

They don't make toy Winchester rifles like they used to. This one had a barrel of solid steel. It was harder than the bone in my right leg, which broke in half when I landed. Essie heard my screams and came running. She didn't know what was wrong, but she tried to calm me down. I remember her asking me if I wanted a tootsie roll. I really loved tootsie rolls, and when I screamed "No! I want my Mommy!" She knew it was serious.

She called my dad at The Rocket Room and by the end of the day, I was wearing a heavy plaster cast on my right leg from my foot all the way up my hip. And it wouldn't come off for three months.

Three months is a long time when you're four years old.

I spent the twelve weeks mostly watching our black-and-white television set. Watching *The Mickey Mouse Club* every day, waiting for *Zorro, Davy Crockett, Spin and Marty,* and other favorites. I watched and was thrilled by George Reeves as Superman. I watched, and I watched, and I watched.

And by the time the cast was ready to come off, I knew where I belonged. I belonged inside the TV just like Zorro and Superman. And I let my parents know it.

And the strangest part of all is: they listened to me.

GRANDPA HARRY
AND GRANDMA
ALMA (LALA).

LALA AND ME.

GRANDMA
DELLA AND
GRANDPA
HARVEY.

ESSIE AND ME (WE WERE
AT A HOTEL IN BAJA,
NEAR SAN DIEGO).

31

Since grandpa Harry and Mom had worked in the entertainment industry, the idea of a four-year-old red-haired, freckle-faced, energetic kid working as an actor wasn't such an alien concept around the Mumy home.

Mom and Dad agreed that as long as Muriel was willing to drive me around to auditions or jobs, and as long as they invested whatever I earned for my future, and as long as I was having a good time, it was okay with them.

The first thing they did was get me on a television program called *Romper Room*. I started on April 21, 1958. Now *Romper Room* was basically a pre-school with a rotating class on television. I don't remember what it took to get on the show, but there were always lots of little kids coming and going on *Romper Room*. Well, I came and ended up staying for several weeks. Miss Mary was the name of my TV teacher. The program was shot on videotape and the set was basically your average-size schoolroom. I remember being a happy little guy there, discovering the multi-colored world of wooden tinker toys - although I must admit, I have no anecdotes from the experience. To the best of my knowledge, no kinescopes or videotapes exist of my debut before the television cameras. I was four years old.

None of the kids got paid for being on the show, and there was no acting involved. We just sat around and played and gathered in a circle and listened to Miss Mary tell stories and learned about "Do Bees" and "Don't Bees." My mother's plan was simply to see how I would react on a set under the lights and in front of a camera. I guess all went fine, because soon after my stint on *Romper Room*, I signed with my first professional agent.

Hazel McMillan was an eccentric agent who handled child actors. That was basically all she did, rep kids. And she represented some of Hollywood's hottest young talent. Hazel worked out of her home on Doheny Drive in Beverly Hills. Her house always freaked me out because you couldn't see it from the street; her foliage was so wild and overgrown that all you could see were these bizarre giant hedges that covered up the small Spanish single-story structure just north of Wilshire Boulevard.

Hazel knew everybody in showbiz and everybody in showbiz knew Hazel, and within a short time I was booked on my first network television show as an actor. It was a 1959 episode of *Riverboat*, a CBS series starring Darren McGavin and Burt Reynolds. I worked two days on the show; we filmed it at Revue Studios on the Universal lot. I had one line: "Thank you," and I was paid $22 a day.

But don't think that my first taste of showbiz was a total cakewalk. Oh no, I must have gone on at least ten auditions after I got that part on *Riverboat* before my next job. Mom and Lala would toss me in the back of mom's brand-new pink 1959 Cadillac and schlep me around town for the auditions. My mother refused to drive the freeways in those days, so it took a while to get from Beverlywood out to the San Fernando Valley, if that's where we were headed. I remember listening to rock & roll music on KFWB radio channel 98 all the time. Ricky Nelson, Jan & Dean, the Everly Brothers - that sort of stuff. There were no seatbelts back then, and I used to climb up on the back console behind the backseat and scrunch up by the rear window next to the magnetic hula girl and put my ear right on top of the speakers in that outrageous ride. I'd make goofy faces and wave at the people in the cars behind us as we cruised around Hollywood.

Then of course when we finally did arrive at our destination, we'd have to wait our turn in the lobby with lots of other kids and their moms. We usually passed the time with coloring books or games like hangman or tic tac toe.

The audition process never was any fun. After waiting and waiting to be seen, watching other nervous actors wait to audition before you, you're finally shuffled into an office where strangers sit and wait to judge you. You've memorized your lines and prepared your performance, but nine times out of ten you stand in their office and perform to the best of your ability while some assistant casting person who can't read one sentence right, feeds you your cues. It's absolutely nothing like working on a real soundstage with other professional actors.

I've always felt comfortable and confident when filming in front of the cameras, but I've often felt uptight during the audition process. Many decades later I had a conversation with my friend, actor/writer/producer and pop star Shaun Cassidy and he said he also felt uncomfortable in auditions, but he had discovered a way to turn it around. Shaun said when he walked into an audition, he immediately pictured everyone there sitting on toilets. I've tried that and it works. But sometimes they ask, "What's so funny?"

But I didn't complain about auditioning in those days because I really wanted to be on TV. I do remember being pretty disappointed a few times when I didn't get the jobs though. Still, after the auditions we'd usually stop off at Super Drugs or Pico Drugs and Mom would buy me a few new comic books to add to my already impressive stack.

Before my big break on *Riverboat*, I had landed a few print jobs, modeling stuff for magazines. They were easy, and I suppose I made some money doing them, but it wasn't exactly the same as being Zorro, if you know what I mean. My goals never were to be frozen in a magazine. I wanted action on the tube! Still, it was showbiz, and if Hazel sent us out on an audition, we went for it.

The decade was coming to a close, just as my career was starting. A few months later we would usher in the 1960s and I would become one of the busiest actors in town.

3. Swingin' Sixties

I was pretty active in 1960. I worked on thirteen episodic television shows, I did voice-over work on four different "Smokey the Bear" animated spots, three national TV commercials, two print jobs (*Saturday Evening Post* and *House & Garden*), one industrial short film for American Airlines, and one feature film *The Wizard of Baghdad* for 20th Century Fox Studios. That was my first job on the lot that my mom had worked at for ten years. Several of her old friends were still working there, and I can honestly say my mother was never a typical stage mother, but she was really proud to show me off to her pals. I played a young Aladdin, a ragged street urchin trying to sell a lamp. It was a small part, but to my mom it was a major event.

I also found time to have the mumps for ten days that year, and my lucky father managed to catch them from me. When you're in your fifties and you get the mumps, it's pretty serious. Thankfully he survived it with everything still functioning properly.

Some of the talented folks I worked with in that election year were: Red Skelton, Loretta Young, Rod Serling, Cloris Leachman, Van Johnson, June Allyson, Tom Ewell, Art Linkletter, Franchot Tone, and Tennessee Ernie Ford.

The first time I received screen credit was in an episode of *The Tom Ewell Show* titled "Tom Puts the Girls to Work." Although I had already done seven TV shows before this, they had all been pretty small bit parts, just a few lines in one or two scenes. In this show I played a real brat named Jeffrey Nelson. We filmed it over a three-day period at Four Star Productions and I was paid $300. Tom Ewell had good comedic timing, similar to Jack Benny. And he was nice to me. I started my autograph collection with his signature.

My very first starring role was in an episode of *The Loretta Young Show*. It was called "My Own Master," and I played a lonely boy named Rennie, who had an imaginary friend he created called Juk. In the story, Rennie's parents, especially his father, weren't really there for the boy, so he escapes reality with Juk.

Cloris Leachman played my mom (something she would do four times), and she was absolutely fantastic to work with. Cloris of course, was an incredible actress. She was very patient with me, and she taught me a lot.

I learned some valuable lessons from her early on. One was that some actors need to concentrate privately before the cameras roll. Here's what happened... Because I was six years old, I couldn't really read well yet, so the way I memorized my lines was by hearing the words spoken aloud. I still have an "audible" memory, and as fate would have it, after hearing dialogue a couple times, I usually retain it for as long as needed.

Back then, I not only memorized my own lines, but I knew everyone else's as well. Since I had memorized the entire script, it never occurred to me that the other actors might not have done the same.

When we were rehearsing a scene, Cloris would occasionally forget her lines. Well, thinking I was doing her a favor I told her what they were. After this happened a few times, I realized that she didn't really appreciate me "helping" her with her memory. She wanted to work things out by herself. And she explained that to me very nicely.

"My Own Master" was a real tearjerker, and I had to cry in it. Rennie was a character with plenty of dynamics, my first lead, and it earned me $480 for the six days of work it took to film. A pretty decent paycheck for a six-year-old back in 1960.

JON PROVOST, LORETTA YOUNG, AND ME. I'M STILL FRIENDS WITH JON. HE AND I SHARED CLORIS LEACHMAN AND JUNE LOCKHART AS TV MOMS.

《〉》

I did quite a lot of commercials as a kid, but I never enjoyed doing them very much. The directors and the crew always seemed stressed and usually there wasn't much serious acting, and you had to do dozens and dozens of takes. But I liked doing Mattel toy commercials because they would inevitably give me the products when the work was over. It was usually toy guns (I had tons of Fanner 50s, Dick Tracey Snub Nose 38s, Jet Power Guns, and Pump Action Water Squirt Guns), but I also remember getting a pretty cool Blaze, the Galloping Horse.

All in all, I did nine Mattel commercials. I was also the voice of Matty Mattel on the animated television series *Matty's Funday Funnies* which featured Bob Clampett's classic *Beany and Cecil* cartoons. That was actually the very first television series I was a regular on, even though it was not an on-camera performance. That series began production in 1961 and ran throughout the 1960s. It was a blast going into the recording studio every few months and performing the voice of the animated character who was host of the show.

My folks invested the money I made from Mattel commercials and *Matty's Funday Funnies* in shares of Mattel stock. It was a good investment. I cashed it out many decades later to buy my wife Eileen a Mercedes Benz.

**MATTY MATTEL LOGO
MODELED AFTER YOURS TRULY.**

4. Random Thoughts

*I*t's 1998. I'm actually having a cell phone conversation with the astronauts on the International Space Station right now while eating brunch at the Mulholland Tennis Club with my family and NASA pilot Charlie Justiz and his disc jockey wife, Dayna Steele. What a trip! *Lost in Space* ended in 1968. Man… people really love that show. I can't believe how many folks have been inspired to have careers in the space program because of *Lost in Space*. How crazy is this? Some things have real staying power. Pass the Tang, please.

THE ROBINSON KIDS (ANGELA CARTWRIGHT, MARTA KRISTEN, AND ME)
ON BOARD THE ENDEAVOUR IN 2001.

≪≫

"So, in the future, when you're delivering dialogue off camera to another actor, remember to always do your best acting. Don't goof around just because you're not in the shot." I'm seven years old and I immediately understand that Cloris Leachman is right. I was goofing around when it was her close-up. She just taught me an important lesson that every seven-year-old busy working actor should know. I'll never forgot this.

I won this argument. Robert Haimer and I, as Barnes & Barnes, have spent this winter afternoon in 1978 working in my home recording studio on our novelty song "Fish Heads" with the intent of sending it to the globally-syndicated *Dr. Demento Radio Show*. We both know this is a very catchy and kooky song, sometimes you just have a feeling about a tune, and this is one of those times. Robert wrote the chorus, the hook, and I wrote all the verses. As with most everything he and I ever do, there's a struggle to come to agreement. It was my idea for us to sing the chorus in a sped up "Chipmunks" style. I always loved Dave Seville and the Chipmunks' records and I felt that recording the chorus that way would put this little ditty over-the-top... but of course, Robert strongly disagreed, until I insisted we at least try it. We did. I was right. Within a few months "Fish Heads" will be a worldwide novelty hit.

My parents are out of town and Joy Bang is naked in my bed. I thought taking the part on "The Party" episode of *Insight* might be kinda tacky and preachy, but it turned out to be pretty cool. I wrote and performed a song for the episode, and my co-star Joy has indeed been a total joy. I really like her. I am eighteen and things could be worse.

But being pulled over by the Los Angeles Sheriff's department for speeding in your 1969 beige MGB-GT on Fountain Avenue between Fairfax and La Cienega is not so good. I was only in second gear. There's no way I was going 53 mph in second gear. I'm about to start arguing that fact with the sheriff who is standing next to my driver's side window and leaning down writing me the ticket when I remember that my girlfriend, who is sitting in the passenger seat, has cocaine in her purse. She always has drugs on her. Never very much, but always enough to make things potentially go from lame to heinous in a few seconds. I accept the ticket and promise to drive slower in the future as I silently remind myself to get a new girlfriend.

Live television is a completely different beast than filming movies or TV episodes one scene at a time, where you have the ability to cut and do it over as many times as needed to get it just right. With live TV, you rehearse it like a play and then you're counted in, the red lights on the cameras are illuminated, and the director and crew are up in a booth looking down and watching multiple monitors to quickly choose which camera to cut to as the show unfolds in real time - live.

I'm seven years old and am part of a scene being broadcast live on a Bob Hope Special. This scene features Bob, actress Jaye P. Morgan, several children, and a dog. We had rehearsed it and now it was being broadcast live across the country.

What I saw onstage was quite different from what the home audiences saw on their black-and-white television sets. As the director up in the booth frantically cut from one angle to another, the scene played out, just as rehearsed, on the home television screens. But onstage, we watched as the dog did a little circle dance and then took a big shit on the stage. You kinda had to be there.

"JOHNNY MADRID
AND THE KID."

5. Horsing Around

"**N**ever deny a stuntperson a check, Billy Person." Jonathan Harris had drilled that into my head for years on the set of *Lost in Space*, but being a kid I liked jumping off high foam rubber rocks and having huge explosions combust all around me so I could look like a superhero on forty million TV screens every week. But this feels different. I'm out on a ranch guest-starring on an episode of *Lancer* with James Stacy and the director knows that I'm fairly competent with horses. He asks me to do a fall. In the scene, I steal Jim Stacy's horse and ride off... Jim Stacy whistles and the horse bucks me off. Hmmmm... "Never deny a stuntperson a check, Billy Person" is echoing loudly inside my skull. I tell them I'm not comfortable doing the stunt. They understand. A stuntman does it while I watch from off camera. He falls awkwardly and breaks his neck. He's taken away on a stretcher (he will eventually regain his full mobility). After a short break, we resume shooting the next scene.

I am fifteen, so no one on the show treats me like a little kid. I'm smoking Marlboros in between filming scenes, and I remember the producer actually makes me shave off my emerging peach fuzz. I must admit, I liked that, and it was the first time I shaved. We shot the episode during the summer, so I didn't have to go to school in between working and I could hang out.

Jim Stacy was probably the boldest and arguably the weirdest guy I ever worked with. The majority of my scenes on this show were with him, and he and I got along and worked together well. It was a good episode. I was paid top of the show, $3000, to play Andy

Cutler. Jim, as Johnny Madrid, delivered a very fine performance and he seemed to be liked by the crew and his fellow cast members. But... man... one day...we both had to film bath scenes. Individually, of course. When filming scenes like that for television, an actor wears flesh-colored tight underwear, which I wore for my bath scene. He was also indeed wearing a pair of undies for his scene. However, when a group of visiting nuns appeared on the soundstage for some bizarre reason, Jim slipped out of his undies and stood up in the tub and waved to the nuns. "Hiya Sisters!" Only a cluster of soap bubbles covered his package. I thought that was a pretty crazy thing to do. But that wasn't the end of Jim Stacy making a powerful and lasting impression on me.

Because it was a western, my dad accompanied me to work. Normally my mother was always with me as my guardian, but my dad, the rancher, enjoyed coming when there were horses and cowboy hats. My father wasn't overprotective of me at all. My mother wasn't either. They pretty much let me experience life as I chose to (within clear boundaries of course). Anyway, I was hanging out in Jim Stacy's dressing room on the last day of filming and the crew broke for an hour lunch. Jim asked me if I wanted to leave the set and grab lunch with him and bring it back. I said, "sure" and my dad was cool about it and said he'd grab something from the caterer. So, I ride with Jim down to Hollywood Blvd. to pick up some hot dogs and burgers. But that's not all we picked up. In 1969, hippies were everywhere in Hollywood and lots of people hitchhiked. Jim picked up two hippie girls who were hitching and brought them back to his dressing room. I'd estimate they were about 18 years old. In the dressing room they asked us if we wanted to drop some acid with them and they produced a handful of LSD blotter acid tabs on paper. I was literally stunned when Jim said "You betcha!" and popped one onto his tongue. Well, that was enough for me. I demurred the offer and left Jim and the two girls and headed back to be with my father. This happened just before the Manson murders. I don't think I ever told my dad that story.

I remember watching Jim Stacy very closely all the rest of that day to see how he was behaving, and he seemed totally normal and professional.

Life after the *Lancer* series ended took some very tragic turns for James Stacy. He lost a leg and an arm in a motorcycle accident that took the life of his girlfriend, and then he ran into some serious legal trouble for molesting an eleven-year-old girl and fleeing the state. He tried to commit suicide but recovered. He was sentenced to six years in prison.

I saw him at an autograph show shortly before he died. He was barely able to talk and seemed quite medicated. We smiled and took a photo together. I chose not to remind him of his behavior around "The Kid."

WORKING WITH JIM STACY WAS QUITE A TRIP!

6. FUN TIMES

*T*he mid-1970s were really the weirdest clump of years I've personally experienced. I was living on my own in Laurel Canyon, co-starring in *Sunshine*, recording soundtrack records on MCA that charted and did well, and found myself at the beginning of transitioning from actor to writer. For recreation, there was the West Hollywood Softball League, made up of half a dozen teams that were all connected to showbiz in one way or another, and my team, Showbiz Kids, had its nemesis, the Hollywood Vampires. I lived on Lookout Mountain and Alice Cooper and Micky Dolenz lived right around the corner on Horseshoe Canyon. Mark Volman of the Turtles lived at the top of Lookout Mountain, next to photographer Henry Diltz, and he would join the festivities. It was a local group of artists and pals competing with bats and gloves and balls.

Admittedly, the Hollywood Vampires definitely beat us most all the time, but the time we did beat them we upped the party level to turbo intensity. The Vampires softball team was different from the Vampires drinking club which included John Lennon, Keith Moon, and Harry Nilsson. Those cats participated in getting wasted and causing trouble in clubs and being in the news for their shenanigans, but they didn't play softball. The Vampires softball team, with David Jolliffe, Davy Jones, Micky Dolenz, Peter Tork, Alice Cooper, and Meat Loaf was affiliated with, but not the same core group that caused serious concern nightly on the strip.

When Showbiz Kids played a game against the Vampires and won, the team celebrated like a Fellini movie. It was over-the-top and out of hand. Lennon and Nilsson never showed up for the softball game celebrations, but Alice, Micky, Peter, Meatloaf, and Jolliffe did. It got quite competitive. We co-mingled the teams upstairs at the Rainbow Bar & Grill for some serious drinking and debauchery as I recall, and everyone was usually pleasant but that competitive sports vibe definitely existed. Harry Nilsson being the wild card that could spontaneously go off on anyone for anything at anytime. Showbiz Kids were the first team in the league to have our own legit cheerleaders... that quickly inspired the Vampires to gather their own crew of vampy sexy cheerleaders... and between us both, the cheerleaders definitely affected the vibe of the games... Winning meant more than just a cheer and a beer. It really was a bubble of time that existed for a brief moment and then combusted and disappeared.

Gerry Beckley, my pal and collaborator from the band America, lived in a fabulous home at the top of Doheny called Flicker Way. It had previously belonged to Mike Nichols. It quickly became the party house where we and a handful of artists like David Crosby, David Cassidy, Harry Nilsson, and Ricky Fataar would often gather. Sometimes for a few hours, sometimes for a few days. I can recall Gerry at his upright acoustic piano, playing a G chord for a solid half an hour. Literally. Just a G chord. Over and over and over. I remember sitting next to him on the piano bench suggesting a change to an A minor 7, and Gerry refusing to budge from the G-B-D triad, explaining with great enthusiasm, "This is PERFECT!" and that one chord being proudly brought to bear for a good thirty minutes.

That's really how things were for a while. And looking back on it... I suppose that wasn't so bad. Who doesn't like a G chord?

«»

Mike McGreevey, Ann Jillian and I are parading around Walt Disney's private office in bathing suits for him to check out. Filming *Sammy, the Way-Out Seal* is one of the most fun projects I've ever been a part of. It's 1962. I'm eight years old and having the time of my life on the Disney lot. Mike is the coolest big brother in the world. Being an only child, I truly wish he was my real brother. I like Ann. She's a good actress and easy to hang out with. "Uncle Walt" (he keeps reminding us to call him that) eventually nods his approval regarding our swim wardrobe and we head back to the stage where they've dug a huge swimming pool in the middle of it, with glass walls for the subterranean camera crew to shoot from as we frolic for days and days in the pool with Sammy the seal. Sometimes it's Corky the seal or Suzie the seal. They're all pretty neat.

ANN JILLIAN, MIKE MCGREEVEY, AND ME FROM
"SAMMY THE WAY-OUT SEAL" – WE MADE A REAL GOOD TEAM.

‹‹›

Jack Kirby, Jerry Siegel, and Bob Kane are sitting in my living room. These men are comic book GODS. They created Superman, Batman, Captain America, and pretty much everyone else. And they're chatting in my living room simply because Eileen invited them over for dinner with their wives, Roz, Joanne, and Elizabeth along with our friends, Miguel and Harrigan Ferrer, Mark and Marilou Hamill, and Robert Haimer.

These three icons of pop culture hadn't been in the same room together in decades. It's 1987. I'm thirty-three years old. I'm writing comic books for Marvel Comics. Miguel and I have created *The Comet Man*. The six-issue series sells half a million copies. The Comet Man interacts with the Hulk, Reed Richards, Nick Fury, and other Kirby co-created characters. Amazing. Jack is telling stories about his experiences fighting Nazis in Europe in World War II and discussing parallel worlds and demons.

Jerry is beyond sweet and sensitive and flattering and kind. Bob is so full of himself it's both funny and somewhat sad. Mark, Miguel, and I have been reduced to puddles of fan boys.

ME, MARK HAMILL, AND MIGUEL FERRER WITH THE COMIC BOOK GODS: JACK KIRBY, JERRY SIEGEL, AND BOB KANE. WHAT A NIGHT!

‹‹›bi›

Brian Wilson is sitting in a chair holding both his arms up and looking at Eileen with a sweet helpless expression on his iconic, handsome, wounded soul face. He needs help getting up. His back hurts him all the time but he doesn't complain about it much. My wonderful and always athletic wife smiles warmly and reaches out to the brilliant architect of the California Sound and grabs ahold of his wrists and pulls him up. We've been hanging out with Brian and his amazing and supportive band for a couple years now. He's made impressive progress in his personal struggles with mental illness. When he's motivated and into it, he still sings beautifully. His range is diminished, and Jeff Foskett now covers those super high falsetto parts that Brian originally sang on scores of Beach Boys recordings, but Brian's in strong voice tonight.

EILEEN AND
BRIAN —
SO HAPPY
TOGETHER.

The Grammy Museum is a cool place to gig. We've been standing next to the stage and watching the set as it's now winding down. Brian and the guys are about to go into the final few songs. Jeff gives me, Gerry Beckley, and Peter Leinheiser the "nod." Come on up! One of the very first 45 singles I ever bought was "Surfin" by the Beach Boys on the Candix label. Here I am, standing at a keyboard onstage, five feet from Brian Wilson and I'm singing harmony on "Barbara Ann" and now I'm actually taking a piano solo! Sometimes I surprise myself. In a minute, I'll pick up a tambourine, walk across the stage and join Gerry, Jeff, and Peter around a microphone and sing harmony on "Help Me Rhonda" and "Fun, Fun, Fun."

Wow.

ONSTAGE SINGING WITH BRIAN. AT THE MIC: GERRY BECKLEY, PETER LEINHEISER, AND ME. WHAT A NIGHT!

I consider just knowing Brian Wilson a little bit to be a blessing, but to share the stage with him and his phenomenal band is truly something very special for me. I see my beautiful wife Eileen smiling and snapping photos below. She's happy because I'm happy. I'm a lucky man.

I was in love with Elizabeth Montgomery. Really. I was also in love with Shirley Jones and Connie Stevens. I'm not kidding here. I legit fell in love with those ladies. Playing Darrin Stevens metamorphosed into a child on *Bewitched* remains one of my favorite roles of all time.

I guest starred on two *Bewitched* episodes, the first was titled "A Vision of Sugar Plums," the first season Christmas episode. Besides finding myself deeply in love with Elizabeth and having her teach me her iconic "nose twitch," I was fortunate to work with the great Cecil Kellaway who gave a most memorable and authentic performance as Santa Claus. But in "Junior Executive," playing Samantha Stevens' husband was really special. We kissed. It was magic.

WITH ELIZABETH MONTGOMERY... IT WAS LOVE FOR ME!

7. School Daze

*T*urning six was a big deal. No more carefree kindergarten days, no sir. Now besides working on television and films, I had the awesome responsibilities of the first grade.

Beverlywood was a nice, middle class, largely Jewish community in 1960. Like all my friends, I went to public school. The Canfield Avenue School. It was a little less than a mile from our house, and I wanted to walk there with my older friends, but for the first few semesters my mother insisted on driving me. She claims it was because of having to cross two busy streets, Beverwil and Beverly Drive. Anyway, mom would drive me and let me out a block before the school so I could walk the final distance on my own.

My first-grade teacher was Mrs. Pritchard, and school was swell. I never was very shy, and I got along with most everyone. Right from the start I was coming and going because of my work, and the neighborhood kids that I went to school with were used to me disappearing for a week or a month at a time, and then returning to the class. No one ever made a big deal out of it, not them, and certainly not me. At least I didn't think they thought much of it, but years later I was told that wasn't always the case and some of the students kept up on my "extracurricular" acting activities.

It never was much of a problem acclimating to public school after being away and going to school with a tutor on a set. Mrs. Pritchard would give my mom the assignments she was going to cover over the period of time I was working, and the tutor would make sure I got the lessons learned. I had a crush on my second-grade teacher, Miss Brownell. She was really cute.

Going to school at the studio however, is nothing like being in "real" school. It's three hours a day, and it can be done all at once or it can be done in increments of a minimum of twenty minutes at a time. You have to have finished your three hours by four p.m.

The tutors that work in the entertainment industry have to be pretty damn smart, because they're required to teach every subject from grammar school through high school.

I must have worked with every showbiz teacher in the business during the 1960s. Some of them were permanently assigned to the studio, and they had a classroom on the lot where I'd join for the day or the week. But usually there was a hot little trailer kept just outside the stage door and a teacher was hired specifically for the show I was working on. As soon as we would finish rehearsing or filming a scene, I was quickly herded back to that little trailer and tossed into the reality of school by an overworked underpaid second assistant director.

Some of the teachers were really nice, and they seemed to understand how hard it was to constantly have to shift your thinking from acting to education. I mean, one minute you're under the hot lights delivering pages of dialogue in an emotional state, and the next you're tossed into a trailer and expected to do math.

That was always difficult for me. I wanted to stay on the set and be with the other actors and the crew. But getting those three hours in was not something anyone could avoid. There's no "ditching class" at the studio.

I never argued with a director or cameraman or another actor when I was a kid. I was taught to listen, hit my mark, know my lines and be polite. But I must admit, I gave some of those teachers a pretty hard time.

I guess a part of me knew that it would be next to impossible for them to seriously cause me any trouble as long as I eventually completed the schoolwork I was assigned before I returned to Canfield. I mean, what could they do? Fire me? Send me to the principal's office?

IN THE PERMANENT FOX SCHOOLROOM WITH ANGE, DARBY HINTON, FRANCES KLAMT, AND ME. FROM THE FIRST SEASON OF LOST IN SPACE

As I said, some of them were really nice, but some of them were truly witches. Horrible, ancient, cranky, old spinsters, who really acted exactly like the terrifying, orphanage-running villains out of *The Little Rascals* shorts. And they probably were the very same ones who gave Spanky, Alfalfa, Buckwheat, and the others an awful time way back then.

There were plenty of times when I was not in the mood to open those books and get back to schoolwork, and I simply refused to do it. However, I was sure to have it done before I returned to Canfield Avenue School, and I pretty much always got Bs.

After school, after work, life was full of adventure and fun.

≪≫

Our little cul-de-sac, Lockford Street, was a great place to grow up. There were kids all around me.

On the corner lived Jeff and David Kalmick; Jeff was two and a half years older than I was, and David was a year and a half younger. Jeff wanted to be a general in the army. He was always the guy who planned the strategy in our neighborhood war games. David, on the other hand was the official boy genius on our block. I remember him spelling "antidisestablishmentarianism" aloud for everyone, whether we wanted to hear it or not, when he was no more than five years old. Jeff turned out to be an animal rights activist, vegetarian, pacifist, and licensed clinical social worker. And I'm still good friends with him to this day. David turned out to be a computer software developer who made many millions of dollars.

Anyway, next to the Kalmick home was the Horowitz house. The Horowitzes were an old European couple and none of us kids ever dealt with them at all, except David and I dug a hole in the ground between their house and mine. We continued to dig that hole for at least four years. It got pretty deep.

Then there was my house: 9712 Lockford Street. We had a big Chinese elm tree in our front yard, and us kids would gather there for group meetings. As a matter of fact, I was told the facts of life under that tree by my neighbor Steve Marshank. Of course, at the time I didn't believe it and swore that if it was true, I'd never participate in such a gross act. I also remember being told that there was no real Santa Claus near that tree. And I can feel the same tears well up inside of me now as I felt then, when I knew in my heart it was the truth, but I swore aloud it couldn't be. That is I believe a major turning point in a person's life, kinda like a bar mitzvah. The breaking of the Santa myth... Anyway, a lot of plans were made under that Chinese elm tree.

My dad had brought back a huge pumice rock from one of his trips to his ranch in Bishop, and it too was proudly displayed in our front yard. When you kicked it, pieces of it would crumble. Although we weren't supposed to, we all enjoyed kicking that rock for many, many years.

The Newmans lived next door to us. Johnny Newman was at least four years older than me. He was one of those perfect kids: a good athlete, a genuine nice guy, a good student, but not a kiss ass. Johnny was kinda like Wally from *Leave it to Beaver*. Johnny was the leader of the kids on Lockford until he stopped being a kid himself, and then the job went to Steve Marshank, until he stopped being a kid, and then Jeff was in charge. Johnny had a brother about two years older than me named Paul Newman. They were both nice guys. Their parents, Phil and Antoinette, were the only parents on the street that my folks socialized with. Phil was a lawyer, who soon became a judge. He and my dad built a cinder block wall between our houses, and they had to build it twice because it didn't hold up the first time around. Anyway, the Newmans were cool and they moved up to Cheviot Hills when I was nine.

Next to the Newmans there were the Van Groves. Leslie and Robin. Two girls, but I don't remember them much, they moved to Beverly Hills when I was about seven and then the Hessekiels checked in. Joe and Arlene. Joe was a year older than me, and Arlene ("Leenie") was a few years younger. They had a scary dog who bit me on the foot one day. Joe became a surfer as I recall. He passed away young.

And then there was the Linden place. Two kids there, too. Tom and Ginny. And like the Van Groves, they moved when I was about seven, and in came the Jakowskis. The father was a Colonel, and as I recall, he was constantly bothered by all the noise us kids would make. Which of course made us crank up the volume. Once again, two kids: Don and Bruce. Don was my age, and Bruce was a few years younger. They were always pretty messy. Bruce, if memory serves me well, used to eat his boogers on request.

Then there was the Marshank house. It was the best house on the block because they had a swimming pool. I remember it as being gigantic, the size of Lake Michigan, but in reality, it was a just an average pool. The Marshank's had two boys: Steve about three years my senior, and Gary, who was a year older than me. When it was hot outside, and the Marshank gate was open, that meant we were all welcome to swim in their pool. I must've spent a million happy hours in that pool playing Marco Polo and other aquatic games. Also, Steve and Gary had an incredibly beautiful young mother. Linda Marshank was a real babe, and when you walked into their living room you were greeted by a large oil painting of her looking very exotic. I don't know what became of them, but they sure had a great backyard.

Next to the Marshank house was Michelle Blonder's place. "Mickey" as we all called her. Mickey was a year older than me and resembled Annette Funicello. She was a good pal, and I remember listening to the great Everly Brothers records in her room that was full of stuffed animals. The Blonders had the first electric garage door any of us had ever seen. There was a little button off the side of the garage that would open and shut that big door and we'd constantly push it and get a genuine kick out of watching that garage door automatically going up and down. Mickey married a kid from around the corner, Joel Marcus. Sadly, Joel was killed in a plane crash not too long after they got married. Mickey moved away from her memories, and I think she became a teacher.

My dad painted a baseball diamond on the street in the middle of the block, and when I wasn't working on a television show or a film, or in school, or in the Marshank pool, or playing ball, or playing war, I was riding with my gang. Yes, there were gangs way back then, and Lockford Street was no exception. We were the "Bearcat Missiles." Johnny, Paul, Steve, Gary, Jeff, Don, and me. We put baseball cards in the spokes of our two-wheelers and rode around the neighborhood like we owned it. And in a way, we did.

Looking back on those early years, life on Lockford was fairly idyllic. Right around the corner there was a gully where we'd capture tadpoles and frogs in coffee tins and play jungle games. Sidewalks seemed to go on forever and no one ever felt wary about venturing out to be with the gang. There was no such thing as drug abuse, or domestic violence, or racial or religious prejudice, or even divorce on our block. At least that any of us kids were aware of. All of the families were different, and all the kids were too, but we meshed in that perfect way that only kids can.

Every once in a while, when I'm near the old neighborhood, I'll drive by my old house. The new owners added a second story to it. They did a good job. The majestic elm is still there and so is my dad's pumice rock. I slowly turn my car around in Mickey's driveway and resist the urge to get out and push the secret button to open her garage door. If I look hard enough, I can still see remnants of the black baseball diamond my father painted in the street. And as I head away, I think of Halloween nights and Christmas mornings and warm summer days when the Marshank's gate was open, and I realize how very lucky I was.

YEAH, I WAS IN A BIKER GANG. GARY MARSHANK, ME, JOHNNY NEWMAN, AND STEVE MARSHANK. I ALWAYS RODE A SCHWINN.

8. WITH MR. MOJO RISIN'

I was in a band named Redwood from late 1969 through early 1975. We were an eclectic, busy, gigging acoustic trio comprised of myself, Paul Gordon, and Gary David. Redwood regularly performed in Southern California clubs like the Troubadour, McCabe's, the Ash Grove, Bitter End West, and The Ice House, among many other locations. Both Paul and I were very much into the Doors and had been in an electric rock group together a few years earlier called Energy (along with my future Barnes & Barnes bandmate, Robert Haimer) that played many Doors cover tunes. Paul, Robert, and I had all seen the Doors in concert. In July of 1969, I had been in the front row of the Aquarius Theater for the afternoon show that resulted in much of their "Absolutely Live" album, where I had shot quite a few photographs of the band in action.

One day in 1970, Redwood had a meeting with a music publisher in the 9000 Sunset Blvd Building on the west side of the Sunset Strip. The 9000 building was the tallest structure on the Strip with an impressive sixteen floors. The three of us got into the elevator in the lobby and were joined by one other person for the ride up to our meeting. I don't remember exactly what floor we went to, but it was near or at the top.

Now, at this point in my life, I was sixteen and I'd been a well-known, productive, professional actor for eleven of those years and a gigging musician for a year. I had worked on over 100 television shows and several feature films alongside some of the most legendary and iconic talents in movie history, so, when I recognized the other guy who was in the elevator with us, I wasn't nervous about it, I just nodded at him and said knowingly, "Jim Morrison."

It was indeed he: "Mr. Mojo Risin'," "The Lizard King." His first response, that he muttered more to himself than to us, was, "I gotta get a haircut." Then he turned his attention to the three long-haired guys in patched blue jeans with two guitar cases and a violin case and asked, "Where are you guys goin'?" I told him we had a meeting with a music publisher. He shook his head knowingly and said, "Yeah... I need to meet with my publisher." We rode up a few more floors quietly and then we reached our destination. As Redwood debarked from the elevator, Morrison said, "Hope you get the job, gentlemen."

We didn't. But hanging with Jim Morrison for a few moments was cool.

ONE OF MY SHOTS FROM THE FRONT ROW OF
THE DOORS' 1969 AQUARIUS GIG.

9. Milestones

*T*urning thirty wasn't so bad at all. Barnes & Barnes rode our novelty hit song "Fish Heads" all the way to Saturday Night Live and several film festivals all over the world to great reviews and acclaim. Bill Siddons, who used to manage the Doors, got us a record deal on Rhino Records and our first two albums were critically well received. Then we signed to Columbia Records and made a cool project that was pretty much a flop, and now, at thirty years old, Robert and I were back on Rhino working on a new B&B album. We'd managed to cross over into the more mainstream pop music world by collaborating as songwriters with our pals Dewey Bunnell and Gerry Beckley of the band America and we had several songs on their last few albums that I'd also played on.

Tonight, while dining at Kathy Gallagher's restaurant, we ran into Dewey and Gerry and Steve Perry. Steve was on top of the world those days singing hit after hit with Journey. He said he was working on a solo album now. Anyway, Dewey and Steve came back to my Laurel Canyon house and we end up jamming and recording together all night. Steve said the Barnes & Barnes track we were currently working on, a science fiction love song I'd written called "Don't You Wanna Go To The Moon," sounded like a hit and asked if he could add a counterpoint vocal to the chorus. Hell, yeah! Man, that cat has some pipes! He and Dewey added some more vocals to it and then Steve sang on a track that Gerry and I were writing together called "Connected to You." Making music and being thirty wasn't bad at all.

<<>>

This is crazy. I've never ever performed music to an audience by myself before and I'm about to be introduced by Art Linkletter to a packed crowd at the Hollywood Bowl! I'm in my very uncomfortable *Lost in Space* canvas silver spacesuit... Ange (my TV sister Angela Cartwright) is in her spacesuit too... God, she's so pretty! We're promoting the series. I'm really nervous. I hope I don't pee. I hope I don't mess up on the guitar. I'm gonna sing and play the Kingston Trio's "Tijuana Jail" I think. I don't know. I'm only eleven. No one's said anything about my song choice. Maybe that's a bad idea? Gotta go... I'm on!

10. Meet The Ricardos

Halloween is one of my favorite holidays. I look forward to putting on a costume and trick or treating all over my Beverlywood neighborhood with my friends and getting a ton of candy. What nine-year-old doesn't like that? It's the summer of 1963. The world feels pretty good right now. President Kennedy and his family are very popular, and I've been super busy working on a lot of different TV shows and films lately. Anyway, I've been shooting this episode of a circus show all week and have been working with Lucille Ball. She's tall. And she's the executive producer of this series. It's called *The Greatest Show on Earth* and Jack Palance is the star. But this episode, "Lady in Limbo," is all about me and Lucy.

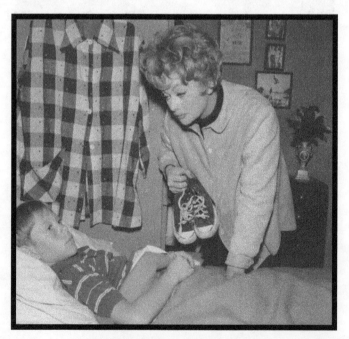

I think she's really cool because today, Thursday, it's Halloween and she wrapped the whole crew out early because she says she knows I'd like to go trick or treating with my friends, and her kids, Desi and Lucie, would like to go out too. So… I guess you can say, I love Lucy!

I worked with Desi Arnaz too. Desilu Studios produced a pilot for a half-hour proposed CBS series starring Pat Crowley, me, Mary Jane Croft, and Barry Livingston. Pat played my mother, a widow, who wrote and illustrated children's books and the unique pitch for the project was that while Barry and I were goofing around like little kids do, Pat would find inspiration from us, and we'd shift from live-action to some animation. It was a fun project that didn't sell. Barry and I had a good time acting together and have remained friends. In fact, we played a few musical gigs together in 2019.

What I clearly recall about Desi was his boisterous laugh. He was on the stage watching us film a bit but you can really hear him laughing in the mix of the soundtrack that accompanied the final cut. *The Two of Us* was shot at Desilu Studios in Culver City back in 1962, but it remained in limbo until it was finally aired as a special in 1966.

The Two of Us and *My Uncle Elroy* were the two pilots I was attached to that didn't sell before *Lost in Space* came along. I enjoyed working on both of those half-hour sitcom type projects, but things work out (or don't work out) for a reason I suppose. Who knows? If either *The Two of Us* or *My Uncle Elroy* had been picked up and become hits, then I most likely wouldn't have been free to play Will Robinson in *Lost in Space*. And let's just say, it's a real good thing that I indeed played Will.

11. KISMET

*I*sn't it interesting how one meeting, one day's work, can lead to lifelong relationships? After filming wrapped up on *Bless the Beasts & Children* in September of 1970, the film needed to be edited and scored and then placed on Columbia Pictures' release schedule.

Producer, director, and all-around good human Stanley Kramer wisely hired the great Stan Freberg to write and direct a television commercial promo campaign for the upcoming film. Stan created a satirical talk-show-type interview, which insinuated a debate about the film between an NRA spokesman and me. It worked well.

We filmed the promos on the Columbia lot on Gower Avenue in Hollywood in July of 1971. School was out and Scott Ehrlich, who had travelled with me as my guardian for the making of *Bless the Beasts* and who had acted in a supporting role in the film, accompanied me for the promo shoot. Stan Freberg had brought his teenage daughter, Donna, and her friend Gina to the set with him. They were beautiful and charming and fun young ladies. I was seventeen and had just been dumped by Angela. Scott was eighteen and single. We chatted with the gals and suggested the four of us get together and have some summer fun. Gina and I had a quick and solid attraction to each other. She gave me her address and we made a plan to have a double date and see each other soon. Scott and I were familiar with Stan Freberg's work, especially his satirical novelty records such as "John & Marsha" and the *Stan Freberg Presents the United States of America, Volume One: The Early Years* album. We also knew that Gina and Donna both lived in Beverly

Hills, a few miles north from us lower Cheviot Hills dwellers. But when we arrived at the address Gina gave me, we were more than a little surprised and quite impressed. Scott and I both lived in nice houses on Forrester Drive in a choice neighborhood. But Gina lived in a mansion. I mean a serious mansion on Mountain Drive just above Sunset Blvd. As soon as we pulled into the driveway, we were stopped by an armed security guard. We identified ourselves and after a quick confirmation, Mike, the security guard, told to continue up the long driveway and to enter the house via the side kitchen door, which was a few yards from where several seriously impressive cars were parked. We could hear a tennis game being played in the large backyard. Scott and I entered the house and were greeted by a beautiful ageless woman with a golden tan and golden hair to match it. She introduced herself as Jeannie, Gina's mom. With a warm smile she told us Gina and Donna were upstairs in Gina's room and they were expecting us. She pointed to the stairway. As we headed up the stairs, we noticed a familiar-looking man sitting alone having a drink at the bar in the den next to an impressive aquarium. It was Dean Martin.

Gina was Dean's youngest daughter. Who knew? Not me or Scott, that's for sure. The other epiphany we quickly learned was that despite her physical attributes, Gina was a few months shy of turning sixteen and Donna had only turned sixteen herself a week earlier. Something told me to tread very lightly.

Within a very short time however, Gina and I were going steady. She had the greatest laugh I've ever heard in my life, and she was smart, quite mature for her age, and very affectionate. To tell the truth, Gina was actually too serious and aggressive for me. I was reeling from the very recent loss of Angela, and Gina was totally ready for a major commitment that I just couldn't make. We spent six months together as a couple, enjoying each other's company very much, but it never progressed to what Gina wanted it to.

Donna, it turned out, already had a boyfriend. His name was Miguel Ferrer, and he was sixteen. Miguel's father was the famed and respected actor Jose Ferrer, and his mother was the amazingly talented singer and actress, Rosemary Clooney. Miguel too lived in his mother's mansion, a short distance from Gina's, but Rosemary's mansion on Roxbury Drive needed a lot of maintenance. It had fallen on hard times. Miguel's parents were divorced, like Gina's, and his father lived outside of California and he was very rarely around. Even though Dean and Jeannie Martin were divorced, Dean was often hanging around the house on Mountain Drive.

I became close friends with Miguel and his siblings, Maria, Gabriel, Monsita, and Rafi, and also with Rosemary. Eventually, Rosemary would record three of my songs, "Roses in the Garden," that I co-wrote with Paul, "Still on the Road," that became the title track of one of Rosie's albums, and "It's a Hard Business," that I wrote with Robert and that became a historic duet between Rosemary and Wild Man Fischer. I truly loved Rosie. She was a strong-willed woman who had gone through a lot in a short time. Her star had shined as bright as any, and then it had waned. Both Miguel and Rosemary had been at the Ambassador Hotel June 5, 1968, the night Robert Kennedy was assassinated. That heinous tragedy sent Rosemary into a deep depression, and it took her a few years to come out of it. Rosie worked hard to make a successful comeback. She played many gigs that were beneath a star of her status and ability, but she never complained about doing them. She continued to tour and gig, and she was out on the road for several months every year. Eventually, she was headlining at places like the London Palladium again and her recording career reached critical and commercial success as her voice matured. Rosemary's talent as a singer was stunning.

In what became an annual ritual, I spent at least twenty Christmas Eves at Rosemary's house drinking the finest champagne, eating the finest caviar, and gathering around the Steinway piano in her living room for sing-a-longs. Rosie's piano had previously been owned by George Gershwin. She welcomed my mother after my father passed away. She loved my wife Eileen and she absolutely adored our children, Seth and Liliana. Those were very special times, and to this day, I miss Rosie.

RECORDING WITH
ROSEMARY.

ROSEMARY IN "HER CHAIR" WITH LILIANA IN 1998,

<<>>

Donna Freberg also lived in a mansion a few houses north of Sunset on Beverly Drive. These new friends grew up only a couple of miles from me and Scott and Paul and Robert, but they lived in a totally different world. I soon found myself acclimated to it. Donna's house was often filled with very late-night gatherings. Stan Freberg was an eccentric man and he welcomed young people all around him at nocturnal hours. We gathered there to play games like The Dictionary Game and charades. We skinny-dipped in their pool late at night. Donna's younger brother, Donavan, didn't have a name until he was five years old. He was simply "Baby." Stan used to take Baby out on the front lawn to play with flashlights after midnight. When Baby was just a toddler, Stan would usher him into the living room where a group of us teenagers were gathered, and Stan would say something like, "Baby, go point to the Frank Lloyd Wright book." And Baby of course would. It was a curious and very loving house. Stan's wife, Donna, was almost always upstairs chain-smoking in her bedroom. She had health issues and although she was very nice to me and all the regulars that invaded her home in the middle of the night, I never really got to know her well. After living room games, a group of us would dash off in a handful of cars around two in the morning to eat at Ollie Hammond's on La Cienega at the edge of Beverly Hills and then we'd return back to Stan's or Rosemary's for more late-night goofing around. We often crashed at Rosie's house in one or more of its many bedrooms.

Redwood continued to gig and record, and all of my new friends came to our performances. Paul became close with Donna. She and Gina were heading off for a two-week holiday in Europe and they literally demanded that Paul and I write a song for them and have it rehearsed and ready to perform by the time they returned. We did as we were told.

<<>>

As 1971 became 1972, Gina was expecting more from me than I could give her. So, we stopped dating and she very quickly moved on to another boyfriend, a younger guy. His name was Shaun Cassidy. Even at fourteen, Shaun carried himself with a swagger and confidence that was impressive. He was very much into "glam rock" and was already writing some interesting songs and singing them to anyone who he could get to listen to him. It was impossible not to like Shaun even though he was now Gina's new boy toy. We became good friends. Shaun lived in Beverly Hills too, in a nice house that wasn't a mansion. He lived there with his two younger brothers, Patrick and Ryan, and his father, actor Jack Cassidy, and his mother...my first true love: Shirley Jones. It was so much fun reconnecting with Shirley. I would constantly remind her how she stole my heart back in 1962 when we filmed *A Ticklish Affair*. Now, ten years later, Shirley was starring in a hit television series opposite Shaun's half-brother, David. The show was *The Partridge Family*.

Although I very much enjoyed being around Shirley, Shaun's house was not a place where the teenagers chose to hang out very often in those days. Shaun's father was an extremely volatile man. I was never comfortable around Jack Cassidy. One minute he'd smile at you like he was thrilled to be in your company and the next he'd combust with anger that felt like it could become violent at any moment. Shirley and Jack divorced in 1975. I'm still friends with Shirley and she called me on the phone twice quite recently to chat.

Shaun's half-brother David had lived with his mother, Evelyn Ward, in Cheviot Hills a few blocks away from me for several years. A couple years older than me, I knew David peripherally. We all hung out at El Rancho Billiards, a pool hall on Pico Boulevard, walking distance from our homes. I'd seen David act on a few episodic television shows like *Marcus Welby* and *Bonanza* and I was impressed by him. In 1970, when I first met with Stanley Kramer for *Bless the Beasts & Children*, I recommended to him that David might make a fine Cotton, the main co-star of the film. But David was committed to *The Partridge Family* by then. Imagine how different his life might have been had he not played Keith Partridge but played Cotton in *Bless the Beasts & Children* instead!

Although we lived in the upper-middle class and safe neighborhood of Cheviot Hills, David was always a bit of a bad boy. Pre-*Partridge Family*, he ran with some pretty tough guys and there was no secret that they had drugs. Uppers and downers. David and I had our ups and downs that's for sure. He sang harmony on a couple of songs Paul and I wrote that the band recorded at Record Plant recording studios. I'll say this: David had a mighty falsetto.

David Cassidy was his own worst enemy. For reasons I can't explain, he just couldn't seem to enjoy reality no matter how much success he achieved. For a while, he was one of the biggest stars on the planet, but in a weird way, David never seemed to accept the fact that he was a teen idol. He acted like he was a peer of John Lennon's or Elton John's. He wasn't. Shaun, who from the beginning wrote many songs on his own hit albums and had more control over his artistic path than his half-brother David did, always understood what he called, "the Joke." Shaun and David both worked insanely hard and what they did wasn't easy by any means. But Shaun saw it for what it was and right from the start, he planned a future path. David never seemed to be able to. He had a biting acerbic wit, but he used it to serve his own ego often.

I remember sitting poolside at Shaun's home one 4th of July enjoying the summer warmth and watching kids frolicking in the pool. My son Seth was in the living room playing chess with David's son, Beau. It was a very nice gathering. Shaun enjoys being the host to family get-togethers. David and I were chatting about Brian Wilson when he turned to me with that teasing smile that he and his father both had, and said "Oh… YOU don't own a piece of *Lost in Space*, do you, Mumy? You know, I, of course, own a piece of *The*

Partridge Family." I just grinned at him and said, "I'd rather be Will Robinson than Keith Partridge any day, David."

I'm no angel. I've done my share of drugs and partying. I did drugs with David. But David was a totally different story. He did hard drugs, and he did them for a long time. Thankfully, I never got too deeply into that stuff, and I never fell into any trouble with the law.

In the mid-1970s, David was making some pretty good albums and playing some small but cool gigs. I went to his run of shows at the Troubadour and was supportive. He asked my good friend Gerry Beckley to produce an album for him and Gerry found a month where he was free of his responsibilities to America, and accepted the offer to produce. Jay Gruska, who was in Paul's and my band at the time, joined them to play keyboards and sing harmony vocals on the album. Jay had recently completed a few tours as a member of Three Dog Night. He had replaced Danny Hutton. Danny eventually returned to that iconic hit-making band. The guys flew to Colorado to the Caribou Ranch studio to record the album. David had some half-finished songs that he'd written and Gerry helped him finish them. Gerry Beckley is the best pop song bridge writer I've ever known. He can create a great middle eight in five minutes. Jay had brought a cassette tape of a new song I had written with him and David Jolliffe called "You Never Saw Me Coming." David dug it and changed the title to "I Never Saw You Coming" and recorded it.

A month or so later, David called me. He told me he'd recorded the song. "Great. I can't wait to hear it." He told me he'd changed the title. "Cool." Then he told me "I need artistic credibility, Bill. With four songwriters listed on the track, I'll lose that. So, although you and Jolliffe will keep half the publishing, and your names will be on the copyright, the song will be credited to only Jay and me." I said, "That's definitely not okay with me, David. I'm glad you cut it, but that's not cool." I then added, "If you want artistic credibility, write your own songs." Didn't matter. The album design and packaging were complete. He had basically phoned to tell me I was being screwed. I never received credit for the song, and I never received a penny in royalties from it. Showbiz.

David and I continued to hang out though. He could be fun and charming. My wife Eileen always liked being in his company. We were often at Shaun's family events together and I let the song credit thing go, but I can't say I truly ever forgave him for that slight.

In the mid-1990s when I was co-starring on *Babylon 5*, I was booked for a weekend at an autograph show called "The Hollywood Show" that was held at the Marriott hotel in Burbank. Lots of major stars were appearing at autograph shows and the promoter who ran the show told me he was close to booking David for the weekend. He knew that I was friends with David and had known him for a long time and he also had heard that David could be "difficult." He asked me if I would sit next to him and help "wrangle" him for the show. I said, "sure." I knew David hadn't done these autograph shows before and he'd certainly be a big draw. Being parked next to him could only bring me more patrons, and he and I always had plenty to talk about and people in common, and maybe we'd have a few laughs.

As soon as David arrived, with a couple of stolid bodyguards, he was on edge. He was jumpy and obviously uncomfortable. He said he wouldn't speak to the fans directly. He would sit sandwiched between his bodyguards and one of them would hand him a photo that he would autograph. Period. His biggest mandate was he was refusing to sign any memorabilia that his fans presented him to autograph. Well, naturally, this upset the promoter. There was already an impressive line waiting for David and they all held items they wanted him to sign. Posters, albums, lunchboxes, magazines, etc.

I was asked to try and talk some sense into him. So, I took David into the green room and we spoke privately. "David, what are you doing? Why are you being so demanding and stubborn?" "Mumy, I know that if I sign a lunchbox or any of that shit, it's gonna be resold on Ebay for more money! I won't be ripped off!" I said, "David, what the hell do you care if one out of 100 fans makes a few extra bucks off your autograph? You're getting paid handsomely to sit there right now and make people happy. They're queued up there waiting for you. David... they LOVE you!" He wouldn't change his mind. He looked me straight in the eye and said something that has reverberated in my head ever since. "Well, they're gonna HATE me!" With that, he returned to the table and sat there and signed his name on the photos he had brought... but only for a few minutes and then he said he had a sore throat and left. I thought it was a very sad scene. David... always his own worst enemy.

David Cassidy was a complicated and talented man, and his passing was very sorrowful. I hope he's found peace.

AT DODGER STADIUM PLAYING A CELEBRITY GAME FOR CHARITY.
BACK: NORM JACOBOVITZ, DAVID JOLLIFFE, JERRY HAUSER, DAVID CASSIDY, RANDY FOOTE, ME. FRONT: TONI TENNILLE, PETER TORK, KAY LENZ, MARK HUDSON.

12. Carrie On

I wasn't unaware of the fact that most of my friends in Beverly Hills had famous celebrity parents. They lived life in the fast lane. I could never compete with any of them when it came to lifestyles and money, but I often reminded myself that whatever I had, I'd earned for myself by working hard from the age of five. That mindset kept me from overspending and attempting to be something I wasn't.

Debbie Reynolds lived a couple blocks away from Shaun and Shirley, and her daughter Carrie Fisher had recently entered the acting world and was climbing the ladder of fame after making an impressive film debut in Warren Beatty's *Shampoo*. Carrie was one of the wittiest, quickest, funniest, street-smart people I ever met.

In early 1977, she had returned from filming *Star Wars*, but it hadn't been released yet. Carrie's brother Todd had recently purchased a 24-track remote recording truck, and to work out the bugs in it, he invited Paul and me to record several new songs we were writing. Todd is an adventurous, easygoing, smart, very nice guy and Paul and I were more than happy to help him figure out and master the ins and outs of his new mobile recording studio, while he in turn generously supplied us with fresh demos of our new songs.

Todd's mobile studio was parked in Debbie Reynolds' driveway for months. Paul and I brought Jay, Jolliffe, Gerry Beckley, Steve Lukather, Mike Porcaro, Willie Leacox, and several other real good musicians to the house to record. Todd would engineer inside the truck and the players would be playing in the living room. Drums, piano, acoustic guitars, etc. were all laid down from inside of the house. Instruments that could be recorded directly like bass and Moog synthesizer and some electric guitar parts were recorded with the musicians playing inside the truck.

Debbie Reynolds herself sang background vocals on a song of Paul's. She came home one night pretty late to find a bunch of young musicians hanging around inside and outside her house while Todd was setting up a vocal microphone in her dining room. Debbie heard us searching for harmony parts and she joined in. She created an "oooh ooooh" type of line, and we all followed her lead and sang along with her. She was toasty and it was a blast and an honor to have the original "Tammy" become a part of our musical history.

Meanwhile, twenty-one-year-old Carrie was never shy when it came to imbibing in a buzz in those days. I was usually up for smoking some weed and on this occasion, she and I headed outside into the night to smoke a joint she produced. Only this joint wasn't a regular joint. It had been dipped in something that made it quite different and slightly psychedelic. Carrie and I started making out like crazy. That was all we did, just made out, but years later it struck me and Carrie both as hilarious and somewhat ironic that Will Robinson and Princess Leia had their sexy moment together. She was a great kisser. Carrie is missed.

13. Getting Lost in Space

Jonathan Harris was beyond happy and grateful. Jonathan had spent decades as a journeyman actor working in supporting roles on television, film, and a huge amount of theater. Landing the part of Dr. Smith on *Lost in Space* and becoming the star of the series was his greatest professional experience and he relished it and he took it very seriously, but always with a twinkle in his eye and a sincere smile. I'm not sure why Jonathan was given freedom to re-write Smith's dialogue, but he certainly did. What the audience heard from Smith on television was quite different from how the first-draft scripts read. Jonathan's love of language and his sense of playing the character over-the-top created an iconic performance of a complicated character that audiences all over the world loved to hate.

There were rituals on our series and Jonathan initiated them. Every day at four in the afternoon, Jonathan handed out Tootsie Roll lollipops to the entire crew and cast. A little sugar bump to keep everyone's energy up and a bit of fun to look forward to. As the show progressed, it quickly focused on three characters: Smith, the Robot, and Will Robinson. That's just the way it was, and I know that one of the reasons that became the dominant trio was because Jonathan, Bobby May inside the Robot, and I were "one-takers." We got those scenes done very quickly and joyfully and that made it easy for the crew and the directors to stay on schedule.

I had to get my schooling done in increments of twenty minutes minimum at a time. Sometimes that was difficult. Our second

Jonathan came up with the "using me as a shield" thing. We did it dozens of times. It aways was funny, even when it was scary. What a team we made. I miss him every day.

The emotional father and son scenes I shared with Guy were scarce compared to the amount of time I worked alongside Jonathan, but I cherished my work with Guy. He was a Hero to me.

assistant director, Doug Morrison, would be waiting right outside the door of the school trailer with a stopwatch counting down the seconds. As soon as twenty minutes went into the books, Doug would pull me out of the school trailer and escort me onto the set and into Jonathan's dressing room where Jonathan would spend five minutes with me discussing the tone of the scene we were about to shoot, and most importantly, tell me what my "new" cues were! Of course, I'd memorized the dialogue that was written in the script, and of course, Jonathan would change his every night at home and so, we'd take a quick minute or three to catch up on what he was going to say. Then we'd comb our hair and the makeup crew would powder our faces and the camera would roll and we'd get it done. Jonathan loved me and I loved him.

Guy Williams had been one of my main two inspirations to go into acting when I was only four years old, watching his dynamic performances as Zorro on our black-and-white television set. I was thrilled to be working alongside Guy on *Lost in Space*. He didn't disappoint. He was very impressive, pleasant, smart, worldly, patient, and he taught me how to fence. Having Zorro in a bright colored velour spacesuit teaching me swordsmanship is something I'll never forget and always cherish. He and June Lockhart were very close, and they spent most all of their time together. When June wasn't with Guy in one of their trailers, she was with me and Angela and she was engaging us in projects to expand our young minds. June loved to play Scrabble and Password and Boggle, games that made you think. She was extremely patient with us and really improved our vocabularies. Scrabble was a game played often on our sets. Marta Kristen would pout and get cranky with me because she would play words that I would often challenge. But don't blame me. They weren't real words.

During our years working together, Marta seemed very happy to have a studio "family." She had been orphaned as a baby and was in

JUNE WAS FANTASTIC TO
WORK WITH. SHE KEPT US
ALL TOGETHER.
A BRILLIANT LADY.

THIS IS WHAT WE DID IN-
BETWEEN TAKES TO RELAX
ON STAGE. OR NOT.

SWEET, BEAUTIFUL, AND A
LITTLE SAD, MARTA
EXPANDED MY AWARENESS
OF POPULAR MUSIC IN A
MAJOR WAY. I'LL ALWAYS
APPRECIATE THAT.

a stressful marriage then. Marta was only twenty when *Lost in Space* started. She and I used to sit and sing songs together. I'd play guitar and we'd harmonize. She often confessed to me that her world at home with her husband, Terry, was far from pleasant. By the time I was thirteen, she'd let me sneak a drag or two off her Tareyton cigarette and then we'd sing Bob Dylan songs.

June Lockhart was really smart. She read constantly. She was a news junkie and had more energy than just about anyone I've ever known. June enjoyed the theater and opera and classical music, but she enjoyed rock & roll just as much, if not more. She once threw a party at her house and hired the Allman Brothers band (at the time they were called The Hour Glass) to play. June then brought Ange and me to the Whisky A Go Go to see them play a full gig along with the Nitty Gritty Dirt Band who The Hour Glass opened for that weekend night in 1967. Ange and I hung in between sets in the Whisky dressing room, and I talked guitars with the great Duane Allman that evening. June also got Ange and me tickets to see Donovan at the Hollywood Bowl and another time to see Simon and Garfunkel, also at the Bowl. Years later, at a personal appearance we made collectively, June told me she carried a photograph of David Bowie with her constantly because she was so enamored with him. I had worked on a film starring Rick Springfield, *Hard to Hold*, and Tony Sales worked alongside me on that project. June knew that Tony had been an integral part of Bowie's "Tin Machine" project and wanted to know all about him because of his proximity to Bowie. June is a fascinating woman.

Mark Goddard was only twenty-nine years old when cast as Major Don West in *Lost in Space*, and he is a one of a kind. I love Mark and he and I bonded right away while filming the pilot. Mark was conflicted during the *LIS* years. He'd done a lot of good work including co-starring in three network series before heading into

I COULD NEVER GET ENOUGH OF BEING WITH MARK. HE WAS GOOFIER THAN ME! BESIDES BEING WILD, MARK IS A TRULY GIFTED ACTOR.

SHE WAS ALWAYS TOUCHING ME. DROVE ME CRAZY RIGHT FROM THE START.

space: the western *Johnny Ringo*, the crime drama *The Detectives,* and a short-lived sitcom *Many Happy Returns*. Mark took acting seriously and sometimes felt like he'd made a mistake signing on to *Lost in Space*, especially when it turned so campy. I just found Mark's energy to be contagious and his antics cracked me up. I often went to lunch with him, off the lot, in his little blue Fiat convertible. We'd go to a nearby dark restaurant called Duke's. In the turbulent, constantly changing decade of the 1960s, it wasn't at all unusual for actors to have a cocktail or two at lunch. Mark enjoyed his martinis. His performances before martinis and after martinis were always top notch. Maybe the booze made Major West a little crankier when it came to dealing with the troubles Dr. Smith created. One day, when having lunch at Duke's, Mark purchased a large canvas sack that was filled with peanuts in the shell. Returning to Stage 11, Mark waited until 4 p.m. when Jonathan handed out his daily Tootsie Roll treats and then… Mark brazenly climbed up the ladder on the side of the stage, crossed over to the catwalk high above where the big lights were always positioned and shouted, "Yeah! I got treats for you, too! I got some treats all right!" And… he proceeded to pelt the entire crew and set with peanuts. They rained down from the rafters as he pitched them and cackled like a junior high school kid who was about to get suspended. It was hilarious. And Mark is nuts.

Angela used to watch it all with me and give me mischievous looks. She wanted to be a part of the trouble making but she was reserved. Her mother, Margaret, who had been a nurse in London during World War II, was a quiet but strict woman. Ange wasn't about to get into trouble when her mother was around. But when Margaret wasn't around, that was a different situation. Ange can be quite bold and up for a challenge. I was hooked on her from the day I met her and I went out of my way to make her laugh and to create situations for her and I that no one else could relate to, like listening to music in my dressing room and exploring the secrets of the studio lot together. She knew all too well the power she wielded over me, but I don't know if she'd admit that.

«<>»

One of my favorite rituals during my *Lost in Space* years came every night when we wrapped. I was usually dismissed at 6 or 6:30 in the evening. I'd dash into my small dressing room trailer outside the stage and get out of my velour wardrobe and put on my regular civilian clothes and then my mom would toss me the key to her car. In those days she drove a gorgeous 1962 Jaguar Mark II. It was a metallic dark brown with sumptuous saddle leather interior and gorgeous burl wood around the dash and the doors. What a boss ride that was. And every night I'd get behind the wheel by myself and drive that Jag all around the Fox lot for about ten minutes. I'd cruise over the bridge that connected the main lot to the back lot while six lanes of rush-hour traffic made their way home on Olympic Boulevard beneath me. The guys at the machine shops on the back lot would wave at me as I circled around the buildings and went back over the bridge and eventually returned to Stage 6 or Stage 11 where my mother was waiting for me. She never let me drive off the lot, but I really enjoyed that nightly ceremonial drive.

I've had a lot of cool cars in my life. Hey, I'm a California kid who grew up listening to Jan & Dean and the Beach Boys, and cars have been a big part of my consciousness. And because of that Mark II of my mom's, I've owned eight Jags. I still keep a nice vintage one in the garage for the occasional cruise. Sadly, it's not around the Fox lot anymore.

"Captain Panther & Fox" heading off the lot into trouble.

My Mom's 1959 Cadillac. They don't make 'em like that anymore!

14. Oh The Pain

A little over four hours! What have I gotten myself into this time? The producer said I'd be in the makeup chair for "about an hour." This is tough. But, I know Eileen was right. I haven't been working much as an actor lately and I've always liked science fiction shows. We're parents now and I'm turning forty in a few months. Sometimes you just gotta cowboy up and do what you gotta do. Who knows? This *Babylon 5* series could be cancelled after six episodes, or it could go for five seasons. Man, in this makeup as Lennier… I look like an eggplant. Goo Goo G'Joob.

LENNIER AND A PUMPKIN PEZ… I SEE THE SIMILARITIES.

《》

*I*n 1998, I was gifted with the opportunity to not only return to the "Will Robinson" character along with Jonathan Harris as "Dr Smith" and Bobby May (and Dick Tufeld) as "Robot," but thanks to producer Kevin Burns, I got to write the scene that reunited the characters and closed the *Lost in Space Forever* TV special which was hosted by John Larroquette. It was a truly great experience that I cherish. Jonathan and Bobby were amazing and the chemistry between the three of us just clicked like no time had passed since we filmed the series, but of course in reality thirty years had passed. Eileen, Seth, and Liliana came to the studio that day, and just like in the old days, Jonathan handed out Tootsie Roll pops to everyone. He really loved my wife and kids and treated them like they were family. Jonathan, Bobby, Dick, and Kevin are greatly missed.

LILIANA, WITH A TOOTSIE POP JONATHAN GAVE HER,
ME, SETH, AND THE GREAT "HIMSELF!"
WILL ROBINSON AND DR. SMITH TOGETHER AGAIN AT LAST!

15. LEGENDS

Working with John Stewart these past few months has been so great! So far, 1970 couldn't be better. Redwood's opened for John at a bunch of gigs and every audience seems to really dig us. It feels like only yesterday when John was in the Kingston Trio, who I totally idolized, and they were playing that gig at Melodyland and he recognized me in the audience and announced that I was there and Scott and I got to go backstage and meet John, Nick, and Bob and have 7-Ups with them. That was so cool. Then John and his girlfriend Buffy came to visit me on the *Lost in Space* set. That was nice too.

But THIS is much cooler. I'm at Crystal Sound Recording Studio in Hollywood playing cowbell on John's brand-new song "Big Joe" for his brand-new album and I'm sitting a few inches away from James Taylor. The basic track is being cut live and James and I just smoked a joint together and I got to play his guitar, an iconic sounding Gibson J-50. The incredible Carole King is a few feet away and she's been playing piano on several tracks. Peter Asher's producing and we're in this cool studio and I'm gonna sing and play on a few other tracks with John and this is exactly what I want to be doing.

Henry Diltz, the nicest guy in the world, is constantly taking photographs during the sessions. Angela is with me. Redwood has contributed background vocals and John's songs are real good.

Everyone's grooving and getting along so nicely. We stopped for an hour to listen to Paul McCartney's first solo album over the big studio monitors. Everybody, especially John, was blown away by it.

James Taylor is really nice and man, can he play guitar. I'm happy.

JAMMING WITH JOHN STEWART IN MALIBU, 1972.
I STILL PLAY THAT MARTIN D-28 ALL THE TIME.

≪≫

Jimmy Stewart is the single greatest guy I've ever worked with. We play catch in between filming all the time. He's super nice to everyone on the crew and in the cast and he's a great actor. I really like all our scenes together. He listens so well. I took cello lessons at the 20th Century Fox lot for a few weeks before we started filming so I could look authentic playing in the music scenes. We're shooting on the lot, up in Sausalito, at the UCLA campus, and in France for the scenes with Brigitte Bardot. Wow, is she gorgeous. I'm not gonna deny it. I've peeked down her blouse more than once. Thank you, *Dear Brigitte*.

Many years after we filmed *Dear Brigitte*, in an interview with *TV Guide*, Jimmy Stewart was quoted as saying, "Billy Mumy was the only child actor I ever worked with who was worth a damn." Needless to say, I was very flattered.

I WORKED PRETTY HARD LEARNING CELLO FOR DEAR BRIGITTE. GOOD THING ERASMUS WAS TONE DEAF!

<<>>

Showbiz is a trip. I used to watch Tiny Tim back in the 1960s and now here I am, many years later in 1990, chatting with him and Robert as we are about to go onstage to play a gig for a television special about Dr. Demento. In normal conversation, Tiny doesn't sound anything like I thought he'd sound like. He sure knows a lot about great old music and he's a really fine ukulele player. Nice guy. "Fish Heads" continues to bring pleasant surprises. Yeah.

PRE-GIG BACKSTAGE PHOTO WITH BARNES + BARNES AND TINY TIM.

16. So You Wanna Be a Rock & Roll Star

A lot of child actors and children of celebrities I knew attended private schools. I was never a private school kinda guy. When *Lost in Space* wrapped up, I went back to public school. I hadn't been a part of regular school for four years and here I was, a pretty high-profile celebrity, marching into the madness of being a senior in the ninth grade in Palms Junior High. I think any fourteen-year-old, boy or girl, has it hard because it's such a limbo age, transitioning from childhood to adulthood. But I honestly believe it was harder being me then.

Sure, there were plenty of kids that I knew in the school, plenty that I'd been in and out of Canfield Grammar School with years ago, but there were countless more that approached and confused me constantly. Girls were flirting with me. Guys wanted to kick my ass. People wanted to be my friend for the wrong reason. I walked a thin line between being cool and keeping my head down and being quiet, which is not my nature. I never thought of myself as being different or more special than any of my other friends and my real friends never acted like I was in any way special or different. I rode my purple Schwinn Sting Ray Deluxe to Palms the same way I'd ridden it to 20th Century Fox when I was going to school on the lot.

By the time I was in Palms amongst "regular" kids in the real world again, I was a certified scuba diver and a very strong body surfer. I was in legit good shape. During P.E. I ran fast and I worked out pretty hard. But there were always guys who are faster and stronger, and I took some bullying on the gym field. I didn't want to be a fighter by any means, but I also didn't want to be a wimp. Finding a balance was tough.

Until I formed a band.

ENERGY, THE FIRST VERSION. ROBERT HAIMER ON ORGAN, ME ON MY RICKENBACKER (STILL HAVE IT), STEVE KESSLER ON DRUMS, AND GLENN HIME ON MOSRITE 12-STRING. TAKEN IN MY BACKYARD ON FORRESTER DRIVE. 1968.

Thank God for rock & roll. At fourteen I'd been playing guitar for four years and was still taking weekly lessons to improve. I'd written at least a dozen songs that weren't embarrassing (at least I felt they weren't!) and my parents had just bought me my first electric guitar and amp. I still have the 1968 Rickenbacker 365 six-string in Fireglow finish and it still sounds boss. I wish I still had that Standell Studio Model amp with four 10-inch speakers, reverb, and tremolo but alas, that got loaned to a friend and disappeared many, many years ago into the Cornfield (an oft-used reference from my classic episode of *The Twilight Zone* "It's a Good Life").

Robert Haimer worshipped the Doors, and he got a Farfisa organ and a Gibson amp. Glenn Hime had a metallic blue Mosrite Ventures model guitar and borrowed someone's crappy amp and Steve Kessler had a nice set of Rogers drums finished in a psychedelic blue swirl. We rehearsed at Robert's downstairs room in his folks' house on Monte Mar Drive opposite the Rancho Park Golf Course. We named the band "Energy." We played songs by the Byrds, the Doors, Buffalo Springfield, Jefferson Airplane, the Rolling Stones, and some originals I wrote, and Robert and I wrote together. "Wicked Woman" and "Pen and Paper Man" were two of the earliest originals. Energy played a few school gigs out on the quad at Palms, and we played a couple of parties and were even hired and paid to play at the prestigious Standard Club on Motor Avenue for some event I can't recall.

When the kids at school heard Energy playing live everything improved for me. I suddenly stopped being "that kid from *Lost in Space*" and became "Mumy in the band with the Rickenbacker." Now the girls were flirting with me for a reason I could relate to. The teen magazines, *Tiger Beat* and *Fave,* wrote articles about Energy and published photos of the band. Soon *16* and *16 Spec* and *Outasight!* magazines were writing about us as well.

It felt great. But this first version of the band didn't feel great after a couple of months.

Drummer Steve Kessler was a real hothead, and he started a lot of arguments and was the kind of guy who pushed you physically if he felt like it. We fired Kessler and chose Ronny Solomon to take his place. Ronny lived a few blocks up on my street, Forrester Drive, in Cheviot Hills. He was a major jazz fan, and he was actually a good drummer at fourteen. Ronny played interesting parts that served the songs well and he also hit the drums hard when we'd asked him to.

Glenn is still a good friend of mine. He's a very successful doctor now and he has a great guitar collection but back then he had a pretty tough time at home, and he didn't really have the time to practice and improve. Enter Paul Gordon.

Everything changed. Paul had a band of his own at the time called Midnight Creation and they were really good. They were much better than Energy on our best day. Paul and I became good friends quickly and we started playing guitars together and writing songs together. Paul, a wiry, small, but quick and strong kid, came to my aid one day during lunch at school and he punched some asshole in the nose who wouldn't stop hassling me. Within a few hours of that, Paul closed up Midnight Creation and became the co-leader of Energy with me.

Robert was "The Haim," Paul was "The Gord," and I was "The Moom." Thus began musical partnerships that have continued to this day.

Energy got better very quickly. Paul and I wrote song after song and Robert wrote with both of us as well. Lead vocals were pretty much evenly distributed between Paul and me. Robert sang some harmony parts. Robert's a great singer but he was shy in those days and Paul and I were definitely not. Paul and I found we harmonized together well, and our voices blended nicely (although they were changing as we matured).

The new and improved lineup of Energy played a few shows in the Palms auditorium that really rocked hard. We played several bar mitzvahs and parties at school and around the neighborhood for a few bucks here and there.

Energy continued to practice in Robert's basement room until one day Paul and I decided we had a pretty decent amount of original songs and both of us were favoring a more acoustic sound.

ENERGY THE FINAL
VERSION... WHEN WE WERE
PRETTY GOOD. RONNY
SOLOMAN, PAUL GORDON
(WITH MY RICKENBACKER),
ROBERT HAIMER, AND ME
WITH MY FENDER PRECISION
BASS THAT I STILL USE
CONSTANTLY.
MY DAD TOOK THIS PHOTO IN
FRONT OF ROBERT'S HOUSE.

Energy disbanded and Paul and I became a duo.

We called ourselves Gully. Within a few months time, with the surprising support and assistance from fellow Irwin Allen TV series child actor, Stefan Arngrim (who had co-starred in *Land of the Giants*, and gone to school with Angela and me on the Fox lot with the beloved Frances Klamt as our teacher), Gully found themselves in a real recording studio. We cut five original songs in that one session produced by Stefan. Paul played guitar and organ. I played guitar, bass, piano, and harmonica. Ronny Solomon returned and played drums. Eddie Eckstein Jr., supplied by Stefan, played bass on one track. Angela and Scott Ehrlich added some background vocals. The songs we laid down that night in 1969 onto a 4-track Studer tape recorder were "How You're Gonna Leave Me When I'm Down," "The Lonesome Dealer," "Yes, You In The Blue," "Denver Thing," and "The H Bomb Song."

That tape, along with some very poorly recorded Energy rehearsals, still exists but has never been released.

AT SCHOOL ON THE FOX LOT:
HOWARD RICE (ROOM 222),
ME, ANGE, STEFAN ARNGRIM,
AND MRS. KLAMT.

A year after leaving Energy for a more acoustic path with Paul as my partner, I brought my red Rickenbacker over to Robert's one night and the two of us jammed, Robert on his Farfisa organ and me on guitar. We played loud electric rock just for the fun of it. After we'd run through some of our old Energy standbys, we started improvising riffs and progressions and soon we were putting some comedy-novelty lyrics to them to try and crack each other up. It was early 1970 and we called it "Barnes & Barnes." Robert and I had been calling each other by the nickname of "Art" for a couple years by then. That started when we went up to San Francisco and made a silent short film on my Super-8 movie camera. We told our friends and parents we were making art films. That evolved into calling each other Art. We chose the name Barnes after a bit on the title track of the Bill Cosby album "Revenge." There's a character in that piece named Junior Barnes and we liked that a lot. So, that's how Barnes & Barnes was officially born.

PART 2

102

17. LOVE AT FIRST SIGHT

I'd been in love before, or at least I thought I had been in love. Shirley Jones, Connie Stevens, Elizabeth Montgomery... I had fallen hard for them all. And I was just now getting over my recent relationship with Brigitte Bardot. But this... This was different.

She was seated across the small waiting room, facing me. She was reading Anna Sewell's classic novel, *Black Beauty*. She wore a multi-colored dress, and she was so... consciously controlled and aware of everything that I was absolutely stunned by her presence.

In the past, I had always gone for blondes but this ivory skinned vision in front of me had long, shining, chestnut-colored hair that cascaded over her shoulders like a royal shawl with a will of its own. It framed her perfect face, complemented by pouty full lips that smiled a tiny dangerous smile as she occasionally looked up from the page with huge soulful hazel eyes that glanced my way sending me silent telepathic messages of playfulness.

This was without any doubt the most extraordinary and beautiful girl I'd ever seen in my entire long ten years of life, and I was instantly smitten by her. And the best part about it was, even though I'd always fallen for much older women, she was twelve.

I was two months shy of eleven and Shirley Jones suddenly seemed ancient.

I knew right then and there my life would never be the same as Angela Cartwright and I waited in Irwin Allen's outer office to meet with the man who had just signed us each to five-year series contracts to co-star in the most ambitious and expensive television pilot in history: *Lost in Space.*

We spent the next six years together.

My relationship with Angela shifted from just friends and schoolmates and co-stars to more than friends in late 1969, and by February of 1970 we were officially a couple. I had secretly been crazy about her from the very beginning, and it tortured me for a long time. I waited five years before "making my move." First of all, I had to be taller than her. Then, I pretty much waited until I could drive and then… it happened.

It was worth the wait. It was wonderful, and it was important, and she and I experienced a whole lot of love and life together. Most all of it included "firsts" for both of us. We were very romantic and wrote each other almost daily. We "slept" on the phone with each other, which was quite an indulgence, but we did it anyway. Ange and I went to countless classic concerts together. We saw the Who, Jimi Hendrix, Sly and the Family Stone, Simon & Garfunkel, Donovan, James Taylor, Joni Mitchell, Graham Nash, John Sebastian, Neil Young, Leon Russell, and many, many more. Ange was also a constant at the countless Redwood gigs during those years. I'd look off to the wings and see her there smiling and taking photographs and that always made me happy.

REDWOOD GIG PHOTO BY ANGE.

We were very strongly connected. One morning upon waking, Ange called and she told me not to smoke when I drove to school, that she'd had a weird dream and she sensed something about fire and the car. We both smoked cigarettes then. She smoked Virginia Slim Menthols and I smoked Marlboros. Anyway, my morning routine would definitely have included firing up my 1969 beige MGB-GT, as well as firing up a cigarette. So, with her premonition in mind, my dad and I checked the car that morning. We opened the hatchback, and a plastic red gallon can of gasoline that I kept under the back hatch, in case I ever ran out of gas, had somehow gotten punctured and had soaked the back of the car with gas. A spark or a flicked ash from a cigarette would surely have been a serious problem. Angela's premonition had been real and by feeling strongly about it, a potential disaster was averted. My dad and I opened up the hatch, removed the upholstery and let it air out. I walked to Hamilton High School that day.

HEADING TO A RENAISSANCE HALLOWEEN PARTY, 1970. PAUL, ANGE AND ME.. PHOTO BY ANGE'S DAD JOHN, TAKEN IN HER LIVING ROOM ON MARIOTA STREET IN TOLUCA LAKE.

After two years, Ange ended our romance. She actually broke up with me the morning of my graduation. That was a really bad day. It was painful and difficult and truly left me partially shattered and depressed for years. It was a very important turning point in my life and that's really all that needs to be said about that. Angela at eighteen years old needed to experience more independent life on her own and that's all that was ever explained. Thirty years later, I brought it up and Ange said, "I couldn't believe you didn't fight for me. Why didn't you fight for me?" And to this day, I don't have an answer to that question.

ANGE AND I... STILL CONNECTED AND CREATIVE TOGETHER

18. REBOUND

*T*hings got weird and took some dark turns right around then. I blamed myself for losing Ange and I got swallowed into a deep depression. I rented a garage apartment a few miles away that was a real dump and I sat there and sulked in the dark. It was such a funky little apartment that it literally shared a toilet with another little dump of an apartment that made up the other half of the garage. And the guy who lived in the other half was an elderly legally blind man and he "missed" the toilet more than he didn't. It was really gross. I only lived there for two months. If you could call that living. If I'm going to be totally honest, I think I only used that toilet twice. I drove back to my parents' house to shower and go to the bathroom most of the time.

Redwood was gigging constantly and that helped me get through my funk in multiple ways. I loved playing and singing with Paul and Gary and audiences dug our songs and our sound. And girls dug guitar players, and some of my sadness was "treated" with the sexual attentions of young ladies who appreciated the band. For a while, I was a bit indulgent in that department and didn't search for a soul mate or someone to go out to dinner and a show with. I simply dabbled in carnal activities to release pent up emotions for a time. Although, I really must admit, I resented myself for doing it and was continually haunted by what I had lost.

The band was not only performing a lot, but we soon began a recording partnership with Mike Stone and Dan Swaggerty as independent producers. Mike was a staff recording engineer at Record Plant, one of the very best recording studios in the world, and Dan fancied himself a producer. They had been following Redwood around for quite awhile attending a lot of our performances and offered us a deal that we thought was a great one. We could go into Record Plant whenever Mike had access to a studio and record and work on our songs. Between Mike, Dan, and the band, we found plenty of top-notch players who would join us for sessions to supplement the arrangements and although Dan and Mike would make suggestions, we were pretty much producing ourselves. We signed the papers and began cutting tracks at Record Plant right away and we ended up, Paul and I anyway, working there with Mike off and on for the next five years.

REDWOOD RECORDING THREE-PART HARMONY AT RECORD PLANT, 1972.
I TIE-DYED THAT SHIRT MYSELF.

Here's how it often worked. We'd get a phone call in the afternoon from Dan, and he'd tell us that "Stevie Wonder is working in Studio C until 10p.m. tonight. Come in at 11, and we'll have the studio to ourselves 'til noon tomorrow." So, we'd decide what we were going to record and work on it at home, MAYBE try to take a nap (ha!), and then we'd head to Record Plant and record all night. For years, we worked around Stevie Wonder's setup. We never touched his keyboards and his drums which were set up and mic'd, but we set ourselves up around his gear and we'd work until midday the next day. Dan would offer us tabs of uppers and Paul and I would take one each and Gary would always pass, and we'd get things done. Record Plant was quite a fancy and hedonistic place as well as being a fantastic studio. We'd see Stevie, Mick Jagger, John Lennon, Phil Spector, Sly Stone, Keith Moon, George Harrison, Graham Nash, David Crosby (who slammed a door in my face, but I still dig him), and other iconic musicians heading to one of the four studios to record or to hang and relax in the galley playing pinball or in the jacuzzi with groupies. We never really mingled much with any of them though. Sly Stone did kick Gary out of the jacuzzi one night… We'd nod at each other, exchange a "how ya doin'?" but we pretty much kept our heads down when passing those iconic stars in the hallways. It was a very cool learning experience and we recorded scores of songs that were quite professional. I wish they'd been released, but as things go with production company contracts, sometimes there can be sticky issues that become red flags later.

Anyway, Swaggerty went to prison and sadly, after I introduced Mike to America and he engineered their second and third albums, "Homecoming" and "Hat Trick," there were studio personnel changes at Record Plant and then Mike got ill and he passed away. Before he got sick, I contacted him and asked if I could buy the master tapes to all the sessions we'd recorded. Mike sighed a heavy sigh and told me they'd all been erased and/or destroyed. That stung. Onward.

Between gigging at clubs where we'd play two sets on weeknights and three sets on the weekends and often be recording all night, our clocks were turned around. I'd sleep until the afternoon and then be up until the dawn. My hair was very long, and I was immersed in making music. Another strange turn of events happened then. Howard Rubin, my beloved mentor and agent, who had guided my career for a decade, decided quite spontaneously, at the ripe old age of twenty-eight, to retire from show business, buy a ranch in New

DANGER, WILL ROBINSON:

Mexico and leave Beverly Hills, and all that went with it, behind. That was a biggie.

MY AGENT AND MENTOR HOWARD RUBIN. WE WERE A REAL GOOD TEAM.
KINDA LOOKS LIKE A WILL ROBINSON ART PIECE BEHIND HIM, BUT... WHO KNOWS?

When Howard announced his decision, I impulsively decided that I too would retire from acting or at least take a couple of years off and dedicate myself to the band 100%. You'd have thought my parents might've sat me down and had a heart-to-heart discussion with me about that, but they didn't.

Looking back, I do think that was a big mistake I made. At the time, I didn't have to audition for parts. Scripts were sent to me. Projects were offered to me. I wish someone had said, "Bill, you can make one film a year to keep yourself in the game. The other forty weeks you can tour and record and gig and write. Trim your hair to McCartney length and you can do it all." But that conversation or advice never came to me. I might not have listened even if it had.

It did come to me as "why didn't I do THAT?" a whole lot later. Whatever. Howard insisted I continue to have representation, so he signed me to an agent that I'd known as a boy, Ronny Leaf, and Ronny pretty much assigned me to another agent named Gary Salt, and Gary would call me once every few months and say, "They'd like you to do a guest shot on *The Love Boat*" and I'd say, "Not my thing. Pass." Occasionally, I'd get an offer to do a violent

120

exploitation film. I was offered the leads in a few of those. I'd read the scripts, which were full of nudity and bloodshed, and I strongly felt that I didn't want to add that kind of work to my resume. I liked what I had done as an actor. I'd covered a lot of territory in terms of characters I'd played, and I'd worked with some of the most iconic and talented people of all time. I felt good about the decision to say, "Thank you, but I'm not interested in those type of films." Even when I was offered a lot of money to star in *The Re-Animator,* I said no. Although a lot of people and reviewers seem to like that film. I just remember reading a scene in the script where the character picks up a bloodied severed head and holds it up to lick a woman's nude breast who's restrained and in bondage… I read that bit and didn't see the humor in it, and I asked myself, "What would Jimmy Stewart do?" I passed. No regret about that.

Anyway, for a few years at least, I was up really late all the time and I was not the happiest guy in town and when I wasn't working with Redwood I was usually hanging around with Scott and a dangerous friend named Gary Krinberg. He is now a talented writer, a college professor, father of four, and a retired Navy deep sea diver. But when he was 18, he was nothing but trouble. Tall, dark, and handsome, quick-witted, funny, and totally fearless, Gary was a trouble magnet. He got into a lot of physical altercations. He pulled out a switchblade knife more times than I pulled out a comb. He initiated chaos and Scott and I let him drive most of the time.

One night, a few weeks shy of me turning eighteen, Scott, Krinberg, and I had shot a few rounds of pool at El Rancho Billiards, then gone to Norm's coffee shop for pie and coffee (usually on the house cuz waitress Doris liked us), and then found ourselves wandering aimlessly in the dark around Rancho Park around midnight. All of these places were basically within walking distance of Scott's and my homes. Gary lived in an apartment in nearby Palms next to the unemployment office. So, here we were, freshly fueled up on coffee with nothing to do. So, we decided to climb up onto the roof of the Rancho Park Recreation Center buildings and play "Ditch" with each other. And I swear, that was our only intention. We were running around the roofs and hiding from each other when suddenly very bright lights illuminated me and Krinberg. "Put your hands up, right NOW!" I clearly remember seeing the barrel of a handgun illuminated in the glow of the flashlight. The police were busting us. "Get your asses down here. NOW!" Gary and I descended to the ground. "TURN AROUND!" Gary and I were handcuffed. "Where's the other one?!" "I don't know. We were playing ditch." "Playing DITCH?! My ass. There's been a series of robberies here lately. Typewriters, office equipment. Looks like we caught you this time." "No! We weren't breaking in or stealing anything! We were playing ditch! I know… that sounds stupid. But it's true." I was the one doing the talking. Krinberg was sneering because they were quite rough handcuffing him. Gary's over six feet tall and he just reeks of trouble. He can't help it, I guess. One of the policemen got up right in his face and snarled, "You got critters living in your hair, boy?" I swear to God that's exactly what he said. I was afraid of what Krinberg might say in response and quickly said, "Look officers, look at my wallet in my pocket. Look at my driver's license. I live two blocks from here. My girlfriend dumped me, and I've been acting like an idiot. But we were just goofing around. We're not thieves!" And then, another officer found Scott and he joined the party… handcuffed of course. Scott's driver's license confirmed we were indeed neighborhood kids acting like fools. And then one of the cops flashed his light in my face and said, "Wait a minute! Didn't I bust you recently?! You look familiar to me!" And I started dancing as fast as I could, "I look familiar to you, cuz I'm Billy Mumy and I grew up on TV and I was Will Robinson on *Lost in Space* and we filmed it right there at 20th Century Fox and I've never been arrested for anything and that's the truth!"

And with that… we were released from our handcuffs and told never to climb around on the roof at Rancho again. And we took that advice quite seriously. That's the closest I ever came to being arrested. Or… close to the closest anyway.

19. PSYCHO

Okay, so he was a genius. Yes, he made some classic movies. Absolutely, he was a master of suspense. He was also a sadistic jerk as far as I'm concerned.

It was the summer of 1961, and it was plenty hot out on the Universal lot. But inside an air-conditioned stage, things were really heating up. I was starring in an episode of *Alfred Hitchcock Presents*. It was the first of three that I would eventually film, but this was the only one that would be directed by the master himself.

Alfred Hitchcock scared the shit out of me. And to this day I remember every syllable he whispered, I can still feel his breath on my face, I can still see his sweaty, puffy jowls as he slowly leaned down toward me with a gleam in his eyes that told me he wasn't kidding.

"Bang! You're Dead" was the title of this episode. The story was simple enough: an uncle returns from a holiday to visit his brother's family and tells his little nephew Jackie (me) that he's brought him a present. The kid is impatient and goes through his uncle's bag and discovers a revolver and a box of bullets. All his friends are outside playing cowboys and they're chasing each other around with toy guns. Jackie assumes the pistol is his present. He grabs a handful of bullets, places a few in the chamber of the gun and puts the rest in his pocket and rushes outside to play with his friends.

The show chronicles Jackie's day as he goes about town adding more bullets to the gun until finally all six chambers are full. During the boy's outing he spins the chamber and pulls the trigger several times.

The audience is in great suspense wondering if and when someone will get shot by this little kid with a deadly weapon that he thinks is a toy. At the same time, Jackie's family has discovered what happened, and they are frantically scurrying about town in a frenzy trying to find the boy and prevent disaster.

It was an excellent show. It won some prestigious television award. Hitchcock paced it perfectly, and the performances he got out of his actors were top notch all around.

An interesting bit of TV trivia is the fact that Marta Kristen was cast as an employee of the grocery store Jackie ventured into, and she and I had a nice little scene together. Marta of course, would later play the role of Judy Robinson, my television sister on *Lost in Space*.

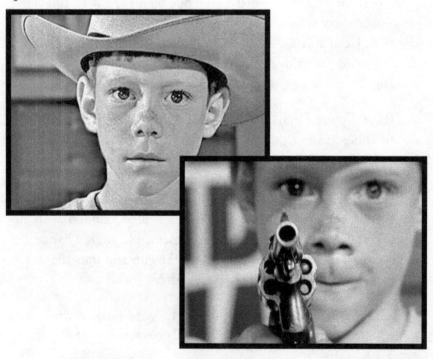

But, regardless of how brilliantly Alfred Hitchcock directed this television drama, he also succeeded in pretty much traumatizing me.

If an actor is over the age of eighteen, you can work him as long as needed, provided you pay the overtime expenses. However, if an actor is a minor, you can only work him eight hours a day. There is no overtime. After eight hours (plus an hour for lunch), the welfare worker pulls the plug, and the child actor goes home.

Well, this drama only took five days to film, and I was in almost every scene in "Bang! You're Dead," so they worked me every day as long as they could. At the end of one day in particular, they wanted to film one last close up of me and they were quickly running out of time. The welfare worker was standing next to the assistant director looking at her watch. Every moment counted.

I had been working hard since early in the morning, and as the DP (director of photography) was trying to light this close-up, I was fidgeting on my mark. I suppose my concentration was slipping a bit, and I wasn't standing as still as they wanted me to.

I was seven years old. I didn't mind standing in for myself at all. But I'm not trained to be a stand-in. I'm an actor. I'm a kid.

So Alfred Hitchcock gets up out of his chair, and ever so slowly approaches me. He was wearing a black suit, white shirt, and black tie. He was sweating. In my memory, he was always sweating. He breathed loud and heavy, and his many chins swayed and jiggled as he headed my way with a very stern look on his very large, pink, sweaty face. He bent down to speak to me so that no one else could hear what he had to say. And this is exactly, syllable for syllable, what he said to me while he looked me in my eyes...

"Little boy... If you don't stop moving about... I'm going to get a nail... And I'm going to nail your feet to your mark... And blood will come pouring out... Like milk... So stop moving!"

I was honestly scared shitless.

I believed he meant every word he said.

I stopped moving.

They filmed the close-up.

Alfred Hitchcock got what he wanted.

I went home. I told my mom what he said to me, and she laughed it off, and said that he was only teasing me. She added that "The British have a different sense of humor than we do. It's just his way of joking." But she didn't understand.

If that was his sense of humor, what a truly sick man he was. Because he certainly knew that joking or not, he was terrifying a little boy. He threatened me with a very visual, real, horrible, physical torture! And believe me, he saw how truly scared I was.

And from that day on, until Alfred Hitchcock was dead, I sent him to the Cornfield. Every time I went to work at Universal, when I had to pass his office which was right on the "main street" of the lot, I walked all the way around several soundstages as a detour because I never in my life wanted to see that sweaty man again.

I've thought about that day many times over the years. All he had to do to make everything right was to tell me he was teasing me after they filmed the close-up. One little extra moment of his busy time to tell a little boy who worked very hard for him that he was only joking. That he would never really nail my feet to the floor.

But he didn't take the time to tell me that.

I worked on two more Alfred Hitchcock shows after "Bang! You're Dead." Another *Alfred Hitchcock Presents* titled "Door Without a Key" which aired January 16th, 1962, and "House Guest," an episode of *The Alfred Hitchcock Hour,* that originally ran in November of that same year. I was seven years old when filming both "Bang! You're Dead" and "Door Without a Key" and a seasoned pro of eight when making "House Guest."

I co-starred with Claude Rains in "Door Without a Key." I clearly recall my mother being quite excited about that fact. She was a big Claude Rains fan. He and I had fine chemistry on camera together and I remember him being a very sweet and calm man. John Larch, who had played my father in the "It's a Good Life" *Twilight Zone* episode, also was featured in this episode and it was nice to be working alongside him again. Connie Gilchrist gave a memorable performance in "Door Without a Key" as well. The good news for me was this episode was directed by Herschel Daugherty and not Alfred Hitchcock.

HANGING OUT WITH CLAUDE RAINS –
A REALLY NICE GUY.

Filmed in winter of 1961, I didn't have a lot of time to hang out and chat with the other actors. Once again, I was in most every scene and the rules required that I attend schooling on the studio lot for three hours every day. So, after we blocked and rehearsed an upcoming scene, while the other cast members were sitting in their chairs or their dressing rooms preparing to film as the set was being lit, I was rushed outside the soundstage to a trailer where I had to put the emotional scene we were soon to film completely out of my mind, and shift my concentration to math or history or english or some other school subject. I always hated that.

My memories of "House Guest" include the fact that I did some fairly serious swimming in the Pacific Ocean off of Malibu at the beginning of the episode that sets the plot up. I was a strong swimmer at age eight and filming those scenes over and over went smoothly enough, although the water was very cold. One thing that I was aware of while working on that episode, was acting with Robert Sterling. Often, because of my young age, I was unaware of fellow actors past catalogues, so I rarely felt intimidated or impressed by them. But Mr. Sterling had co-starred in the television series *Topper* as the ghost George Kirby opposite his real-life wife, the lovely Anne Jeffries who played Marion Kirby, the "Ghostess with the Mostess." Well, I loved *Topper* as a kid and watched it as often as I could with Lala, my grandmother. So, working with Robert Sterling was pretty cool to me.

20. LAUREL CANYON ON MY MIND

Laurel Canyon, just above the Sunset Strip, has been a legendary mecca to artists and musicians forever. I have lived in the canyon since 1973. My old agent, Howard Rubin, was a co-owner of Café Galleria, a hipster restaurant that rested just under the iconic Canyon Country Store. It's been through many name changes and owners since 1969, but it hasn't really changed very much. When I was fifteen, I'd played Howard several of my original songs and he "booked me" to perform at the Café. Outside of my very first gig at the Hollywood Bowl five years earlier, it was the first time I'd performed in LA as a solo artist. I played my acoustic Gibson B-25N and had a harmonica holder around my neck and swapped out various harmonicas. I performed a little over thirty minutes worth of original songs and I tossed in a couple of cover tunes. The gig went fine and after that, I was sure that Laurel Canyon was where I wanted to live.

Redwood had been managed for three years by Cort Casady who also managed John Stewart, Jennifer Warnes, and the We Five among others. So Redwood was often booked as opening act for them. Sometimes we played fourteen sets a week for $250. It's called paying your dues and getting your shit together. During the years that Cort managed us, he was dating a gorgeous blonde named Alison Wickwire. When they broke up and Cort stopped managing Redwood and my relationship with Angela ended, I very luckily started dating Alison. She and her roommate Linda shared a house on Lookout Mountain Drive in Laurel Canyon.

Alison was a long, tall, blonde beauty with a great smile and a worldly, wicked sense of humor. She worked in the promotion department of Warner Bros. records. Alison had a constant supply of tickets to every gig in town and she also had some great drugs that may or may not have been intended for sharing with acts on the label. Alison was six years older than me, and I was extremely happy being her boyfriend for seven months. We had incredible sexual chemistry together and I don't remember a single argument or unhappy time. For the very first time since my relationship with Angela ended, Alison removed her from my mind. My best friend Scott started dating her roommate Linda and nights in the Canyon were blissful.

I could tell from the beginning that my relationship with Alison wasn't going to last for the rest of our lives, but while it lasted, it was fabulous. I was cast in the feature film *Papillon* and was headed out of the country for a few months to work. When I returned, the romance with Alison had ended. She and Linda were moving out of the Laurel Canyon house at 8529 Lookout Mountain. So Scott and I took over the lease and moved in.

In 1974, the two-bedroom, two-bathroom, two-car garage house with a "bonus" room added (dubbed the "Room of Fear") cost a whopping $330 a month. The Room of Fear was a cinder block add-on that held a king-size waterbed, a set of drums, and two amps and an assortment of instruments.

Shaun Cassidy had just gotten his driver's license at the time, and he used to regularly show up in his funky dark blue Cadillac accompanied by various unbelievably gorgeous women and request some time in The Room of Fear. This was before he was a television star or a rock star. In those days he was just David Cassidy's little brother. But man, did he pull the chicks! Scott and I always welcomed him in.

After a year there, the landlord, a nice cat named David Romero, put new carpets in and painted the house and raised the rent to $400 a month. Scott, who was working regularly as a background actor on the series *Welcome Back, Kotter,* felt $200 a month was too much for him, so he moved into an apartment building his parents owned. The girl I was dating at the time, actress Janit Baldwin, moved in.

IN A PHOTO BOOTH WITH ALISON. IT WAS GREAT WHILE IT LASTED.

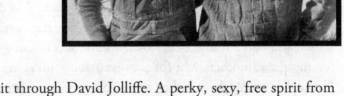

WITH JANIT IN MAMMOTH FOR THE SNOW.

I met Janit through David Jolliffe. A perky, sexy, free spirit from Kansas City, Janit was a working actress and she had shot a pilot for a television series with Jolliffe's mother, Gloria. The pilot didn't sell, but Gloria fixed Janit up with David and they were a couple for a few months. I found her very attractive, and she seemed to flirt quite seriously with me. David and Janit stopped dating for reasons that I can't remember now, and I asked him if it would be alright with him if I asked her out. He gave me his blessing.

Janit and I stayed together for a total of four years. Looking back on them, I can't say they were very happy ones. There was a lot of drama and a lot of drugs and a lot of infidelity. We probably never should have lived together, but we did.

Two new houses were being built right around the corner from the Lookout Mountain rental and at the age of twenty-two, I decided to buy one of them. I liked the fact that no one else had ever lived in it and I also liked the fact that I could literally just walk all my stuff over to it.

I've been there ever since.

Within a year of me buying my house, my grandmother died at age eighty-three. I remember Paul and I were recording at Frank Wolf's "A Little Night Studio" and close friend Debbie Shapiro (who became Broadway star and Tony award-winner Debbie Gravitte) answered the phone and interrupted the session to tell me my mom called to say my grandmother, Lala, had just died from a brain aneurysm.

Not long after that, my parents sold the impressive Cheviot Hills home they had built and lived in for twelve years. My dad was never particularly happy living in Los Angeles, but he stayed until I was settled and had a house of my own and he was no longer responsible for my grandmother. My folks moved forty miles up the coast to Camarillo, where the weather was nice and it had a much more rural vibe which pleased my father, the old cowboy.

I REALLY WAS A LITTLE COWBOY, AND OF COURSE
I STILL HAVE THAT HAT.

ALWAYS COWBOYS.
MY DAD IN 1941, AND THE TWO OF US IN 1993.

21. Tractors and Other Tales

"Lonesome George" Gobel was hysterical and really nice. I worked with him twice in the early 1960s. Both projects have rarely been seen. "*Scooter Deere Day*" was a film that was financed and made for the John Deere tractor company. It featured George Gobel and John Carradine, and starred me as Scooter. It was filmed in bright color and featured fantasy sequences of young Scooter surrounded by giant amounts of cotton candy, ice cream, hot dogs, popcorn, etc.... As the fantasy progresses, Scooter's stomach grows huge. They fit me with several different prosthetic rubber stomach pieces, belly buttons included, that continued to increase in size until I looked like a beach ball boy! It all turned out to be a dream. George Gobel played my dad and John Carradine played the doctor who treated me for a stomach ache when I awoke.

Honestly, I can hardly believe I remember that much about it. I don't remember ever actually even seeing it. It was an "industrial film," so it didn't run on national television. I do remember that we filmed it in Chicago and instead of flying there, my parents and I took the train. It was a few days of riding the rails and seeing the country as the click-clack of the wheels on the track laid down a steady groove that was soothing. I passed the time drawing superheroes with crayons and trying to sell the artwork to passengers on the train. I guess I hustled up enough scratch to buy some new comic books when I got to the newsstand in Chicago.

I have no idea how John Deere tractors figured into this production.

<<>>

My Uncle Elroy was the other project I co-starred in with George Gobel. It was a more traditional half-hour sitcom family pilot produced by Joe Connelly and Bob Mosher who produced *Leave it to Beaver* and *The Munsters*. We didn't travel by train to shoot it. It was made at Universal but since it was a TV project, it was technically Revue Studios. I played Buzz and George played Uncle Elroy, a daydreamer who would doze off into various funny fantasy bits. We shot it in a week back in 1961 but *My Uncle Elroy* didn't sell so it has lingered in TV limbo for over sixty years now. I'd love to find a copy of it. I'll bet it's a crackup. I'd also love to have one of the super rare Gibson "George Gobel" model L-5 electric guitars. They only made a few of them and they were thinner than the regular L-5's with a deep burgundy finish. David Crosby had one.

<<>>

Barbara Parkins played my older sister in *My Uncle Elroy*, and she and I hung out a few years later when we were both working at 20th Century Fox. Barbara was co-starring on *Peyton Place* and I was doing *Lost in Space*. My agent, Howard Rubin, also represented Ryan O'Neal who was also working on *Peyton Place*. The main outdoor square of *Peyton Place* was ten feet from the great Fox commissary and most everyone who was working on the Fox lot ate in there almost every day. The food was great and the atmosphere was always friendly. You'd see folks dressed up as apes from *Planet of the Apes* having lunch or aliens and spacemen and superheroes, folks in military outfits, etc.... A lot of cool TV shows were filmed on that lot in the 1960s. *Lost in Space, Voyage to the Bottom of the Sea, Batman, The Green Hornet, Peyton Place, Daniel Boone, 12 O'Clock High, Time Tunnel, Land of the Giants*... the list goes on and on. Because I had worked with Barbara and knew Ryan, and because I was a friendly and somewhat fearless guy who was ridiculously comfortable on the Fox lot, I would sometimes go join the *Peyton Place* cast members for lunch at one of the big round corner tables in the commissary. For a while I got in the habit of sitting next to the lovely Mia Farrow, who would introduce me as "her boyfriend." I enjoyed that. But as soon as Mia started dating Frank Sinatra, her vibe changed suddenly and dramatically. She cut her long blonde hair super short like Twiggy and she stopped eating with groups of people. In fact, she was rarely seen in the commissary after that.

MY UNCLE ELROY WITH GEORGE GOBEL, PAULA WINSLOWE (I THINK), AND BARBARA PARKINS. I PLAYED BUZZ.

22. In the Zone

In December of 1960 I was fortunate enough to take a very interesting journey into a dimension of sound... a dimension of sight... a dimension of mind...into a land of both shadow and substance... of things and ideas... crossing over... into *The Twilight Zone*.

It is my opinion that Rod Serling created the best dramatic science fiction and fantasy television series that has ever existed, with classic stylized writing, wonderful direction, great music, and stellar performances by some of the finest actors ever to grace the television sets. I am so very grateful and proud to have been a part of his wonderful project.

"Long Distance Call" is a great Muddy Waters blues song. It's also the title of the teleplay written by William Idelson and Charles Beaumont that became the fifty-sixth episode of *The Twilight Zone*.

It was the last of a short-lived experiment CBS had insisted the series try during its second season. It was shot on videotape, like a live television show, as opposed to being filmed. The budget on the anthology series was extremely expensive for the time, approaching $65,000 per episode, and videotape, being cheaper than film and requiring zero developing time, seemed like a good idea.

Whether this journey into a dimension of tape was a success or not, I'll let others decide. It does however make the six episodes that were shot on tape instead of film, true rarities in the 156 episodes that were made.

"Long Distance Call" focuses on a dying old woman and her passion for her grandson, Billy (me). At the opening of the story, she gives Billy a toy telephone for his fifth birthday present. Shortly after, she dies. Billy begins to spend all his time chatting away on the toy telephone. The boy says he's talking to Grandma, and she wants him to come keep her company. He walks into traffic and almost gets killed by a speeding car... He throws himself into the fishpond and nearly drowns... His mother picks up the toy phone and hears breathing on the other end... In a dramatic climax (brilliantly executed by Phillip Abbot), Billy's father picks up the toy telephone and pleads with his mother to let his son live. Let him grow up. He says if she truly loves the boy, she won't let him die. And... Billy lives.

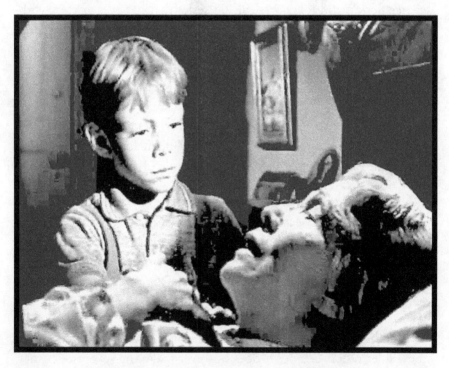

WITH LILI DARVAS AS "GRANDMA" PREPARES TO DEPART REALITY PRIME.

Rod Serling was on the set when the ending was being shot and he didn't like the original speech. While we all sat around and waited, writers Idelson and Beaumont dashed into an office and rewrote it with Serling's guidance. Rod was absolutely right, and very hands-on with his series; the change made it much stronger.

THE PHONE TO HEAVEN... OR MAYBE HELL? OR PURGATORY AT LEAST!

Working on "Long Distance Call" was interesting. My mother almost refused to let me do it. She was very nervous about the suicide attempts. I guess she thought it might put some strange ideas into my young head, and I might try a stunt like that at home to get something out of my folks. Even though I was a very good swimmer by then, my mother was also very anxious about the pond scene. Although it barely ended up on camera, I can remember floating face down in that little pond like I had drowned. It didn't bother me at all, I enjoyed it, but Muriel was really upset by it.

I'm sure glad it all worked out. If I hadn't have made "Long Distance Call," I might not have made "It's a Good Life" or "In Praise of Pip," and those were powerful shows.

"Long Distance Call" added $650 to my savings account. We worked on this episode at CBS on Fairfax and Beverly right next to the Original Farmers Market. We rehearsed it for four days, like a play, and then taped it over the next two days.

I remember Rod Serling being around quite a bit and feeling very comfortable with him. Everyone on the crew stayed relaxed when he was there. That's certainly not always the case when the creator of a program comes on the set. I recall him telling me some jokes, and of course he always had a cigarette going. We got along swell. It's not like we went out for pizza and beer together, but obviously he liked me since I worked for him three times. I wish he were still with us today. His writing was so great, so singular.

Both "Long Distance Call" and "It's a Good Life" were beautifully directed by James Sheldon. He was a real pleasure to work for, and he communicated his ideas to me with patience and clarity in a very comfortable manner. He had kids of his own, and I remember running into him and his family at Disneyland one day, and we strolled around the Magic Kingdom together, which seems to have an odd symmetry to another world of fantasy: *The Twilight Zone*.

Of all the roles I've been fortunate, or unfortunate enough to play, two seem to stand out in the minds of everyone. The first is Will Robinson from *Lost in Space*, the second is Anthony Fremont from "It's a Good Life," the fifth episode of the third season of *The Twilight Zone*.

Teleplay by Rod Serling based on the 1953 short story by Jerome Bixby, "It's a Good Life" is one damn scary little tale. A monster in the form of a six-year-old boy, Anthony Fremont (me), has unlimited mental powers. He has used his unfathomable ability to separate his little rural town of Peaksville, Ohio from the rest of the known universe, and since then has slowly but surely reshaped it and whittled it down to his liking.

ANTHONY FREMONT - THE MOST POWERFUL MUTANT IN THE UNIVERSE!

Anthony didn't like electricity, or automobiles, or any machines in general, so by using the God-like power of his young mutant mind, he took them away. This monster can read thoughts, any kind of thoughts, animal or human, and if he's displeased by them, he responds with swift retaliation; he either transforms them into hideous things, like a jack-in-the-box with their own face, or he sends them away to a limbo world known only as the "Cornfield."

The entire population of Peaksville lives in constant fear of little Anthony. Regardless of his actions, they must applaud and approve, lest he turn his attention their way. Everyone goes around telling him, and themselves, that, "It's real good you did that Anthony, it's real good."

We filmed this classic episode at the wonderful old MGM studio in Culver City (before it was sold and became Sony Pictures Studios). It took five days to complete it in May of 1961. I was paid $720.

Once again, the mighty Cloris Leachman played my mother, and once again she gave a perfect performance. Everyone in this program gave excellent performances: John Larch as the guilt ridden father who knows he should murder his son, but is afraid to try; Alice Frost as Aunt Amy who at one time had more control over Anthony than anyone else until he heard her singing aloud one day (Anthony doesn't like singing, so he gave her a mental lobotomy). Don Keefer, Jeanne Bates, Casey Adams, Tom Hatcher, and Lenore Kingston all turned in stellar performances as unified, terrified, residents in Anthony Fremont's private hell.

I loved playing Anthony. Who wouldn't? Total power! He made Zorro seem meaningless. He could've wished Superman and the

CLORIS WAS ALWAYS BRILLIANT. I LOVED ACTING WITH HER.

Lone Ranger and Davy Crockett into the Cornfield if he'd wanted to, and none of them could've stopped him.

The capable and affable James Sheldon once again directed me with one simple plan: whenever Anthony was using his powers, I was to make my eyes as big as possible and never blink. Well, I had big eyes to begin with, my face has more or less grown into them over the years, but you use what you've got. It's fun to look scary when you're seven years old.

Anthony has never really gone away. I've always kept him alive inside of me (or he's kept himself alive). When I was a kid, I used to practice using Anthony's powers to turn the traffic signals green, or to open up the gate to the Marshank's swimming pool, and to this day when someone pisses me off, I still send them to the Cornfield! They may not know I'm doing it, but I really do. I <u>do</u> it.

Not that it works, but it's a release for me.

If I had to pick only one television show from my youth to proudly show as an example of my work, it would undoubtedly be "It's a Good Life."

The first three seasons of *The Twilight* Zone were produced by Buck Houghton, a tall, slender man who resembled Lee Marvin. Mr. Houghton was a master craftsman, and together he and Rod Serling had made the project what it was... an unparalleled television accomplishment.

As the third season ended, the show was late in finding a sponsor for its next season, and without warning, CBS slotted another series in its place. Suddenly the future of *The Twilight Zone* was unsure. As the powers that be attempted to work something out, the creative forces behind the series were going through some changes of their own.

Buck Houghton left *The Twilight Zone* and accepted a very attractive offer from Four Star Productions, and Rod Serling accepted a teaching position at Antioch College, effective September 1962 through January 1963. The series was eventually picked up as a mid-season replacement. For its fourth season, CBS transformed the show from a half-hour to an hour. *The Twilight Zone* continued, but with less input from Rod Serling, and without Buck Houghton's production skills.

For its fifth and final season the series returned to its original length of half-hour episodes. The show was now produced by William Froug and Bert Granet. "In Praise Of Pip" was the first episode of the season.

Written by Rod Serling, it was a touching, frightening drama that focused on a man's love for his son. It was also, to the best of my knowledge, the very first mention of an American casualty in Vietnam.

Jack Klugman plays Max Phillips, a two-bit bookie who has made a complete mess out of his life. The only thing he ever managed to do right was raise his beloved son, Pip. Max learns that Pip, now a soldier (played by Bobby Diamond), has been critically wounded in South Vietnam. In an attempt to straighten out his crooked life, Max ends up with a bullet in his gut. He stumbles, bleeding, through a closed amusement park he used to take his son to. Suddenly, young Pip (me) appears to him. Somehow the mortally wounded soldier has been transformed into a young boy again. The amusement park comes alive, and the father and son have a happy reunion reliving past pleasures.

Suddenly Pip turns to his father with a stolid look and runs away. When Max finally finds the boy, Pip explains that he's dying and starts to fade away. Tearfully, Max pleads with God to take his life and let Pip live. It's a beautifully acted scene by Jack Klugman as he collapses to the ground and dies. Pip lives. He returns from Vietnam and walks through the amusement park remembering his "best buddy"... his father.

A VERY EMOTIONAL MOMENT CAPTURED. JACK KLUGMAN TOTALLY COMMITTED TO HIS FEELINGS. WORKING WITH HIM WAS A GIFT TO ME.

Filmed June 18 through the 24th at the Pacific Ocean Park amusement park in Santa Monica and at MGM, Pip was my last journey into the original *Twilight Zone*. For my role as young Pip, I earned $937.50 and the respect of Jack Klugman. It's a wonderful feeling when an actor you admire tells you you're doing good work. And Jack Klugman was indeed a great actor.

Both my parents had come out to watch me film at night on the creaky boardwalk that was home to the now-long-vanished Pacific Ocean Park. This was no Disneyland. P.O.P was an old-fashioned amusement park, complete with creaky roller coasters, haunted houses, and countless arcade games and shooting galleries. There was something very spooky about that place at night with no one there except two actors and a crew.

In one scene, as Max was pursuing a fleeing and dying Pip, I had to run through a real house of mirrors. They had placed tiny little pieces of tape on the floor for me to use as a guide for where to turn, but of course I couldn't really look down at them as the camera rolled. It was pretty scary running through that house of mirrors; I bumped into several of them before we got it right.

IN THE REAL HOUSE OF MIRRORS...
A SCARY PLACE TO RUN THROUGH AND SHOOT IN.

In the scene where Max first sees Pip, he gets so excited to see his son as a little boy again that he passionately swept me up in his arms and gave me a big, slobbery kiss. Well, Jack knew how he wanted to play the scene, and I remember him taking me and my father and my mother aside and talking to us about the way he wanted it to work, and he warned me that he was going to really kiss me, and he hoped that me and my family would be okay about it. Of course we were. I understood completely and so did my folks. But it was really nice of him to talk to us about it.

The Twilight Zone was such a high-quality show in every respect that it's no wonder it has endured in global syndication nonstop. To this day, the *Twilight Zones* I was a part of remain career highlights, shiny memories like trophies I can still dust off and watch with a proud smile.

I LOVE BEING ACTION FIGURES. HIGHLY COLLECTIBLE.

23. That's Rock + Roll

1978 was a major year in my life. My longtime good friend Shaun Cassidy sold ten million records within a little over a year and had become a huge star. He was prepping a full-scale summer tour of arenas and the band he put together included some of my best friends. Jay Gruska on keyboards and harmony vocals. David Jolliffe on percussion and harmony vocals. Carlos Vega was on drums. Jay and Jolliffe had been in Paul's and my band for a year. Carlos' very first recording session was at Record Plant backing me and Paul on a song we'd written called "Isn't It Easy." Jolliffe and Jay both played and sang on that recording as well. I wasn't too surprised when I got the call and was asked if I would join the band for the tour playing rhythm guitar. I quickly accepted the gig. Filling out the band was Jimmy Greenspoon, from Three Dog Night, on organ and Joey Newman on lead guitar. Bass was handled by the great Dennis Belfield. Saxophone was played by Michael Altshul and later by George Englund, Cloris Leachman's son.

We rehearsed at S.I.R. in Hollywood for ten days before hitting the road. It was truly an amazing experience. Everything was first class. It felt like we were in *A Hard Day's Night* (without the Beatles music). Every gig was sold out. Fifteen to twenty thousand screaming kids freaking out from the beginning to the end of each show.

The performance started with Carlos on drums by himself laying down the groove to Eric Carmen's "That's Rock n Roll," which was a gigantic smash hit for Shaun. After a few bars, I started playing the

MAKING MUSIC WITH SHAUN CASSIDY HAS ALWAYS BEEN FUN...

WHETHER IT'S TO TWENTY THOUSAND SCREAMING FANS IN AN ARENA OR A COUPLE OF HUNDRED IN A CLUB.

guitar riff and then Shaun jumped through a hoop with pyrotechnics and the full band kicked in and from then on to the final chord of "Da Doo Ron Ron," the place went crazy. For me, my responsibility in the band was to help groove the songs along on my 1973 tobacco burst Gibson Les Paul. It wasn't too hard. Shaun was always a total pro, and the tour went smoothly. The road manager was Al Wilson, who had served in that capacity for Elvis Presley. He knew what he was doing. At the end of each gig, the band would race to several waiting limousines that would speed off in different directions. Shaun was usually hidden under a blanket so he wouldn't be spotted by the hordes of young girls wanting a piece of him.

Was there also 1970s rock & roll backstage and hotel debauchery? Yes. There was.

《》

When the tour ended, so did my four-year relationship with Janit Baldwin. But instead of accepting the fact that it probably would have been best for both of us if it had ended three years and six months earlier, I bemoaned and wallowed in sorrow.

My friend, music publisher Brian Greer, moved into my Laurel Canyon house when Janit moved out and he helped me a lot because besides being a good pal and fine company, he was an excellent joint roller. A lot of weed was smoked.

Creatively, I was in a very good but quite eclectic place. Paul and I had stopped performing together, but we were still writing songs together and hanging out almost daily. Brian, Paul, and I started writing a screenplay to resolve the cliffhanger ending of *Lost in Space*. It seemed like a natural thing to do and an easy sell to CBS as a TV movie of the week. We worked hard on it and it was coming along nicely. Tone-wise, it resembled the very earliest episodes of the first season of the series. We collaborated on it for over a year.

Thirty-five years later it was made. Showbiz.

Musically, I was very inspired in 1978 and I was writing a lot of new songs. The summer tour in Shaun's band was truly one of the most enjoyable experiences of my entire life and I had spent months bonding with and playing with excellent musicians. My electric guitar chops were up. I booked time in a cool recording studio in Hermosa Beach called Media Arts and started work on an album's worth of new songs with my friends from Shaun's band, Carlos Vega on drums, Dennis Belfield on bass, Jay Gruska on keyboards, and me on guitars. That was the core that laid down over a dozen basic tracks. They all generously agreed to collaborate with me on the project and for that, I will always be grateful to them. Frank Wolf engineered and the arrangements fell together by feel as we worked out the songs. Paul and I had written three new strong tunes that made the cut and another was a collaboration between Jay and me. David Jolliffe and I had written a mellow song that Carlos and Jay turned into a reggae groove. The rest I wrote myself. The sessions were nothing but enjoyable and the tracks were strong. We smoked weed and drank beer and Amaretto and ate Mexican food from a joint called El Yaqui every day. I added two Gretsch guitars to my arsenal, a Country Gentleman and a Tennessean, both made in 1967. For the recording sessions I relied on the Gretschs, my Les Paul, and my Martin D-28.

«<>»

At the same time my solo project was coming together, Robert and I started rekindling our Barnes & Barnes novelty songs and we recorded them anew on my four-track Teac 3340-S tape recorder in my living room. They had a great, crazy, smart, unique thing about them, and Robert sent some of the songs to Dr. Demento.

Dr. Demento had been on the radio for about ten years at this point and his show was huge. It was syndicated all around the world on hundreds of stations. In LA, he was heard every Sunday evening from six until ten on KMET, one of the biggest rock stations in town. Well, you just never know what's going to be a hit. By the end of 1978, "Fish Heads" was the biggest song in the history of the Dr. Demento show and was getting airplay and attention all over the world.

Through my relationship with Janit, I was close friends with Sissy Spacek and her husband Jack Fisk. They lived in Topanga Canyon, and I spent a lot of evenings at their house. One night, David Lynch was there, and he was screening a 16mm print of his film, *Eraserhead*. What a trip that one is! It was a small group that night that included a young wannabe filmmaker from Texas named Bill Paxton. Bill had recently moved to Santa Monica from Texas with his young wife, and he was assisting Jack on some projects. After we finished watching *Eraserhead*, the conversation turned to "Fish Heads," which was very popular with the "outsider" crowd at the time. Bill very passionately exclaimed that "Fish Heads" should be turned into a short film and that he should direct it. Everyone embraced the idea. Bill was so excited, and he campaigned so dramatically that Robert and I quickly agreed to finance a "Fish Heads" film that Bill would direct. Cinematographer and fellow Texan, Rocky Schenck, Bill's best friend and super talented artist, was assigned the gig of DP.

It was guerilla filmmaking at its best. Shot on a hand-cranked Bolex 16mm camera that Barnes & Barnes bought from Janit's brother Don, and a cheapo cheapo Super 8 camera of mine, the "Fish Heads" film came together slowly but surely. Instead of a crane, we pushed Rocky around in a shopping cart. Bill would go to the Santa Monica fish market and buy heads of fish that he'd keep in his freezer until they literally disintegrated. Joan Farber, who had designed the first Barnes & Barnes "look" and had done the layout and artwork on our first two albums, was drafted as makeup artist. It was Joanie who applied false eyelashes and lipstick onto rotting fish heads. Ahh, how we suffer for art.

Bill Paxton not only directed the film, but he also starred in it. His supporting cast included Barnes & Barnes and Dr. Demento. The film is several minutes longer than the "Fish Heads" single and Robert and I had fun scoring the ancillary bits.

Everyone was very pleased with the end result. It has a creepy beauty to it. It's funny and it's dark. It works.

THE LATE GREAT
BILL PAXTON.

I TOOK THIS PHOTO
WHILE WE FILMED "LOVE
TAP" IN A REAL FUNERAL
HOME ON HALLOWEEN
NIGHT!

Bill's passion and determination were unsurpassed. I never knew anyone with as much drive as Billy had. With absolutely no management behind the project, no appointment booked, or even a phone call ahead in advance, Bill flew to New York with several video prints of the film and promptly headed to the offices of *Saturday Night Live*.

The "Fish Heads" film (an edited version) ran on *SNL* the following week.

Rolling Stone magazine named it the fifty-seventh greatest rock video of all time.

It ran in film festivals all over the world.

It was featured in an episode of *The Simpsons*.

"Fish Heads" was used in a Quizno's sandwich commercial.

MTV named it the number one novelty video of all time.

In 2020 it was featured in the Netflix film, *The Babysitter 2*.

More than forty years later it remains the most requested song in the history of the Dr. Demento Show (which is still in production).

"Fish Heads" has been very, very good to me. Yeah.

BARNES + BARNES ON-SET FILMING "SOAK IT UP."

<<>>

*I*n 1987 Barnes & Barnes gathered a very eclectic and impressive cast of iconic talents to create a "mockumentary" that included all of our short musical films. Titled *Zabagabee*, Rhino released it on video to commercial limbo and critical success. The project features America, Janit Baldwin, Mark Mothersbaugh from Devo as "Booji Boy," Annerose Bucklers, Shaun Cassidy, Rae Dawn Chong, Rosemary Clooney, Eileen Davis Mumy, Dr. Demento, Jose Ferrer, Miguel Ferrer, Flea, Wild Man Fischer, Mark Hamill, Jonathan Harris, Teri Hatcher, Woody Herman, Shirley Jones, Gwen L., Bill Paxton, Jerry Siegel, Stephen Stills, Kate Vernon, "Weird Al" Yankovic, and of course Robert and myself as Art & Artie Barnes. It was quite ambitious and with a cheapo, cheapo budget and the editing skills of Dusty Ebsen, Buddy Ebsen's son, we got it done.

BARNES + BARNES WITH THE GREAT DR. DEMENTO, BARRET EUGENE HANSEN, WHO I CALL "BEH." HE LAUNCHED OUR CAREER.

CH 24. UNCLE WALT

"**M**ickey Mouse Lane"... "Donald Duck Drive"... "Goofy Road"... The names of a few streets on the beautiful Disney Studios lot in Burbank, California.

I did not know Walt Disney very well. But I did know him. I made three films for his studio while he was alive, and one after he died.

In 1962, I co-starred in *Sammy, the Way-Out Seal*, a delightful diversion written and directed by Norman Tokar, who was one of my very favorite directors. Excellent with children, Norman had directed countless episodes of *Leave it to Beaver*. He was also the voice of Henry Aldrich on the popular radio show *The Aldrich Family* for two seasons.

Norman had a very simple way of getting the best out of child actors. Just before the camera would roll he would walk over to me and very quietly but intensely look me in the eye and whisper one simple word: "think." And it worked. Still does. I often tell myself to "think" to help me get things focused while working on the set.

So much for the secret of my acting "technique!" "So Bill, did you study Strasberg, or Stanislavski? Grotowski, or Uta Hagen? What technique do you use to prepare for a role?" "Well, actually I picture Norman Tokar in my mind, he directed lots of *Leave it to Beaver* episodes, and I can hear him tell me to 'think.' That's what I do."

Yikes.

Norman was a small man, about five feet four inches, with a sunny face and a crew cut, usually hidden underneath a floppy hat of some sorts. He had a great dry sense of humor. I would work with Norman again in 1968 when I starred in *Rascal*, another Disney feature.

As the years passed and I grew up, Norman and I became friends. One night, after he had returned from directing a film in Kentucky, I went to his house in Hollywood with my pal David Jolliffe for dinner. Norman was dating Jolliffe's mother Gloria at the time. Norman, David, and I shared a bottle of homemade moonshine liquor he had received as a gift from someone on the hillbilly location. We sat on the front porch of his Hollywood home and reminisced about the old Disney days as the bootleg booze blurred our vision... Man, that stuff was powerful!

Anyway, back to 1962... Kennedy was in the White House, comic books were going up from ten cents to twelve cents, and I was working opposite a seal.

Sammy the Way-Out Seal was about two young brothers, Arthur and Petey (me), who find a wounded seal while on their beach vacation and manage to smuggle him back home and into their garage, where they proceed to heal him, train him, and get into some wacky trouble in town with him.

SAMMY, MIKE MCGREEVEY, AND ME.
JUST ANOTHER DAY ON THE BEACH.

My brother Arthur in this film was played by an actor named Mike McGreevey. Mike's father was a very successful screenplay writer, and Mike was absolutely super to work with. He was four years older than me, which would have made him all of twelve at the time.

I loved working with Mike, and we really looked like brothers. After working as an actor for many years Mike went on to follow in his father's footsteps and he became a prolific screenwriter. I still talk with him often and I always call him "Big Bro" and he calls me "Little Bro."

ME AND MY "BIG BRO."

I'm often asked about actors I've worked with who were not pleasant. Well... Robert Culp played my father in *Sammy the Way-Out Seal*, and all I can say about him is that he wasn't very friendly. He didn't seem to enjoy being there at all, and I don't think he ever said a single word to me when the camera wasn't rolling. Oh well, I suppose he didn't have to. And he sure was great in *I Spy*. I really loved that show.

The next summer I returned to work at Disney, again teamed with Mike McGreevey. This time we made two hour-long episodes of *The Wonderful World of Disney*: "A Taste of Melon" and "Treasure in the Haunted House."

It was a simple rural setting; Mike and I played two country boys on top of the world. The mischievous red-haired, freckle-faced brothers, J.D. (Mike) and Freddy (me) spent the summer stealing watermelons and getting into mischief. In the show, J.D. has a crush on the little girl down the road, Willadean (Terry Burnham), and she liked him just fine.

In one of the first scenes in "A Taste of Melon," Mike and I had to bust up a watermelon that we had just "snitched," and hungrily devour it. Well, we had to do that scene many, many times and Mike and I must have eaten at least a dozen watermelons that day.

It took twenty years before I had any desire to eat watermelon again. Even now, a little goes a long way.

"A Taste of Melon" presented a very laid-back way of life. Up in our fortress/treehouse, school was out, and life was swell until a wealthy city boy, Harley (Roger Mobley), and his family moved in down the road.

Harley is given his own horse, and this impresses Willadean, and J.D. gets jealous and dares Harley to steal a gigantic prize seed melon that the cranky old farmer neighbor has been growing for years. And Harley, wanting to impress Willadean and not look like a chicken to J.D. and Freddy, does it.

Well, things get pretty wild after that and eventually the kids end up in a deserted (so they think) old abandoned house that rumor has it is haunted. Inside, after a sequence of scary and funny events, they meet an old hobo (Ed Wynn), and learn a little bit about life.

We shot a lot of these two shows out at the Disney Ranch. It's a huge, magnificent piece of land. As big as the Ponderosa, I imagine. The only drag was the Disney ranch is a long way from Beverlywood and our shooting calls were very early, seven or eight a.m., so I'd have to wake up around five in the morning.

That part was never any fun.

Still isn't.

Ed Wynn was a real joy to work with. A one-of-a-kind actor, too. What a nice man! When we finished production, he gave everyone on the show a leather wallet that said "Thanks, Ed Wynn" inside in gold letters. I carried that wallet for many, many years. He was a real mensch. We worked together again on a feature I starred in with the amazing Jimmy Stewart called *Dear Brigitte*, and I received another "Thanks, Ed Wynn" wallet.

WORKING WITH THE ICONIC ED WYNN WAS A JOY. HERE'S THE CAST OF "TREASURE IN THE HAUNTED HOUSE." ME, TERRY BURNHAM, ED WYNN, MIKE MCGREEVEY, AND ROGER MOBLEY. WE HAD A BLAST!

The last project I acted on camera for the Disney studio was *Rascal*. It was filmed in 1968, two years after Walt Disney died. It was adapted from a classic book by Sterling North, a story about his own childhood. Norman Tokar directed it, and I felt very fortunate to land the leading role of Sterling. I was fourteen at the time, and it was the first feature film I made after working on *Lost in Space* for several years.

RASCAL. *I REALLY BONDED WITH THE RACOONS INCREDIBLY.*

Sterling and his traveling salesman father, Willard, are out in the country enjoying an apple pie, when they come across an abandoned baby raccoon. The part of Willard was beautifully played by the talented Steve Forrest. Steve had played my father years before in an episode of a dramatic hour-long western television show called *Wide Country*. It was a good script called "The Royce Bennett Story" about a rodeo rider who is losing his sight.

Sterling decides to bring the orphan raccoon back home with him, and soon the two are inseparable. Willard's work keeps him on the road, and for most of the summer, Sterling is on his own.

A few things happened while filming *Rascal* that I'll never forget. One: Steve and I had to eat fourteen apple pies during the very first day of filming, and again, it took twenty years before I could even think about eating apple pie...

Two: Towards the end of the film, there's a scene where Rascal has grown up into a mature raccoon, and he's no longer content to stay inside as a pet. He's clawing at a window to pry open the screen and Sterling plucks him up off the windowsill to reprimand him. In the scene Rascal turns and bites him. This is a dramatic turning point for Sterling because he realizes he must set his beloved pet free. Anyway, when we were filming it, everything went exactly as scripted. Everything. The raccoon really bit me! We finished the shot, and then the crew realized I was bleeding! It was no big deal, and I loved working with the raccoons. I wish the raccoon hadn't been such a "method" actor, but it sure made that scene "real!"

Three (saved the best for last): There's a moment very early in the film where Sterling is sitting in his father's car and he picks up the tiny raccoon and holds him up to his own face and looks at him and declares, "I'm going to call you... Rascal!" Well, during the first take, I picked up the raccoon pup, and held him up to my face, but the dialogue went a bit different than scripted: what I said was, "I'm going to call you... SHIT!" Because the lovable little creature did exactly that, all over my face as I held him in my hands! Baby raccoon shit bears a strong resemblance to mustard in case you're interested in the sordid details. I don't suppose the outtake of that scene was saved, but I wish it was! It would be a highlight in my library, that's for sure!

Rascal was a nice story. Sterling learns a lot about responsibility and so does his father. And we learn that the bond between man and nature is a delicate one, and not something man can ultimately control. It's a fine little movie. A real "Disney Family Film" in the truest sense of the phrase.

We filmed *Rascal* on location up in Lake Arrowhead, at the Disney Ranch, and on the Disney lot. When it was released, it was quite successful, and made a decent amount of money.

THE ONLY COONSKIN CAP FOR ME IS A LIVE ONE!

《》

When Walt Disney was alive, the Disney lot in Burbank was without a doubt the coolest lot of all the studios. It was truly a happy place. Outside the commissary there were several ping-pong tables and after eating folks would play table tennis and if you won you got to hold court and keep going. We had a table at my house (still do), and I was a pretty good ping-pong player back in those days. I have fond memories of games there. As you walked into the commissary there was a gift shop that, of course, sold Disney stuff. I used to buy little figurines all the time and in fact I still have a couple of them around the house. I also had one of my most embarrassing experiences in there when I was only eight years old.

There was a commissary dining room and there was also a cafeteria. We always ate at the cafeteria. I pushed my red plastic tray along and when I got to the soda machine, I filled my glass up with Pepsi and then squirted a large dab of whipped cream into my beverage. That was just something I always did when working at Disney. Then I moved my tray along the line and got a cheeseburger and French fries. As usual, my mom and I were eating with my "big bro" Mike McGreevey and his mom. I distinctly remember my mom offering to carry my tray for me and me strongly saying, "No, I can carry it." Then, of course I dropped it and spilled my Pepsi and whipped cream and burger and fries all over the cafeteria floor. I was mortified and really humiliated. But I got over it.

So, Mike and I are walking back to the set together. Our moms had gone on ahead of us. Walt Disney stops us. "Hi Mister Disney!" "You mean, Uncle Walt." "Right. Hi Uncle Walt." He leans down and tells me he hears I've been falling asleep on the set and says he wants me to get more sleep at home.

"Huh?!"

Mike and I exchange puzzled looks. I have no idea what he's talking about. I have more energy than a bear with a bucket of honey. I've never fallen asleep on the set. But I don't tell him that. I don't know what to say. He just smiles and says, "See ya later, boys" and walks on down Mickey Mouse Lane, the path filled with squirrels and flowers.

Well, this really confused and bothered us. So, we told Mike's mom about it and in a short time, she solved the mystery. While we were shooting *Sammy, the Way-Out Seal* one of the other features being filmed on the lot was *Mary Poppins* and Matthew Garber, the red-haired young boy in that film, had been sleeping on the set. So, I guess all of us red-haired kids looked pretty much the same to "Uncle Walt."

I remember the moment I heard he had passed away. I was on stage in front of the lights filming a scene during the second season of *Lost in Space*. It really made me sad. And trust me, everything that bears the name "Disney" has changed dramatically since he's been gone.

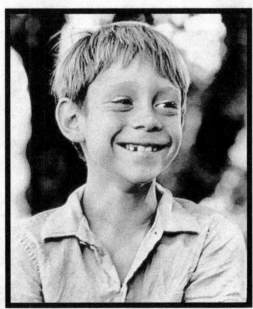

THE DISNEY PROJECTS I WORKED ON
WERE NOTHING BUT HAPPY TIMES.

WHAT HAVE I GOTTEN MYSELF INTO?
LENNIER... A VERY INTERESTING CHARACTER.

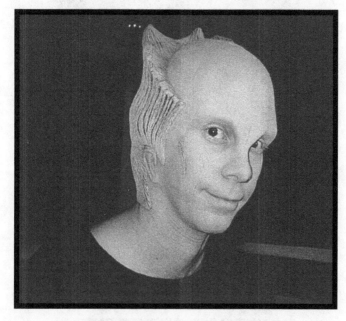

I AM THE EGGPLANT... GOO GOO G'JOOB.

25. Back in Space

Babylon 5 lasted for five seasons. 110 episodes were produced. That was the intended course that Joe Straczynski, the creator, writer, and producer designed it to be. Although Warner Bros. would have renewed it for further seasons, Joe felt it was a novel with a clear beginning, middle, and end. He didn't want to compromise his vision and after five seasons, the series concluded.

I started working on *B5* from the beginning, in late 1993, and I was still there on the final day of shooting when it wrapped in 1998.

There are so many memories, equally positive and negative, that make up my *B5* experience that it's difficult for me to open those files in my head sometimes. The highs and lows are extreme. Interestingly, they balance each other out, which leaves me feeling almost numb when exploring them.

The day I turned forty, my four-year-old son Seth came to visit me on the set and I just happened to be filming a martial arts fight scene at the time where my character, Lennier (up until this moment thought to be a very quiet and sensitive spiritual pacifist), combusts with unexpected energy and skill and he literally kicks ass. Lennier's first "superhero" type moment was captured on film while my son smiled and applauded. That's a wonderful memory. My daughter Liliana was born during Season Two and that is, of course, another very happy recollection. But my father died during Season Three. And that hit me hard.

It was not unexpected. My father, age ninety when he died, refused to be put on dialysis. He had been in extended care for a while. I spent the day at his side. I remember moments from then like a dream. My mother, who adored my father, asking him if he wanted some water and him replying "No. I want a kiss." (I'm actually crying right now remembering that.) Finally, I had to go. I had a very early call the next morning and was in every scene on the call sheet. I told my dad if he had to ride on ahead, that I'd catch up with him later. I kissed him and drove forty miles home, alone.

My mother couldn't bear to watch him pass, and completely drained and exhausted by then, she went home. My remarkable wife Eileen stayed with my father and cradled him in her loving arms as he exhaled his last breath. >Poof<. Charles William Mumy was gone. I didn't have a dad anymore.

But I did have a 4:15 a.m. call the next day and Lennier was in every scene on the shooting schedule. I woke up around 3 a.m. and called the hospital to ask how my father was doing and I was told he had expired a few hours earlier. I froze for a few moments and then I did the only thing I could do. I drove to work.

I didn't want to draw attention to it, but people knew my father was close to dying and I shared the news with the good people of the Optic Nerve makeup crew as they applied the Lennier makeup on me. It soon was known around the set. There was nothing to do but do the work and in a way, I was grateful for it because it took my mind away from constantly thinking about me never being able to talk with my father again.

But the human body is a fascinating thing. Although I was handling it pretty well, for the entire day, my right eyelid twitched uncontrollably. While we were shooting, I had to quickly turn my head profile as if I had seen something off camera to avoid having to film many retakes. I guess my soul just had to release the stress somehow and that's how it was channeled. That was a very tough, sad day.

I always knew Joe Straczynski was writing a brilliant multi-chapter, well- plotted-out-in-advance huge novel for television and I was proud to have contributed to the arc not only as an actor but also as a writer. When *Babylon 5* began production, I was writing the *Lost in Space* comic book published by Innovation Comics. For the second year I had plotted a big thirteen-issue story that juggled multiple locations and character arcs that led to major advancements in the *Lost in Space* saga. It was called "Voyage to the Bottom of the Soul" and has since been collected as a graphic novel. Joe is a comic book guy and he and Harlan Ellison, legendary writer who was a very involved creative consultant on *B5*, were both reading my comic book as each monthly issue was released. They complimented me on the work and accepted me as a fellow writer and not just one of the actors. So, as Lennier's story was beginning, I made some suggestions to Joe regarding his arc.

I told Joe that I thought Lennier was actually deeply in love with Delenn and that it haunted him and would be the underlying passion that controls his destiny. Joe listened and said, "Let me think about that over the weekend." The following Monday, he and I talked and he said, "Yeah. Let's do that. He'll be like Lancelot with Guinevere. But we won't reveal it for a while. But yeah. Let's go with it." And we did. And we didn't drop that card obviously for almost a full season. But if you look back through the previous episodes, it's definitely there. That was cool.

I honestly never acclimated to the physical makeup process of becoming Lennier. It was uncomfortable. It took hours. The makeup team couldn't have been nicer, and they did everything they could to make it better and quicker. They eventually got it down to two hours in the chair. But it was still difficult for me to have all that rubber glued onto my face and neck. I could never really see correctly because there was a piece that was glued down on the bridge of my nose, and I always felt somewhat cross-eyed. It was very difficult to hear with the "Minbari Bone" covering my ears. It became impossible to scratch the back of my head or really even twist my neck around much. It looked good and I developed quirky ways to "use" the alien shape to show emotions with a tilt of my head, but... let's just say I'd much rather have played a human instead of a Minbari for five years.

To remove the rubber and paint that was glued to my head and face every day required my skin absorbing very harsh chemicals that I knew were causing damage to my pale complexion. Five years of that takes its toll on your skin. Yet, until the fifth and final season, I loved playing Lennier despite the physical discomfort because he was a very intriguing multi-layered impressive character. He was also the opposite of Bill Mumy. Lennier was always centered, calm, capable, steady, and powerful. I tend to be impulsive and somewhat goofy.

The fifth and final season of *Babylon 5* was absolutely a drag. The entire cast and crew were treated very differently by the producers. The budget was reduced. The shooting schedule was cut by a full day per episode. Actors left. I found my own contract being reduced from appearing in all episodes produced to acting in only six episodes and writing one. Take it or leave it. That stung.

Peter David (my ofttimes writing partner) and I wrote the script based on Joe's logline and we turned it in. Joe praised it and said he had almost nothing to tweak. And then... the studio threw it out. We were paid for writing it, but it wasn't filmed. That really, really stung.

The business affairs people at Warner Bros. were super tough regarding talent. There was never any room for renegotiations.

Although it was a Warner Bros. series, *B5* was not filmed on the studio lot. We worked out of a converted hot tub factory in the deep San Fernando Valley. A fairly impressive makeshift studio was created there, complete with wardrobe, makeup departments (alien and humans were separate teams), props, special effects, etc. All of it was packed together in this isolated space a few yards from a freeway. Throughout the entire run of the show, no one ever left the facility to go to lunch or run errands. We had caterers set up in the parking lot and rows of benches under a huge tent-like umbrella where we waited for everyone to gather and eat together every day. No one received any "star" treatment. Didn't matter if you were Bruce Boxleitner or if you were an intern production assistant, you ate what they served, and you ate together. We all had the exact same size dressings rooms, and they were quite nice. No one ever complained about them. We each had couches and a desk and a makeup station and a little bed, a television and stereo, and a bathroom. All our trailers were properly air conditioned and heated. The only time the cast members didn't eat outside under the canvas overhang was when weather was either too cold or wet or too hot. In those cases, we'd retreat to our dressing rooms for meals. The food was always decent, and we always had several choices. I haven't eaten meat since New Year's Eve 1977-78. Pastas, salads, veggies, fruit and sometimes a little fish served me fine.

Babylon 5 had an excellent crew, mostly young folks starting their careers. The bulk of those who started at the beginning of the series were still there when it ended. It was produced very well. Unlike most hour-long science fiction projects, *B5* hours were consistent and manageable. I don't believe there was ever a forced call (a violation of the union's mandatory rest period between shoot days) on any actor. We rarely worked later than seven thirty at night. Of course, for those of us who were the regular "alien" cast members, 7:30 p.m. seemed late enough as our arrival time to head into the makeup chairs was something like 4:45 a.m.

Some wonderful actors appeared in guest roles on *B5*. I really enjoyed working with Brad Dourif, Bryan Cranston, and Walter Koenig -- the latter did several episodes and was wonderful as "Alfred Bester." Michael Ansara, who I'd worked with on *Lost in*

Space, Majel Barrett from *Star Trek*, Theodore Bikel, Jeff Corey, David McCallum, Lois Nettleton, and many others appeared in strongly written episodes. June Lockhart, who of course played Maureen Robinson (my mother in *Lost in Space*), guest-starred in a first-season episode of *B5* called "Quality of Mercy." How great to be working in space with June again! But our characters were not written into any scenes together and that was a disappointment. So, I went to Joe and asked him if we could simply put Lennier in one of June's "walk through the hallway" scenes where we'd pass each other and perhaps pause for a second, tilt our heads and then continue. He laughed and we were going to try to make that happen until the 6.7 Northridge earthquake happened on January 17, 1994. It was a major shaker and it was followed by thousands of aftershocks.

You need to understand, *B5* was not filmed on a traditional huge soundstage built like a military Air Force hangar out of solid concrete. We worked out of a little converted hot tub factory. The aftershocks shook our building like crazy for weeks. The entire crew and cast would evacuate and wait in the parking lot to see if the structure might collapse. It was scary working in that building after the quake. So there was no time for frivolity. No time to set up a little "ha ha, nudge nudge, wink wink *Lost in Space* joke." We just did what we had to do and moved on as quickly as possible. June and I posed for a publicity photo and that was it.

The *B5* cast was close. We were all constantly flying around the world making personal appearances to promote the show and everyone got along fine. There were extreme personalities... extreme political differences... extreme senses of humor... but like a good big band, we all grooved together nicely.

WITH MIRA AND BABY LILIANA. THE FIRST TIME SHE VISITED THE B5 SET.

SETH GOT TO PLAY AN ALIEN IN AN EPISODE OF B5. I LOVED IT WHEN EILEEN WOULD BRING THE KIDS TO VISIT ME AT WORK.

163

I honestly cannot think of any other series in the history of television that has lost so many of its main cast to premature deaths. It's hard for me to even write about it now. These were comrades I worked alongside of for five years. I knew their joys and their frustrations and their plans for their futures and their families.

Richard Biggs. Tim Choate. Jeff Conaway. Jerry Doyle. Mira Furlan. Stephen Furst. Andreas Katsulas. Michael O'Hare. All series regulars. All gone now.

THE WHOLE CAST. SO MANY GONE. RICK, ANDREAS, JEFF, STEPHEN, JERRY, AND MIRA... IT'S BITTERSWEET.

As close as I was to all of them, Mira and I were super close. I used to drive her home after work when we wrapped out together. In the many years after the series ended, Mira and I often spoke on the phone and we always went to lunch with each other, just the two of us, at least once every six months. We dubbed our ritual get-togethers "Getting Gloomy with Mira & Mumy." We would talk for hours about politics, our families, our projects, art, and music and we always made each other laugh. Mira was a very dramatic person and she was brilliant.

When Mira was bitten by a mosquito in her own lovely backyard, a mosquito that carried the West Nile virus, and when she then fell into a coma and never regained consciousness for many months and then died… I was absolutely shattered. I don't expect to ever fully accept or get over that tragic loss.

I simply can't enjoy *Babylon 5* without feeling the sorrow attached to the loss of so many.

As my character, Lennier once stated: "Faith manages."

BSERS AT THE 2015 SAN DIEGO COMIC CON. PHOTO BY EILEEN.

26. WAITING NO MORE

Not everything I worked on in 1962 was as pleasant as *Sammy, the Way-Out Seal*. I spent a few weeks working on Stanley Kramer's feature film, *A Child Is Waiting*, and I have to say, that was a difficult and pretty unpleasant experience. It's a film about mentally and emotionally disturbed children and the institution and school they are in. A new teacher joins the staff and has issues with the administrator regarding his teaching methods. The movie stars Burt Lancaster, Judy Garland, Gena Rowlands, and Steven Hill. Stanley produced it and it was directed by John Cassavetes.

There were a few professional child actors like myself in it, but the bulk of children who appeared in the film were truly mentally challenged kids who were bussed in every day. They were always kept separate from me and only came onstage when filming was imminent. That itself became a recurring problem from day one.

Judy Garland was going through a very rough time then and I clearly recall more than several occasions when she just wouldn't come out of her dressing room. We'd all be brought onto the set and be at our places or on our marks under the hot lights, and then we'd wait. And wait. Eventually we'd be sent back to our various holding places until she actually did come onstage. When Judy Garland was working, her performance was so real and so impressive and so sensitive, it radiated powerfully from within her. She was nothing but sweet to me, but she was obviously extremely troubled and although I was only eight years old, I felt very sad for her.

THE SENSITIVE BUT SAD, AMAZINGLY TALENTED JUDY GARLAND
LOOKING INTO MY YOUNG SOUL.

Burt Lancaster was as fine and professional and as easy going as you could hope for on an uneasy project.

I am a fan of several John Cassavetes films, but I did not enjoy working for him at all. He was a yeller. He yelled all the time. He yelled at the crew and he yelled at the kids and he yelled at the cast. I learned that he and Stanley Kramer had very different thoughts on what the tone of the film should be and they struggled to collaborate. Cassavetes seemed to be constantly very stressed out, for good reasons I'm sure, but he made an already uncomfortable undertaking much tougher.

When it comes to on-set schoolteachers, I had the very worst of the worst on *A Child is Waiting*. If memory serves me well, she was known to us child actors as "Missy Lau," and she was ridiculously strict, completely devoid of humor, seemingly ancient, and mean as a junkyard dog. I can't say I was at ease anywhere during my time on the film. Not on the stage and not in the school trailer.

It felt strange right from the very beginning. I was never encouraged to mingle with any of the kids who were bussed in and I remember feeling uneasy because they were kept isolated and treated so differently. Of course I understood that some kids had disabilities and I was sympathetic and curious but I was never comfortable.

I wasn't cast in a truly essential role in the film and after a few strained weeks when I'd filmed a handful of my scenes, my mom knew I was miserable. My agent asked if I could exit the production early and it was granted. *A Child is Waiting* is the only project I ever left before my initial contracted work was complete.

GROUP SHOT FROM *A CHILD IS WAITING*

27. Voyage to the Bottom Of the Studio

*F*rom 1964 until 1968 I was pretty much the "Little Prince of Fox." There wasn't an inch of the lot that I didn't know like the back of my hand. My workload on *Lost in Space* was certainly heavy and I had to get my schooling done, but I still found plenty of time to cruise around and discover all the secrets the Fox lot could surrender to a young, adventurous, and very inquisitive Billy Mumy. I knew exactly what candies were stocked in what candy machines in what building on what floor. You wanted a Zagnut bar? I knew the only place you could get one.

No one ever seemed annoyed that the kid from *Lost in Space* was hanging around. When a sign on a stage door said "Closed Set," that didn't apply to me. I dragged Angela with me most the time on my explorations. She really was a very good girl and she always worried about being somewhere she wasn't supposed to be or doing something she wasn't supposed to do and getting into trouble for it. I wasn't like that at all.

One day in 1966, we ventured into the closed set where they were filming *Fantastic Voyage,* which was a film about a group of people shrinking down to microbe size and traveling through a human body on a medical rescue mission in a tiny submarine. Ange and I bounced around for a while on what was supposed to be a stomach. Raquel Welch was one of the stars of *Fantastic Voyage* and we used to see her around the lot all the time. Pretty lady. The film was based on a short story written by Jerome Bixby who had written the original short story "It's a Good Life" that became "my" classic *Twilight Zone*.

Lost in Space had shot on Stage 11 and Stage 6 and sometimes around the Fox lot on various locations like the pond and caves or the back lot where the machine shops were and a full-size Jupiter 2 was usually parked. Between Stage 11 and the Prop Department building there were doors across from each other that were always locked. I wondered what was behind those doors. One day, I turned one of the doorknobs and it opened.

Having read most all of the *Hardy Boys* books by then, I made sure that the door would remain unlocked behind me and I ventured inside. A long concrete stairway heading down a full story awaited me. The walls were thick concrete, and I found a light switch and turned it on. The path became illuminated. I walked down the stairs and found myself at the bottom staring at another thick door. It too was unlocked. Again, I continued on. Again, I made sure I wasn't going to be locked in and again, I found a light panel on the wall and switched it on.

WHOA.

It was like a giant retro high-tech Bat Cave down there. I was inside a really huge concrete bunker-type chamber with a tall ceiling and pipes running all around it. Scattered in corners were giant fans and generators and machinery whose purpose I had no clue about. Twenty feet ahead of me was a small concrete step up to a huge round tunnel big enough for a grown man to stand upright and maneuver through. I walked up the steps and again switched on a light that illuminated the tunnel, which seemed to stretch on ahead of me into infinity. What a find!

HELLO... ANYBODY DOWN HERE???

I turned all the lights off and closed the doors behind me, making sure they remained unlocked, and resurfaced back where I entered and ran to get Ange. I had to talk her into it, and once she saw the steep stairway heading down into this mystery she came close to bailing, but she didn't. She followed my lead and soon we were down in this strange labyrinth of weirdness that lurked underneath the studio above us that we knew so well. Again, I illuminated the lights in the tunnel and she and I ventured forward like Penny and Will Robinson exploring an ancient abandoned alien underground civilization. You could hear a hissing sound in there and the farther we walked the hotter it got. We held hands. Actually, I thought it was kind of sexy. I was glad she was down there with me. The tunnel finally ended only to be cloned at the exit into another huge chamber with another tunnel ahead of it. Ange had had enough and convinced me to retreat back to Stage 11 and not to mention it to anyone because she feared we'd get in trouble. I agreed to the first part of her request, but I quickly found Mark Goddard and told him about it. A couple of days passed before Mark and I went below and explored the underground further. We went down there several times and it was always spooky yet always exciting. Ange got her courage back up and she and I eventually explored more of those subterranean tunnels. They continued on and on, one after another, each chamber seemingly of the exact same design, leading all around deep beneath the Fox lot.

One day, quite some time later, I checked the door and it was locked. Moving a few stages down and across the path where I knew there was another door, it proved to be locked as well. Same everywhere I checked. I don't think those doors were ever supposed to be unlocked and I just got lucky that first time and then had kept them unlocked until someone noticed and locked them all again. That was the end of our underground adventures.

However, I do believe I've come to understand one of their purposes besides just storage space, generators, and piping. My mom worked on the Fox lot from 1941 through 1951. She was there every day during World War II. She explained to me that during that time, the government would not allow the big studios to camouflage their huge soundstages. Why? Because they resembled airplane hangars, and if the Japanese or the Germans tried to bomb Los Angeles, the government would prefer the studio lots got bombed instead of the actual military hangars where the real war planes were being made and stored, and those were indeed camouflaged. So, in the case of an air attack, the people who worked at Fox would have access to these underground, heavily fortified, concrete subterranean bunkers. Makes sense in a weird way. I don't know if that's ever been confirmed, but that's my story and I'm sticking to it.

Mark, who was thirty at the time, was really just a big kid. His real full name is Charles Harvey Goddard and mine is Charles William Mumy Jr. We call each other Charles Harvey and Charles William. My mom used to call him her "other son" and scolded him for being so goofy all the time. She'd shake her head and roll her eyes and say, "Mark, I love you, but you're a fool." She used to say that to me a lot too. My mom was quite a character. Mark was very spontaneous and sometimes I felt like I was actually the older brother. He and I were the pranksters on the *Lost in Space* series and once in awhile we did some pretty goofy stuff, like the time we commandeered a golf cart and drove it up to the back lot pond and straight into the water until it sunk. We both knew we shouldn't have done that, and we both knew it was stupid and we've both laughed about it for over fifty years now.

ANGE COULD REALLY SCREAM!

28. You Should Be Dancing
(Yeah!)

1-2-3-, 2-2-3-, break step, 1-2-3-. As if I wasn't busy enough working every day on *Lost in Space*, my mother was talked into signing me up for Cotillion. Mrs. Paul Henreid's Dance Cotillion, which was held on Sundays at the Beverly Hilton hotel.

Oy.

Darby Hinton, who co-starred on the *Daniel Boone* series went to school on the Fox lot with me and Ange during hiatus. All the shows with minors had school trailers parked outside their sets with assigned teachers for each individual show, but Frances Klamt was in charge of all of them and she ran the permanent schoolroom on the lot. So, when we weren't filming, we all went to school with Frances. Whom we all loved. Frances had been on the Fox lot since Shirley Temple was first signed. Some of the kids who joined me and Ange for weeks at a time in the classroom were Stefan Arngrim from *Land of the Giants*, David Jolliffe and Howard Rice from *Room 222*, Cristina Ferrare who was working on the feature film *The Impossible Years*, and Veronica Cartwright (Ange's sister) and Darby Hinton from *Daniel Boone*.

Darby is a great guy with a very big personality. He's always been full of confidence and good humor. He and his sisters and his mom, Marilyn, lived in Beverly Hills and they seemed to know everybody and everything. Marilyn was a very impressive and boisterous woman. She was quite large and somewhat loud, but full of fun. I remember she always wore bright colored mumus. She had her kids enrolled in Cotillion and somehow, despite my whining, Marilyn Hinton convinced Muriel Mumy that Cotillion would be a smart thing for me to be a part of.

So, for about a year, on Sundays, I had to put on a suit and go to Cotillion. At first I really hated it. Yeah, there were a lot of kids there and you could run around the halls of the Hilton hotel and get into a bit of trouble once in a while but being all dressed up took most the fun out of that. I mostly remember being in that ballroom and learning various dances. The one and only dance that I actually liked and got good at was the Swing. I was lucky to have a lovely partner, Anona Peck. "Noni" was cute as can be and very sweet. She was about a year younger than me and dancing close with her never made me nervous. We won some swing contest together and I liked the classic old time rock & roll groove that we could swing dance to.

Years before my pal "Weird Al" Yankovic became famous, I wrote and performed a parody of "These Boots Are Made For Walkin'" at Cotillion. Of course it was "These Shoes Are Made For Dancing." Sheesh.

As much as I enjoyed my dance partnership with Anona, I didn't enjoy Cotillion much and after two "semesters" of it, I'd had enough and refused to let my mother sign me up for additional rounds.

Although… there was another girl from Beverly Hills who went to Cotillion named Diana Boos. Diana, a spunky cute blonde, was a few months older than me. I always go for the older women. Diana was my first real make-out kiss. Our young tongues wrestled. It was exciting. That made Cotillion worthwhile.

I still chat with Diana on social media once in a while and remind her she was Numero Uno in the smooch department.

29. WEEKEND LOVE

Some broken hearts take a long time to mend, others heal quickly. After wrapping up MGM's *A Ticklish Affair* in 1962, I pined over Shirley Jones. I had fallen hard for her. But I went straight into another feature film, *Palm Springs Weekend* for Warner Bros., and my amorous dreams quickly shifted from Shirley to Connie Stevens. Can you blame me? Connie was the quintessential "Queen of the Scene." She was gorgeous and very perky with a sexy purr of a voice and excellent comedy chops. I had enjoyed watching her weekly on *Hawaiian Eye* as Cricket before I met her, and I was familiar with her hit record "Sixteen Reasons" too. I was already a fan by the time we worked together. I hadn't planned on falling in love with another leading lady so quickly, but it happened.

Palm Springs Weekend was easy and fun to make and it was a hit. Directed by Norman Taurog, we filmed it at the Burbank Warner Bros. studio and on various locations in Palm Springs where production took over a hotel for several weeks. I played Boom Boom Yates, the son of the hotel manager, played by Carole Cook. Boom Boom was a trickster and a manipulative brat, but he was also really funny and I enjoyed playing that role. Besides the awesome Connie Stevens, there were a lot of cool people in the cast, including Troy Donahue, Stefanie Powers, Robert Conrad, Ty Hardin, Jerry Van Dyke, Jack Weston, Andrew Duggan, and even an appearance by the Modern Folk Quartet featuring Henry Diltz. Everyone in the cast was young and easy to work with, with the exception of Robert Conrad who was cranky and got into some fights while we were on location in Palm Springs.

The script was written by Earl Hamner Jr. who went on to create and write *The Waltons*.

Palm Springs Weekend is one of those period pieces that takes you right back to the carefree days of the early 1960s. It's goofy, campy, and cute. It seems to run on various networks often and people always enjoy talking to me about Boom Boom and his antics, such as pushing Jerry Van Dyke into a pool covered in soap suds. I remember shooting that scene clearly. Jerry had to be careful counting his steps because there really was no way of seeing exactly where the patio ended, and the pool began. It worked out fine.

After a couple months, *Palm Springs Weekend* wrapped production and Connie gave me her current 45 rpm single, "Mister Songwriter." It's a good song. And she inscribed a nice note on the red label to me. I still have it. In 2011, we were at an event together and I sat down with her and we laughed and shared memories of that kooky, fun little film we'd worked on together almost half a century before. We took a photograph, and she still gave my heart the flutters.

Palm Springs Weekend opened in theaters on November 5, 1963. In less than three weeks, President John F. Kennedy would be assassinated and the world that resembled the tone of that movie would never return.

WITH THE LOVELY CONNIE STEVENS... REUNITED AND IT FEELS SO GOOD!

30. Space Wars

Lost in Space premiered on CBS September 15, 1965 just shy of a year prior to the launch of *Star Trek*, which debuted on NBC September 8, 1966. Almost from the start, fans acted like there was some type of competition between the shows. I never understood that. Was there competition between *Leave it to Beaver* and *Father Knows Best*? Was there competition between *Bonanza* and *Gunsmoke*? Why, just because both series were set in the future and off of Earth, should there be a rivalry? *Lost in Space* was a show about a family. *Star Trek* was a series about the military. They both had some great science fiction episodes and they both had plenty of silly campy episodes. Me? I watched 'em both.

I was very pleased to become a part of the Trek television world when I was asked to guest-star in an episode of the seventh season of *Star Trek: Deep Space Nine*. My friend and Laurel Canyon neighbor, Ira Behr was the executive producer and main writer on *DS9* and he called and offered me a role in a very dark and gritty war episode. In "The Siege of AR-558" I played an exhausted Starfleet Engineer, Lt. Kellin, who dies in battle at the end of the episode. Ira was visiting the set when we filmed my death scene. Once the shot was in the can and the director, Winrich Kolbe, said, "that's a print," Ira announced to everyone on the Paramount soundstage, "Ladies and Gentlemen… *Star Trek* just killed Will Robinson!"

"The Siege of AR-558" aired on November 16, 1998, a mere nine days before the final episode of *Babylon 5*, "Sleeping in Light" aired.

There was, and continues to be, fan competition and rancor between *DS9* and *B5* fans as both series dealt with space stations and both series featured multi-season war stories.

I say: "Live long and prosper. Beam me up, Scotty. Danger, Will Robinson!"

THE DOOMED LT. KELLIN ON *STAR TREK DEEP SPACE NINE*.
PHOTO BY EILEEN.

31. Kinda College

*I*magine during the turbulent transition of adolescence to adulthood, an oasis… a Shangri-La for young artists to thrive in. That's exactly what the home of Leo and Sylvia Wolf was to many during the late 1960s,1970s, and beyond. My grade in school fell between their brilliant son, Frank, and their amazingly talented daughter, Tanya, and I bonded for life with both of them as well as with Leo and Sylvia. Their Cheviot Hills home was open to many young aspiring artists and political activists. We would gather in their living room and take turns performing newly written songs on their Steinway baby grand piano and then give and receive appreciated feedback. We would stay up all night passionately discussing politics and spiritual paths. It was a magical and positive refuge for many. My life would be very different if not for the love, nurturing, and generosity of Leo and Sylvia Wolf. May they rest in peace.

<<>>

*T*he food truck that served the Fox lot was nicknamed "The Roach Coach" and it was driven by a blonde-haired young man in his twenties named Teddy. I used to know exactly where the Roach Coach would be at any given time. Carrot cake, sweet rolls, and cold roast beef and cheese sandwiches were my favorites for a year or so. I used to sit inside the Batmobile and the Green Hornet's Black Beauty car when they were parked and not being filmed. I remember telling Bruce Lee how cool I thought the hard plastic masks he and Van Williams wore as Kato and the Green Hornet were. Bruce let me try his on. He also taught me a few kicks and moves. I thought he was really amazingly cool. He and I did a personal appearance together for charity at Santa Monica City College in 1968. I wish I had a photograph from that. A few years later, I'd be a student there.

«<»

Santa Monica City College is a nice campus and it's close to the beach. It was easy to be enrolled there and I chose to further my education like most of my friends were doing. Paul Gordon was studying music at LACC downtown, Gary David was studying music at Cal State Northridge, and in 1972, at the age of 18, I was a college man studying music at SMCC.

I took Diatonic Harmony, Musicianship, Musical Theatre, History, and English classes. But it became clear to me almost from the very beginning that I wasn't interested in anything beyond improving my musical theory knowledge. I went to the History class once. I never even went to the English class. The Musical Theatre class was not at all what I thought it might be and for a few months, Scott Ehrlich and I found ourselves cast in the chorus of a production of *Fiddler on the Roof.*

Oy.

I had my little apartment at Mediterranean Village off the Sunset Strip, was driving a new Camaro, Redwood was gigging often and recording at Record Plant, there were lots of college and rock & roll girls to party with, and I was far from broke, so you'd think I would have been enjoying myself. But I wasn't. I was still reeling from losing Angela. I was writing dirge tempo, depressing songs and shall we say, being less than cautious in my lifestyle. I'd stay stuck in this quasi-party depressed groove most of the year until Alison and I became a couple. She made me a very happy man and everything that was self-indulgent and sorrowful and sad about me shifted into a grateful, happy, and positive mode. For a little while, anyway. Thank you kindly, Alison Wickwire.

Anyway, I did learn what I set out to learn from the Diatonic Harmony and Musicianship classes. I quit the rest of the courses, stopped going to *Fiddler on the Roof* rehearsals and never showed up for a single test or final. So, basically my year in college is nothing but official "incompletes" but I was indeed there, although most of that is a blur to me now.

Francie Schwartz was a writer from New York who went to London in 1968 and became Paul McCartney's girlfriend for a while. She sang background vocals on "Revolution 1" and then was hired to create press releases for the Beatles' newly created Apple company. Francie is best remembered for being the reason Jane Asher broke off her engagement to Paul when she discovered her in bed with her fiancé. After leaving England, Francie relocated to Los Angeles and moved into a high-rise apartment building overlooking Venice Beach.

There used to be a small but very cool club in Venice with a good sound system and a nice stage called Attica. Redwood played there at least once a month back in 1971. Attica was walking distance from Francie's apartment and she happened upon the club while Redwood was having a particularly good night. Francie had a lot of chutzpah and drive and within a short amount of time, she became our publicist and wrote a pretty artistic press release for the band that got us more gigs and more press. She and I had a fling, which was fun. By the time Redwood was recording at Record Plant, Francie had moved on to other projects. I don't imagine if I were chatting with Paul McCartney, I'd bring up the Francie connection. Probably best to just let it be.

32. Coming to America

The first time I heard "A Horse With No Name" in November of 1972 I thought, like many others, it was a new Neil Young track. It's an undeniably contagious tune that draws the listener in to a surrealistic visual ride. It was written by my good friend and collaborator, Dewey Bunnell, and performed by Dewey and his bandmates in America, Gerry Beckley and the late Dan Peek. Dewey just happened to have a vocal tonality similar to Neil's and there's no denying this young trio was influenced by Crosby, Stills & Nash.

America happened quite suddenly in the LA scene. One minute they had a hit single out of the blue and the next, their debut album was top of the charts, and they were booked into the Whisky A Go Go on the Sunset Strip for a week. One of the first, and perhaps the only, acoustic trios to ever play that hard-rocking room. I lived in an apartment a few hundred yards south of the Whisky in a building named Mediterranean Village on Larrabee Street when America first came to town. A friend of mine, Paul Markowitz, a fine guitarist and singer, had gone to high school and jammed with them when he lived in England. Paul was on their guest list and he invited me and David Jolliffe to accompany him to see his friends the first night of their week-long gig.

I ended up being there every night and every set. I quickly became good friends with all three of the guys.

One of the most peculiar experiences I've had was with America at the Whisky gigs. Brian Wilson was there a couple of the nights.

Brian is a huge hero of mine and that cannot be overstated. Even as the Beach Boys' popularity had dropped, I remained a true Brian fan. America had opened for the Beach Boys in Europe before coming to LA and they were well acquainted with Brian. Late 1972 found Brian Wilson to be quite manic. The upstairs headliner's dressing room at the Whisky A Go Go is a pretty big space. A grand piano was in there and although there were a decent amount of folks hanging around, it was never super crowded. I clearly recall the night Brian stood in front of the entire room and with a pointer and a blackboard, gave a very zippy and passionate speech about the benefits of vitamins and health foods and then immediately began offering amphetamines to everyone. Man, he was jumpy.

A short time later, I was sitting at the piano and noodling a little bit and Brian came over and sat next to me on the piano bench and said, "You write songs?!" I said "I do." Brian commanded me to play for him the most recent song I had written. I remember this so clearly. I was working on a new song at the time and I played him what I had of it, "It's called 'I Don't Drive the Canyon Anymore.'" Well, you'd have thought I played him "Let it Be." He jumped up and shouted, "That's an amazing song! I love that song! I'm going write a song called 'I Don't Drive the... FREEWAY anymore!!'" You couldn't help but smile and feel good around this genius who was combusting with good vibes like a giant puppy.

Another night at the Whisky that week, Brian was again very shall we say "up" and he was pacing the dressing room as America was finishing up their first set of the night. "Love, Love is the Way!" He kept repeating *something* like that and he enthusiastically grabbed me (don't ask me why I was elected) and told me he wanted to go onstage and play a few songs before the guys' next set. He wanted to play this new "Love, Love" idea. Well, I thought that was fantastic. Brian Wilson wants to make a solo guest performance at the Whisky? How cool is that?! So, as requested by the man himself,

I set out to make that happen for him. I quickly found Mario Maglieri, the owner of the Whisky, and I told him the good news. "Brian wants to go onstage and play a few songs. He's got a new idea he wants to share." Mario, without missing a beat, shrugged it off and said, "That maniac isn't getting on my stage. No way. He's nuts." I felt really bad. I thought, even if Brian had gone onstage and been less than great, he would still have been Brian Wilson and I was sure it would have been interesting and musical. But Mario walked away, cranky and busy. When I returned to the dressing room, Brian was still anxious and still wanted to be onstage. I fibbed to him to not hurt his feelings and told him "Mario appreciates it, Brian, but there's a union thing and it's not going to happen tonight." Within two seconds, Brian had accepted that and was zipping off to another idea. I had a plethora of feelings blending together inside me that night. I realized that yes, Brian was high on speed, but there was such an innocence and pure sweetness about him that you wanted to protect him from having his feelings hurt and yet you also could see he was deeply damaged, but you also didn't want to talk down to him or obviously placate him, because he deserved the truth. It was complicated.

America reminded me in some ways of my band, Redwood. We were also an acoustic trio that sang in three-part harmony and Redwood had been gigging around Southern California for almost three years. Redwood was recording at Record Plant with house engineer Mike Stone engineering and co-producing us at that time. When the Whisky gig ended and the America guys had a little down time, they all came to some Redwood recording sessions and liked what they saw and heard.

America decided to record their second album at Record Plant and to use Mike Stone as their engineer. All three of them also liked the new apartment building that David Jolliffe was living in on Kings Road in West Hollywood and so they all got apartments there. Sessions for the sophomore America album *Homecoming* yielded the smash hit single "Ventura Highway," another song written and sung by Dewey, and I attended many of those sessions.

Next up for America was a world tour. They needed a rhythm section to back them up. They were a solid acoustic trio live but they also wanted to plug in and rock hard. For the *Homecoming* sessions they had relied on legendary session players Hal Blaine and Joe Osborn for drums and bass. Now they needed their own guys. Jolliffe, who was co-starring in the television series *Room 222* as Bernie, a skinny white kid with a huge bright red afro, had been writing songs and recording some demos with the rhythm section of David Dickey on bass and Willie Leacox on drums. Gerry, Dewey, and Dan heard those tapes and ended up using David and Willie for their tour and the two of them stayed with the group for many years. Willie and Dickey are both gone now, but they were a very cool rhythm section.

Besides jamming and hanging with the guys, I began collaborating on writing songs with them and we've played and sung on each other's records and sessions often. By the time they had a hit with "You Can Do Magic," I was a regular co-writer with both Dewey and Gerry and over the years have written dozens of songs with them, co-produced their recordings, and played guitars, bass, and provided background vocals on America records. I have also joined them onstage many times as a guest guitarist and vocalist.

Dewey and I sang and played the National Anthem at an Angels baseball game in 2001. That was quite an experience. I had worked out a folky arrangement for the two of us to sing in harmony while I played guitar. It went great, but what I hadn't accounted for was the delay and slapback from the sound system in the massive ballpark. It was quite something, but we pulled it off nicely and my son Seth was super impressed, and he and Liliana and Eileen were there and it was a real nice family experience. In the 1990s I was invited to join the band on bass to tour, but my contractual commitment to *Babylon 5* made that impossible.

Dan left the band in 1977 and passed away in 2011. Gerry and Dewey remain close friends of mine. I still write songs with Gerry fairly often. But I never call them "Dewey" or "Gerry." I always call them by their middle names. Gerry's is Linford and Dewey's is Merton. We've seen a lot of crazy life together.

As for the horse with no name? Dewey and his wife Penny adopted a wild horse a few years ago and named her Noname, pronounced "no nah may." La la la la la la la la…

ONSTAGE WITH THE BOYS SOMEWHERE IN THE 1980s (ABOVE) AND IN 2002 (LEFT). GOOD TIMES. GOOD MUSIC. GOOD FRIENDS. PHOTOS BY HENRY DILTZ.

33. I Love a Parade

I guess many people would be honored and would enjoy riding in a parade. I'm not really one of them. I rode in many parades as a kid. I was in the Rose Parade a couple times and the Hollywood Christmas Parade and dozens of others all over the country. I remember my face hurting from holding a smile for hours and waving as the float or the open car or the truck slowly made its way along the route where thousands of people were staring at you, snapping photographs and yelling while one marching band's music was fading out and another's was fading in. Many times, Angela would be next to me in the parades and we'd try to crack each other up as we passed the people by and waved.

But honestly, and I know this is telling about the way my mind works, I was always on edge in those parades because I would find myself thinking about President Kennedy being assassinated and I'd constantly be searching the roofs and windows for maniacs with rifles. Sad, but true.

There were exceptions to the rule though, and a couple of parades remain treasured and beloved memories of mine. The first was the annual Bishop Labor Day Parade. My dad had been "Big Man in Bishop" and before I was a recognizable child actor, I would ride on horseback alongside my father down the main streets of Bishop and I was so proud. My dad would be dressed in his finest and fanciest cowboy outfit, waving a Stetson hat to his friends who would cheer. When I was four and five years old, riding next to him in those parades I felt just like a junior Roy Rogers. I really loved that.

And then in 1996, Jonathan Harris and I were "Grand Marshalls" in a parade at Disney World in Orlando, Florida. Jonathan and I sat next to each other up high in the back of an antique fire truck and smiled and waved as we slowly made our way through the Magic Kingdom. That was a real good time. I always enjoyed working with and hanging out with Jonathan as an adult. He was so clever and so funny and he absolutely loved being a celebrity. His memory for names and details from the past was remarkable. Jonathan would giggle and cackle and it was contagious. So, yeah, I got joy being in a few parades, but in general I didn't dig them.

CRUISING THROUGH THE MAGIC
KINGDOM AS MARSHALLS OF
THE PARADE, JONATHAN AND I.
WHAT FUN WE HAD TOGETHER.
I LOVED THIS.

RIDING DOWN THE MAIN STREET
OF BISHOP WITH MY DAD IN THE
LABOR DAY PARADE, BEFORE I
WENT INTO SHOWBIZ.
I WAS JUST A LITTLE COWBOY
SO PROUD TO BE WITH MY DAD.
I'M RIDING MAGGIE, MY PINTO,
AND MY DAD IS ON BONNIE. HE
WAS BEAMING.

I'M THE VERY SERIOUS "LIEUTENANT FLEMING"...
WATCHING THE BIRTH OF CAPTAIN AMERICA.
WE SHOT THIS IN YUGOSLAVIA.

34. MARVEL-OUS

*I*t was the caped adventurer, Zorro, and the ultimate superhero, Superman, that inspired me at such a young age to "get inside the TV" and I have always enjoyed any opportunity offered me in that realm. I've always considered Anthony Fremont from *The Twilight Zone* to be the most powerful mutant ever and Will Robinson was pretty much a young superhero in my mind. I modeled Will after a comic book character created by Jack Kirby and Joe Simon: Bucky Barnes, Captain America's young partner. When I was filming *Lost in Space*, Jack Kirby and Stan Lee were putting out World War II Captain America and Bucky stories every month in *Tales of Suspense* comics and Bucky, for some reason, always just hit me harder than other young comic book characters that I could relate to somewhat. So, I indeed played Will Robinson with Bucky Barnes in mind. I was also in the first *Captain America* feature film.

I was excited about working on Marvel's *Captain America* film. I was friends with the great Jack Kirby at the time and I genuinely was hopeful it would be a successful movie. I flew to Yugoslavia to work on the film for several weeks. However, this was the 1990 version, not the 2011 film, and it quite honestly just isn't very good. Directed by Albert Pyun, it's a bit of a mess of a movie. Matt Salinger played Captain America and he was committed to the role and delivered a fine performance, but he's no Chris Evans. The script took a lot of liberties with the origin story, going so far as to make the Red Skull an Italian instead of a German. I played Lieutenant Fleming, a not-too-trustworthy World War II military man. The Fleming character was portrayed in "modern day" by

Darren McGavin in the film. An interesting side note here was that my very first acting job ever was with Darren on an episode of *Riverboat*, a TV series he starred in, filmed back in 1959. Unfortunately, Darren, Ned Beatty, Melinda Dillon, Ronny Cox, Michael Nouri, and all the other respected actors could not turn the *Captain America* movie into a success. The rubber ears on the Cap mask certainly didn't help.

Matt Salinger's wife, Betsy, traveled with me from Los Angeles to Yugoslavia. To say she was tightly wound would be an understatement. She insisted I listen to NWA's first album *Straight Outta Compton* on her Sony Walkman several times during the flight. It's certainly powerful urban folk music, but it's not relaxing stuff. Then she gave me a pill to help me sleep and I don't know exactly what it was, but I found myself tired and itchy for the next eight hours, but not sleepy.

Being on my own in Zagreb, Yugoslavia was interesting. I walked for hours and hours all over the city on my days off. This was before everyone had a cell phone of course and as usual, I brought my Nikon camera with me. I've always enjoyed photography. The camera becomes your travelling companion. Like a friend, you share your experiences with it. You tell it a secret or a story, and it tells it back to you later in a different way that keeps it alive. I didn't get into many, if any, conversations with strangers in Zagreb. Having the Nikon with me kept me from feeling lonely.

Zagreb was clean and although it was politically unstable, I felt safe there. I visited museums and little shops and I found a fantastic pizza restaurant called Pinocchio's a few miles from my hotel near the railroad tracks and I ate there several times. I spoke zero Serbian or Croatian, but it never ceases to surprise me how English seems to be pretty well known wherever I've traveled.

A few years later, when I started working on *Babylon 5*, one of the things that helped me bond quickly with Mira Furlan were my recollections of my time in Zagreb. That was her hometown. She was a huge star there and she laughed in wonderment when I mentioned Pinocchio's pizza to her. It was one of her favorite spots.

It's difficult to be objective when you're in the thick of working on a film. You become friends with the crew and your fellow actors and like a musical group, you want to groove and harmonize. While shooting *Captain America*, I remember thinking everyone was doing a good job.

Sometimes the ingredients are right, but the recipe is wrong.

I have guest-starred on other "super" shows such as *The Flash*, *Ultraman*, and *The Adventures of Superboy*. I did three episodes of *Superboy* playing Tommy Puck, a genius arch-villain of the Boy of Steel.

GERARD CHRISTOPHER MADE A GREAT SUPERBOY. I DID THREE EPISODES AND ENJOYED EVERY MINUTE OF IT.
SO COOL TO BE A SMALL PART OF THE OFFICIAL SUPERMAN SAGA.

35. IF YOU CAN HEAR MY VOICE

*F*rom the very beginning of my career, voice-overs have been a part of my work. What a great arena of showbiz that is. I've been blessed to have had a prolific voice-over career that has covered the spectrum of animation, commercials, announcer, and narration. Way back in 1960 I did a series of animated "Smokey the Bear" public service announcements, working alongside the legendary "Man of a Thousand Voices" Paul Frees. Shortly after recording those I began working on the *Matty's Funday Funnies* cartoon series featuring Bob Clampett's *Beany & Cecil*.

I had some more "super" adventures working on *Batman: the Animated Series, Rescue Bots* (I did three of those and played a robot!), *Ben Ten*, and... I was fortunate to team up and work with Jonathan "Dr. Smith" Harris again on two episodes of Disney's *Buzz Lightyear of Star Command*. John Lasseter was in the studio with us when we recorded our scenes together and he giggled seeing us acting up a storm as space people again.

As always, it was great to work with Jonathan. The chemistry between us clicked in a wonderful way and we laughed and got it done quickly, just like in the old days.

I also worked in animation with June Lockhart in a fantastic episode of *Ren & Stimpy* titled "Blazing Entrails." That was really great. Jonathan and I also supplied voices for an animated short titled *The Bolt Who Screwed Christmas*, and that project featured my "Robinson sisters" Marta Kristen and Angela Cartwright as well. *The*

Bolt turned out to be Jonathan's final voice-over work. I'm grateful we were together once more. *Scooby Doo, Roswell Adventures, Holly Hobbie & Friends, The Oz Kids*, and *Animaniacs* are some of the other animated projects I've worked on.

<<>>

My daughter, Liliana, has had an amazing career in animation that makes mine look like a piece of nothing! She's done thousands of episodes on long-running hit television series and feature films as a voice-over artist. I have been lucky enough to have worked alongside my multi-talented daughter on several animated series including *Holly Hobbie & Friends, Bravest Warriors* (I did eleven episodes of that one and played Liliana's father), and *The Loud House*.

<<>>

Narration is another appendage of voice-over work that I found a successful niche in. For the acclaimed *A&E Biography* series I narrated over fifty episodes featuring an impressive array of subjects: Jane Fonda, Steve McQueen, Dustin Hoffman, James Dean, Paul Newman, Betty White, Carol Burnett, Elizabeth Taylor, Harrison Ford, Mark Hamill, Natalie Wood, Andy Griffith, Ron Howard, Ava Gardner, Jayne Mansfield, Tippi Hedren, James Brolin, Sir Alec Guinness, Sharon Stone, Bernie Mac, Will Smith, Susan Sarandon, Faye Dunaway, Keanu Reeves, Linda Blair, Blake Edwards, Jane Withers, Mary Martin, Donna Reed, Tim Robbins, and Carolyn Jones. There are more, but you get the picture. It was a good gig. A real good gig.

A&E also hired me to narrate TV-themed episodes of *Biography* and those included: *M*A*S*H, The Mary Tyler Moore Show, The Wonder Years, Cheers, Happy Days, Laverne & Shirley, Batman, Charlie's Angels, Home Improvement, The Partridge Family, That Girl*, and *The Love Boat*. Henry Winkler produced several of those.

Henry's one of the sweetest guys in showbiz. Back when "Showbiz Kids" and "Happy Days" had teams that competed against each other in the West Hollywood Softball League, Henry used to pitch for the "Happy Days" team. His pitches were pretty easy to hit.

For a short while I was the announcer for the WB network as well, but one day after finishing up a long session recording promos at Warner Bros. I barely made it back home before Laurel Canyon was flooded due to a huge rainstorm. The roads were covered with a foot of cascading water mixed with tons of mud and big rocks. It was a huge mess. I pulled my 1986 Porsche 911 coupe (that I'd purchased from its original owner, Don Henley of the Eagles) into my garage and sought shelter from the storm inside my house. As soon as I got inside, my answering machine was blinking. It was my voice-over agent. WB had forgotten to record one more promo and wanted me to come back as soon as possible. Well... I said I'd be glad to if they'd send a car for me. They didn't, and that was the end of my being an announcer for the WB. Showbiz.

I've provided voice-overs for dozens of commercials over the more than sixty years of my career, but perhaps the greatest gig I ever had was being "the voice" representing Farmers Insurance. I held that job for eleven years. I would drive to a recording studio, receive a few pages of copy, view a rough cut of a new commercial if it was for television, and go into the booth and record anywhere from two to eight commercials in less than an hour. "Farmers... Gets you back where you belong." I recorded that line hundreds of times. And it sure got my family where it belonged. Those Farmers spots ran all the time on national TV, on the radio, on the internet... What a fabulous job! Doing voice-overs for Farmers put my kids through private middle schools and high schools and helped me pay off my house mortgage ten years early. The teams that produced those spots changed over the years, but they were always smart, prepared, cool people who were easy to work for and gave excellent direction.

Like most everyone in the world who was alive then, I recall the morning of September 11, 2001 clearly. Eileen and I watched in horror as it unfolded on our television. I was booked to record several Farmers spots that afternoon. No one called to cancel them, so I drove to the studio in Santa Monica and showed up for work. The vibe was awkward. Everyone in the studio had difficulty focusing on the task of creating funny 30-second commercial spots that centered on reversing time. I read my lines and then left. A few weeks later, we re-recorded all those commercials.

My Farmers' gig lasted from 1995 through 2006, eleven years. I remember the day my agent, Mary Ellen Lord (David Jolliffe's wonderful wife), called me and said, "Well, Farmers is changing the campaign and they're going in a different direction." Losing the Farmers' gig meant losing the bulk of my income, but I was grateful it lasted as long as it did.

WORKING IN THE RECORDING STUDIO DOING A VOICE-OVER GUEST SHOT ON NICKELODEON'S *THE LOUD HOUSE* ALONGSIDE LILIANA AND THE HUGELY TALENTED CAST. I PLAYED A FOOD CRITIC.

36. ROBOT TALES

Yes, the story is true. Mark Goddard and I once locked Bobby May inside the Robot and left him trapped in it alone on Stage 11. It happened sometime late during the third season. Bobby worked insanely hard, and he created ways to give the Robot a unique and quirky character. He'd raise the bubble up, he'd pull his arms in close to his body and lock the Robot arms in place and spin the entire torso around like Linda Blair's head in *The Exorcist*. It was Bobby who came up with the Robot waving his arms around like crazy when there was "Danger! Danger!" He also had to memorize and deliver all the Robot's dialogue. To do so, he had to push a button inside the Robot's claw for every single syllable he spoke. That illuminated the neon on the Robot's chest in sync with the rhythm he delivered the dialogue in. Dick Tufeld re-recorded the Robot's dialogue in post-production because he had an amazing voice and tone and also because Bobby's delivered dialogue sounded like it came from a guy inside a fiberglass box: because it did.

Bobby May loved being inside that claustrophobic, dangerous prop. He'd literally spend hours in it sometimes and never ever complain. I think he actually truly liked being inside it. He certainly never complained, even after taking a couple of hard falls and being knocked nearly unconscious. Bobby was sweet, a real trouper. He came from a legendary vaudeville family. Bobby was the grandson of vaudeville comedian Chic Johnson, half of the Olsen and Johnson comedy team. However, Bobby's never-ending enthusiasm and cheerleader-like energy could get a bit tiresome. Bobby went over-the-top often. He painted his chair silver. He painted stuff in his dressing room silver. He never ever did or said anything maliciously, in fact, quite the opposite, he tended to overdo his camaraderie. Anyway, Jonathan, who of course brilliantly turned Smith's relationship with the Robot into a hugely successful bit, often rolled his eyes at him.

One day, after wrapping up a master shot just before breaking for lunch, Bobby had been especially trying. Our effects team, led by Stu Moody headed out to unlock the Robot so Bobby could get out, and Mark and I exchanged a look and said, "You guys go on ahead to lunch. We'll let Bobby out of the suit." You see, there was no way Bobby could extricate himself from inside the prop. The bubble top had to be unscrewed and removed and then there were bolts at the bottom of the torso that needed to be released and only after that had been done, could Bobby climb out of the rubber legs section.

The crew all left the stage and Mark and I just grinned at each other, and we also left the stage, abandoning Bobby inside the Robot in the sand surrounded by foam rubber rocks. It was our original intention to actually go to lunch and then come back to let him out, but honestly, we only got 100 yards or so outside the stage building when we looked at each other and knew we couldn't go through with it any longer. It just wasn't fair to Bobby not to let him eat. So, we strolled back onto Stage 11 through the wide-open huge door and what we saw was terrifying. The Robot, which was a good fifty feet away, had smoke coming out of it! You have to understand, that prop had multiple batteries inside of it and many wires and various electrical systems. If something had sparked, a short of some kind with Bobby trapped inside it, with no one on the stage to hear him cry out for help, it could have been a deadly accident. Mark and I sprinted over to the Robot, and we unlocked the top as quickly as we possibly could. We were both afraid we'd remove that bubble and find Bobby May fried to a crisp! Instead, and I swear this is true, we discovered Bobby smoking a cigarette! He had pulled his arms in close, locked the Robot's arms in the torso, held a small pen sized flashlight in one hand, had a lit cigarette in his mouth, and he was reading the *Hollywood Reporter*.

"Oh. Hey, Mark buddy! Billy. What's up? How come you're getting me out?"

Mark and I couldn't believe it. He was totally unaware that we'd locked him in there for several minutes and he was happy as a clam. He didn't get the joke. Years later Bobby would tell that story at conventions, but he exaggerated it to say he was smoking a cigar and that it was Irwin Allen himself who rushed to get him out of the suit.

See? He could be annoying.

BOBBY MAY WAS THE HARDEST WORKING GUY IN SHOWBIZ.

THE ORIGINAL "HEAVY METAL" BAND!

MARK HAMILL AND I AS "JIN AND PEL: THE FERNAHERNA" ON MY NICKELODEON SERIES, SPACE CASES. MARK IS A TROUPER!

CELEBRATING MARK GETTING A STAR ON THE HOLLYWOOD WALK OF FAME. UH... I WANT ONE!

37. The Force is Strong

Speaking of space… Mark Hamill is a longtime good friend of mine and we've worked together on several projects. Mark guest-starred alongside me in an episode of my Nickelodeon series *Space Cases*. "A Day in the Life" was the title, and he and I played silver-faced alien air traffic controllers who were about to blow up the Christa spaceship and its crew. We spoke in Liverpudlian accents and made it a Beatles-type joke. Mark had a bad reaction to that silver makeup, but he was a great sport about it. Then I did a comical bit for an independent film Mark made called *Comic Book: The Movie*. Mark also did a very funny cameo bit in Barnes & Barnes' *Zabagabee* video compilation and he and I wrote an ambitious movie pilot script together that we shopped around a bit but didn't sell. Perhaps we should polish that one up and try again? Hmmmm. Food for thought.

Mark and I are insane comic book collectors and fans of the Golden and Silver Age books. We used to go to comic conventions together, along with Miguel Ferrer, who was also addicted to vintage pulp collecting. The three of us would always find some cool books to add to our collections and then go back to our houses together and gently open the mylar bags, withdraw the books, smell them (it's an intoxicating scent!), and turn the pages and read the stories before gingerly placing them back in mylar. I recall the time Mark bought *Superman* Number 1 through Number 100 at once. That was impressive. Between the three of us, we had/have excellent collections.

Even though we were often recognized at comic cons, rarely were we bothered. The problem begins when you stop and start signing a few autographs and taking photos with a few people, then it quickly becomes a lot of people and a lot of autographs and that's flattering, but can certainly put a dent in your quest for books.

"It's Luke Skywalker, Will Robinson, and that Robocop guy!" The three of us had a lot of fun together. I recall a small convention in Hollywood, it may still be going, it was run by Bruce Schwartz and sometimes I'd show up as an invited celebrity guest, but most of the time I'd just go with Miguel and Mark, and we'd wear baseball caps and shop and then leave.

MUMY, MARK, AND MIGGY...
COMIC BOOK HUNTERS.

For a while I got into re-purchasing the old Aurora model kits I'd had as a kid. I saw a vintage, sealed-in-shrink-wrap Robin the Boy Wonder kit at this particular Bruce Schwartz con and I bought it. I'm pretty sure I paid $60 for it. When we got back to my house, Mark's eyes got as big as saucers when he watched me open it up. "Mumy! What are you doing?! That's shrink-wrapped!" "I'm gonna make it and paint it." He thought I was crazy. Mark has the excellent habit of usually buying two of most everything he likes; one to play with and one to put away unopened. Well, my wallet's not as fat as his, so I just bought the one Robin kit and I opened it, made it, painted it, and I enjoyed it. Until we had a small earthquake that rattled it off the shelf it was perched on, and it broke into too many pieces to glue back together. No regrets.

Is it just me? Or does the trio of Luke Skywalker, C-3PO, and R2-D2 remind anyone else of Will Robinson, Dr. Smith, and the Robot? Hmmm? Or does that not compute?

38. MUMY + THE MUNSTERS

The Munsters TV series ran for two seasons from 1964 to 1966 and has retained a passionate fan base ever since. Butch Patrick played the role of Eddie Munster, somewhat of a werewolf boy, and Butch did a great job. However, the part was originally offered to me. We passed on it because the makeup seemed like it would be difficult and a drag. Thirty years later I experienced plenty of serious makeup reality playing the alien Lennier from the planet Minbar for five years on *Babylon 5*.

I did work on *The Munsters* though. I guest-starred in an episode titled "Come Back, Little Googie." It was the 25th episode of the first season and originally aired on the CBS network, March 11, 1965. I played Googie, a friend of Eddie's, who was a real brat and a trickster. Googie convinced Grandpa Munster, brilliantly played by Al Lewis, that he had turned me into a chimpanzee.

That show has run continuously for well over half a century and I hear from fans to this day about how much they love *The Munsters* and what a little jerk that Googie was. I take that as a compliment.

Al Lewis guest-starred on a second season episode of *Lost in Space* and between him and Jonathan Harris, I felt like a piece of cheese between two big slices of ham. They both were super over-the-top with their comedic performances and tried to upstage and outdo each other on the set. They had a blast working together.

I have no regrets about passing on the opportunity to play Eddie Munster. If I had taken that gig, I wouldn't have ended up playing Will Robinson on *Lost in Space*.

Butch remains a pal and he and I speak fairly often.

EDDIE AND GOOGIE.

BILL AND BUTCH.

39. Home on the Strange

When I returned from filming *Papillon* I moved back into my parents' house for a while. I'd moved out of my apartment on Larrabee just off the Sunset Strip when I left on location for a few months. The Mediterranean Village apartment was a month-to-month rental and the one-bedroom space came fully furnished, so leaving it was easy. I had some good times in that place.

Moving back with my mom and dad and LaLa, my grandmother, wasn't so easy but it was okay for a little while. My parents let me be as "hippie-ish" and as "modern" as I wanted to be, but when I was staying in their house I had to live by their rules. No girlfriends could spend the night in my bedroom. If a date did sleep over, she had to sleep downstairs in the guest room, which to me was always "Essie's old room." Of course, they would never for a nanosecond have tolerated any weed being smoked in their house and that was fine with me. I wasn't smoking very much marijuana in those days anyway. I'd imbibed enough ganja in Jamaica to last me awhile and besides a little herb, I wasn't doing any other drugs at all.

I'd been a professional musician gigging with Redwood for several years already, so coming in very late after third-set gigs was always understood and was fine with my folks. They only requested that if I was not going to be coming home at all some nights that I call and let them know that. It didn't matter if I phoned them at 2 in the morning. They were cool about it. They just wanted to know I was safe.

When my kids, Seth and Liliana, were over eighteen and living here, I was the exact same way. Just please check in and let us know you're okay whatever the clock says. Parenthood is the most important, and rewarding, and stressful, never-ending gig of all.

《<》》

Papillon wasn't a very positive experience for me. I knew it would be a big movie and I'm glad I stuck it out, but in the end... it was the first time since I'd been five years old that I'd been reduced to such a small role in a project, and I didn't find any joy in that. I came home with a weird buzz cut and I grew a beard.

Redwood had been on hold for a few months, and I was anxious to get back onstage in the studio with Paul and Gary. While I had been on location, although I had my guitar with me constantly, I didn't write any new songs. Paul had been writing alone while I was gone, and he was overflowing with new material and it was quite theatrical, complicated, impressive and... different. We started rehearsing with a largely new set list in mind. Paul's new songs were great, but you couldn't dance to them or even tap your foot to most of them. They were quite difficult to play on guitar and the harmony parts were more complex than ever. Because Paul had written them, it made sense for Paul to sing the lead vocals on them, but that greatly reduced Gary's lead vocals. Gary hadn't written any new songs and he was feeling the pressure of Redwood not achieving what we all felt we should have by then. I started writing a batch of new songs to keep up with Paul and he and I wrote a couple good ones together, but for the very first time in our musical partnership, we began consciously TRYING to write songs that we thought would take us to that next level.

We'd watched America somewhat step into our template and continue to have huge success and whether we were really aware of it at the time or not, we started trying to write more "America-type" songs, more "Eagles-type" songs, more "Randy Newman-type" songs… and that's when our downward slope started. Redwood, for three years, had been an eclectic, unique, acoustic trio featuring two guitars and a violin (or sometimes a piano, guitar, and violin or a guitar, banjo, and violin) and we rotated lead vocals evenly and sang in three-part harmony a lot. People really dug us. We had a solid following. They dug our "Tree Music" sound that wasn't out to emulate the hits of three months ago in any way shape or form. Now… we started reaching so hard for the brass ring that we were falling off the horse.

REDWOOD… 1972. PAUL, ME, AND GARY.
PHOTO BY JANIT BALDWIN.

40. Sunshine on My Shoulders

My agent got me an interview for a new Universal film called *Sunshine*. The movie was a true story based on the written and audio diaries of a young pregnant hippie girl, who sadly is dying of cancer. Her boyfriend, not the biological father, is a musician in a folk music trio along with his two band mates (both draft dodgers) living in Vancouver, Canada. She makes the best of her fading days and leaves her baby daughter in the care of her boyfriend and his bandmates when she dies. It's a tearjerker and it was beautifully made.

George Eckstein produced it. George was a showbiz veteran and a very kind and open man who knew how to assemble an excellent team. His career started back when mine did. He wrote and produced many television shows such the final two-part episode of *The Fugitive*. He produced and wrote the sci-fi series *The Invaders*, *Banacek*, and many others. Perhaps George is best remembered for giving Steven Spielberg his first major job directing a Universal Movie of the Week about a mysterious demonic truck chasing Dennis Weaver. It was called *Duel* and it was based on a story written by *Twilight Zone* alumni Richard Matheson. My first *Twilight Zone* "Long Distance Call" was based on a Richard Matheson short story.

Sunshine was directed by Joe Sargent. Joe was one of the best. His list of credits was extensive and impressive. Best of all, he was always focused and nice and communicated with his actors with clarity and great positivity. He was always open to suggestions and Joe had boundless energy. After the disappointing time I had working for Franklin Schaffner on *Papillon*, I really appreciated working with a director like Joe, who cared about his actors and what they were questioning or struggling with choice-wise.

Carol Sobieski wrote the *Sunshine* teleplay based on the life of Jacquelyn M. "Lyn" Helton. Carol was very involved with the casting and the continuation of *Sunshine* beyond its initial film. She was enthusiastic and a cheerleader for all the *Sunshine* projects. Carol very much encouraged us to contribute to the characters.

I met with George, Joe, and Carol in George's Universal office to audition for the film as a musician. They were all familiar with my acting resume, but they wanted to cast the singing and guitar-playing parts with strong actors who could really play instruments and sing so that the music scenes would be authentic and not obviously overdubbed and recorded by others. I remember being very comfortable in that initial meeting. My hair was still quite short, but my beard had grown in thick and was quite a bright orange-red. I opened up my battered guitar case, extracted my 1968 Martin D-28 and proceeded to play and sing James Taylor's "You Can Close Your Eyes" for them. A little over two minutes later, we were discussing the character I would go on to play. His name was Weaver, and he was the cousin of Kate, the dying young mother. Weaver was pretty much an insensitive, draft-dodging, dope-dealing, banjo-and-guitar-playing, self-absorbed biker. I tried to make him a little likeable, too.

The lovely and talented Cristina Raines was cast in the starring role of Kate. A stunningly beautiful flower child and fine actress, Tina was a doll and we got along great. At the time, she was living with Keith Carradine out in Malibu, and they came up to my Laurel Canyon house and we jammed and hung out a few times. I haven't seen or heard from Tina in many decades now. But working with her and just being around her positive energy was a joy.

Cliff DeYoung was cast in the other starring role as Sam Hayden who marries Kate and takes on the responsibility of raising her infant daughter, Jill, who was played by twin toddlers Lindsay and Sidney Greenbush who later starred on *Little House on the Prairie*. Cliff had an impressive musical career before becoming a successful actor. He'd been lead singer in a band signed to Elektra Records called Clear Light and they'd toured with the Doors, among other top acts in the mid-1960s like Janis Joplin. Cliff had also been successful on Broadway playing the lead in *Hair*. (Angela and I saw *Hair* here in LA at the Aquarius Theater in 1969.)

Cliff gave a solid performance. He sang lead on all the songs in the film with the exception of "Take My Home, Country Roads" which I sang. The project featured the songs of John Denver. Good, solid, heartfelt, folky country music.

Corey Fischer, all six feet and seven inches of him, was cast as Givits, the third member of the trio. Corey and I instantly became good pals. Our characters were almost always in scenes together and with Corey towering a foot above me we made a pretty interesting sight in our tight two shots. Corey had been in the feature film, *M*A*S*H*, and had done lots of theater. He was a songwriter and guitarist with a deep baritone voice. He and I played guitars naturally and well together. After many years of working with Paul, I was very comfortable finding different inversions and melodic arpeggios to add to the John Denver simple progressions. Corey played the first-position rhythm parts and although Cliff was supposed to play a third guitar part, he didn't really play much guitar and most of the time it was just Corey and me with Cliff strumming along a little. Being in Redwood, a trio that sang three-part harmony, I pretty much worked out the vocal arrangements for the *Sunshine* songs and they fell together quite easily. Cliff sang the melody, Corey sang the bottom harmony, and I either sang above Cliff or in between him and Corey. We blended fairly nicely.

Surprisingly, Universal released a *Sunshine* soundtrack album and a single. "My Sweet Lady," credited to "Cliff DeYoung with Bill Mumy and Corey Fischer," reached Number 17 on the *Billboard* Hot 100 pop charts and the album went gold in Australia.

Meg Foster and Brenda Vaccaro completed the main cast. They are both not only terrific actresses, they're both funny and very strong-willed women who I enjoyed working with.

We shot most of *Sunshine* up in Vancouver, a city I truly like.

WEAVER – NOT THE NICEST GUY, BUT I TRIED TO MAKE HIM
LIKEABLE. I WAS TWENTY ONE YEARS OLD HERE.
TIME IS A BIZARRE RIVER.

Released to critical and commercial success as a feature film overseas, *Sunshine* originally aired domestically as a two-and-a-half-hour *CBS Friday Movie of the Week* on November 9, 1973.

When it first aired, *Sunshine* was the most watched made-for-TV film in history.

Because of the critical and commercial success of *Sunshine*, George Eckstein and Carol Sobieski received the nod of approval from Universal to adapt and evolve the characters into a weekly half-hour comedy-drama television series. Can you imagine that "pitch?" "Yeah, three draft-dodging hippies up in Canada who are in a folk rock band and living just under the poverty level are raising a dead woman's young daughter." Seems like a natural. Or not. But it happened, and it was a very unique project. Cliff, Corey, Meg, and I starred in the series and young Elizabeth Cheshire was cast as Jill. The series took place three years after Kate's death and it focused on this unconventional "family" raising her.

Again, we went up to Vancouver to shoot the pilot and some ancillary bits that would be inserted into several episodes as establishing and exterior shots. Although the original *Sunshine* film had aired on CBS, the 1975 *Sunshine* series was on NBC. We were up against some serious opposition with *The Waltons* and *Barney Miller*. We managed to make and air thirteen episodes before the network cancelled the series due to less than stellar ratings.

John Badham directed the pilot. John's sister, Mary Badham, had starred in *To Kill a Mockingbird* as Scout, and she and I were pals on the Universal lot back when she worked on that classic film. John was a fine director and I enjoyed reconnecting with Mary through him.

George Eckstein and Carol Sobieski always welcomed and encouraged the cast to be creatively involved with the show. Corey and I wrote a couple of songs together that were used in a few episodes and then we took their offer to heart and he and I collaborated on writing a script together. We titled it "Leave it to Weaver." The plot was simple. My character, Weaver, grows frustrated because Sam is too busy parenting Jill to really be serious about the band and when Weaver gets an offer to join another commercially successful group... he must make a hard decision.

Carol and George liked our pitch and our treatment and approved the script. Corey and I wrote a strong first draft and Carol polished it and we were all set to film it. "Leave it to Weaver" was the first television script I ever got produced, but it wouldn't be the last.

Now, the job of casting the other musicians in the episode that tempt Weaver away was once again, pretty much a gift from George to me. After a quick meeting and audition for George, Paul got the part of the keyboard player and Brian Greer was cast to play the bass player. Finding the drummer was both easy and hard.

Miguel Ferrer, who had been a close friend of mine for several years by then was a fine, well-trained, professional drummer and he had a cool rocking look and attitude. Miggy had played not only with rockers like Keith Moon, but he'd toured with his mother, the legendary and super-talented Rosemary Clooney, and he'd also backed up Bing Crosby. His father was the Academy Award-winning iconic actor, Jose Ferrer. Miguel was perfect for this. I told him that I'd written the episode, that Paul and Brian were doing it, and that he had to play the drummer. It was only a few speaking lines and it would be a blast. Miguel said, "No way, Mumy. I'm not an actor! That's my father's gig." I told him, "Well, your father's too old for this part. You have to do it!" I insisted. I really twisted his arm. He continued to resist, but he agreed to go to Universal and meet with George Eckstein and me. George was super nice and generous to Miguel. He told him how much he respected his mom and dad's work and that he'd be honored to have him do this part. George told him he'd consider it a personal favor. Besides, all the guys were gonna make an easy $500 each for the day's work.

Miguel agreed.

Just consider me a Doctor Frankenstein. From then on, Miguel Ferrer dedicated his life to acting and although he still played the drums, his great rise to fame as an actor started because I pushed him into it.

Paul, Brian, and Miguel all slept over at my Lookout Mountain Laurel Canyon house the night before filming the scenes together for *Sunshine*. We drove onto the Universal lot very early the next morning and went straight into the recording studio and laid down the backing tracks for the scenes. Couldn't have gone any smoother. Paul on Wurlitzer electric piano, Brian played my 1968 Fender Precision Bass, I played my Gibson Les Paul, and Miguel laid down the groove on a set of white Ludwig drums. As far as the on-camera acting scenes went, they too were completed fast and easy. Each of the guys had a few lines and they delivered them like pros. I felt great to be able to give my friends some work on my network TV show. I also got Scott Ehrlich a supporting acting gig on an episode of *Sunshine*. That's what friends do.

One thing that's always been frustrating for me is the fact that I never saw most of the thirteen *Sunshine* episodes when they originally aired. I was gigging, or in the studio recording with Redwood, when they were broadcast and so I missed seeing them. When the series ended and the final episode aired at the end of May, NBC never ran the thirteen *Sunshine* episodes again. The series wasn't transferred to digital and the prints remain locked up in Universal's film vault somewhere. A lot of people remember watching it fondly.

I wish I'd seen it.

While filming *Sunshine*, I had a very nice dressing room on the Universal lot connected to the stage we filmed on. It had a shower, bed, makeup table, and television. I had brought a stereo record player there and had a fairly large collection of vinyl I kept there as well as a few changes of clothes and toiletries.

After getting the not-so-good news that the series was over, I drove up to the main gate with the intent of clearing out my dressing room. "Hi Scottie." "Hi Bill." "Did you hear we got cancelled?" "I did. Sorry, Bill." "Well, I'm gonna go get my stuff out of my dressing room." "I'm sorry, Bill. But you don't have a drive on anymore." "What? Are you kidding me, Scottie?" "I wish I was, Bill. You don't have a drive on." Now, Scottie had been manning the main gate at Universal for many years. I'd known him since I was a child. Here I was, twenty-one years old, in my new black Mercedes Benz 280-C that I'd just gifted myself for my birthday, looking at him with a confused expression that clearly was not a happy one. I'd worked on the Universal lot off and on for fifteen years at this point in time. After a few silent seconds passed, Scottie opened the gate and said, "Try and make it quick, Bill."

Showbiz.

Well, you'd think that would be the end of the *Sunshine* story. But 'twas indeed not. George and Carol had yet more stories in mind for Sam, Jill, Weaver, Givits, and Nora and in 1977 we all returned to those characters yet again for another movie-of-the-week. This time we were working on a Christmas-themed story simply called *Christmas Sunshine*.

The plot revolved around Sam taking young Jill on the back of his motorcycle from Vancouver to Texas to visit her grandparents for the holidays. Sam's relationship with his parents, especially his conservative father, is rife with negative history and while there, his parents try to convince him to let Jill stay with them and be raised in a "normal" environment. Sam also reconnects with his high school sweetheart and almost agrees to surrender the freedom and artistic life he lives and loves in Canada to settle down in Texas for the betterment of his young seven-year-old daughter. That is until Weaver, Givits, and Nora trek down to Texas and snap Sam out of it and teach his traditional father that a loving family can be many things, including a trio of long-haired musicians and a hippie girl.

Sunshine Christmas had a really strong supporting cast beyond us regulars. Barbara Hershey gave a soulful and deeply emotional performance as Sam's old girlfriend, Cody Banks. The great Pat Hingle, whose acting was multi-layered and strong, brilliantly played Sam's stubborn father, Joe. Eileen Heckart was cast as Bertha Hayden, Sam's mother, the salt of the earth who wanted only what was best for her husband, her son, and her granddaughter. Glenn Jordan directed, and most all of it was filmed on location, in Claude and Amarillo, Texas.

We weathered a few weeks of pretty wild storms while down in Texas working on *Christmas Sunshine*. Production stopped for several days because of the intense rains and lightning. When the sunshine returned on *Christmas Sunshine*, we were treated to a big weekend party at the iconic Cadillac Ranch, owned by eccentric millionaire Stanley Marsh III. Ten various Cadillac models, spanning the years of 1949 through 1963 were submerged, nose down, into the ranch as art pieces with their iconic tailfins on display. I thought it was very cool and since my mother had driven a pink 1959 Cadillac for several years, I began to appreciate that old ride more than ever.

I did one of the stupidest things I've ever done that sunny afternoon at the party. I remember it like it happened yesterday. Although I've always been quite capable of making small talk and schmoozing with strangers, I've never really enjoyed that sort of thing. We were hanging around outside, enjoying the food and having a few beers, when I noticed that several horses were gathered close and they caught my attention. I grew up with horses and I feel very comfortable with them. I started talking to an impressive handsome sorrel that stood approximately sixteen hands tall. We seemed to have a nice connection. So, I thought, "Wouldn't it be nice to have a little saunter around the ranch?" Talking calmly to this glorious creature, I pulled myself up onto his back and straddled him. Now, there was no bridle or saddle or anything like that at all on this horse. I didn't know anything about him and here I was sitting on top of him. Well, he turned his neck around and looked me square in the eye and telepathically sent me a very clear message, "Who the hell do you think you are? Did I invite you to sit on me? Hell NO!" And then... BAM! He took off like a bullet fired from a Winchester rifle. In a split second I realized what a fool I was and all I could think was, "If this horse bucks me off and I get seriously hurt, like break some bones, it's going to wreck production and they're gonna kill me!" I raised myself up and leaned forward into a jockey position and gripped that horse with my knees as hard as I possibly could, and I grabbed on to his mane with both hands as tight as possible. He bucked and he kicked, and he ran straight towards several huge low-hanging branches intent on extricating me from him. But I was determined not to get hurt. I clung on and kept talking to him until finally, after what felt like twenty minutes, but was more likely closer to twenty seconds, he acknowledged that I was worthy of the position I had so brashly taken, and he stopped trying to buck me off. I immediately dropped off him, thankful that nothing negative came from my spontaneous audacious stupidity. It all happened so fast that I don't think any of the *Sunshine* cast and crew were even aware of it.

We wrapped up the film successfully with no further drama and after four interesting and creative years, the *Sunshine* projects came to an end.

I saw Cliff a few times after that. He and I performed a musical set together at Royce Hall on the UCLA campus for the Special Olympics and that was cool. We sang songs from the *Sunshine* movies and the series, and a Beatles tune or two. Years later, he came to a gig of mine. It was nice to see him.

Corey and I stayed in touch throughout the years. He moved up to Northern California and continued his work in the theater. He visited me in Laurel Canyon in 2019 and the two of us jammed on guitars and sang the old songs and had a lovely day just catching up. I was shocked and saddened when he passed away in June of 2020, age seventy-five, after suffering a brain aneurysm. Corey was a true artist. He loved the theater and he never stopped creating. One of his art pieces hangs in my bedroom.

THE BAND. SAM, GIVITS, AND WEAVER.
WE PLAYED AND SANG IT ALL OURSELVES.

The guys with the mesmerizing Meg Foster.

Shiver me timbers.

We did a houseboat episode, filmed on the Universal backlot.

221

PART 3

WITH THE LOVE OF MY LIFE, EILEEN.

41. SOUL MATE

Everyone knows that my wife Eileen is the best thing that ever happened to me. It just took me a while to fully understand that. Sarah Taylor, the very talented singer and longtime good friend, brought Eileen to a gig of mine in late 1979. I was performing at the Bla Bla Café in Studio City with the Igloos and sharing the bill with Paul Gordon and his solo backup band. The club was packed, but Eileen made a quick, strong impression on me. It turned out that she lived in the same apartment building as Sarah, the Park Beverly, off La Brea and Beverly. Eileen and I exchanged phone numbers and quickly started a late-night phone relationship. At that time, I was not looking to be in a committed relationship. After four years of living with Janit, which were four years of a few ups and a lot of downs, I just wanted time to myself and experience being single again. But I kept being drawn to Eileen.

We came from very different worlds. Eileen grew up with very little financial security in Detroit. Her father, Irving, was a World War II veteran who sold insurance and had a shoe store. Her mother, Friedel, worked in her parents' bakery. Eileen grew up in a very observant Jewish family. Her mother, uncle, and grandparents barely managed to make it out of Hitler's Germany, arriving in America in 1937. Several of her relatives were not so lucky and perished in Nazi concentration camps. In Michigan, as a child, Eileen worked in the family bakery with her mother. Her two older brothers, Bill and Mark, were not exceptionally close with their gorgeous, energetic, hard-working little sister. Eileen spent a lot of time on her own as a child. Her family couldn't afford luxuries like birthday parties and her material possessions were few.

After graduating high school, Eileen got a scholarship to study drama at the Goodman Theatre at the Art Institute of Chicago. She appeared in many plays there and did commercials and print ads. She got her bachelor's degree in acting and then moved from Chicago to New York and became a traditional wannabe actress. Eileen received no financial help from her family back in Detroit and she worked countless waitressing, babysitting, and other odd jobs to support herself. She appeared in several off-Broadway plays, a few soap operas, a few commercials, and print work, but the brass ring of showbiz eluded her grasp. She fell in love and moved to London expecting something that dematerialized very quickly. She picked herself up and moved to Hollywood.

Eileen was a board member of the Ensemble Studio Theater, and my friends and I all went to see her perform in several plays such as *Bird Bath, The Cherry Orchard, A Coupla of White Chicks Sitting Around Talking, Hot L Baltimore, Fool For Love,* and *House of Blue Leaves.* She was excellent. Really impressive. Her performances were authentic, and she tackled very difficult roles. I have done a lot of acting in my life and I've done a lot of live music gigs but working in the theater never called to me. I prefer learning a script, shooting it scene by scene, and then purging it and moving on. The dedication to performing a play night after night and keeping it fresh and dealing with all the little things that can go wrong during a performance is not my thing. But it certainly was Eileen's and she shined onstage.

Eileen has more energy than anyone I've ever met in my life. She is constantly on the go, and she is a genuine people person and a giver. If someone is sick, Eileen always makes them chicken soup and brings it to them. We used to talk on the phone for hours late into the night. I remember she was modeling shoes at a "shoe show" in downtown LA one week, and it was about 2:30 in the morning and she had to be there at 8 a.m., I apologized for keeping her up so late, but she just shrugged that off and we kept talking. Laurel Canyon had been through a crazy rainstorm and literally tons of mud had fallen down into my yard from the acreage above it. It was a huge mess. I complained on the phone to Eileen that I had to drive downtown and get a permit to build a retaining wall. She quickly said, "I'm going to be right there. I can get the permit for you." I thought that was insane. Who'd volunteer to wait in line to get someone they hardly knew a building permit? She absolutely insisted. Eileen brought the permit over to my house the next day and basically has stayed ever since.

Honestly, Eileen never pressured me about getting married. Years passed and things between us continued on a smooth path. Every year we'd fly to Kauai and rent a house on the beach in Hanalei for three weeks. Often Eileen would travel with me to personal appearances around the country. We had a nice life. We had our beloved dog, Molly, and two cats, Dinah and Gretsch, in our Laurel Canyon home that was constantly filled with friends and music. It wasn't that different from Graham Nash's classic ode to his life in Laurel Canyon with Joni Mitchell, "Our House." (Graham's magnificent home on the beach in Hanalei was our very favorite house that we stayed at with our kids when they were really little.)

In 1986, Eileen's beloved grandmother had taken ill, and Eileen was flying to Michigan often to be by her side. On one of those trips, while I was home alone, I simply realized I never wanted to lose Eileen. When she came home from that journey, I picked her up at LAX, popped in a cassette tape of a new love song I'd written and recorded for her while she'd been gone and said, "I think it's time we got married." She agreed. We got bean and cheese burritos at Taco Bell on La Cienega and 3rd Street to celebrate.

CRUISING UP THE NAWILIWILI RIVER TO GET MARRIED.
WHAT COULD GO WRONG?

I didn't want to wait, and I didn't want to deal with inviting 100+ people and all that huge weddings entail. We picked out a nice diamond ring and a wedding dress, called our parents and booked a wedding ceremony in the Fern Grotto at sunset on our favorite island of Kauai with a few weeks advance notice. We included Eileen's parents, Irv and Friedel, my parents, Charles and Muriel, Eileen's best friend Frances, and Paul and Robert. That was it.

You couldn't imagine a more lovely sight. We cruised up the Nawiliwili River with torches lit along the gorgeous grotto as the sun began to set. Several native Hawaiians accompanied us on our private boat and played and sang beautiful traditional Hawaiian songs. I borrowed one of their guitars and serenaded Eileen with "our song," Buddy Holly's "True Love Ways." It was all going great. The boat docked and the nine of us slowly walked up to the natural rock area for the ceremony. The sky was pink and purple. The smell of orchids filled the dusk air. Torches were lit everywhere. Our closest friends and our parents were with us to witness us joining our lives.

And then Jesus crashed our wedding.

As I explained earlier, Eileen is Jewish and she has always enjoyed celebrating the Jewish holidays, speaking Hebrew and... being a Jew. I am one-quarter Jewish, my grandfather Harry was a Jew, but I have never felt connected to any religion of any kind. Nature is my religion. I don't subscribe to any form of religious dogma. In my opinion, a lot of damage has been done and way too many wars have been fought in the name of religions. So, of course, we made absolutely certain that we were having a non-denominational wedding ceremony. We booked a native Hawaiian minister, a woman, Reverend Kalama, to perform our nondenominational service. We met privately with her before the ceremony and confirmed that. But not long after she began speaking, Reverend Kalama paused, she looked up to the sky and took in a slow deep breath and then passionately said, "... and in the name of Jesus Christ and the blood he shed on the Cross...." And as fast as you could say, "Oy Vey," our wedding ceremony was in the Twilight Zone. Eileen's mother gasped so loud you could have heard her in Honolulu. My parents started squirming. Paul, who served as my best man, looked at me wide-eyed as if to say, "what's happening?" Robert shot it all on video. Eileen turned white. I don't think either of us heard much more of what Reverend Kalama said after that. I remember whispering to Eileen, "Do you want me to stop this? I'll do whatever you want. Just tell me what you want me to do, and I'll do it." And my beautiful soul mate just turned to me with the slightest glint of tears in her gorgeous eyes and said, "I don't know. I don't know."

We stood there and looked at each other until the reverend pronounced us man and wife and then... something absolutely beautiful and wonderful and perfect happened. Irv, Eileen's father, immediately stepped up to us and took our hands and married us in Hebrew. I get chills remembering that. I absolutely loved Irv for doing that. He made everything that went wrong turn right. Eileen's parents truly loved their daughter and welcomed me into their family with open arms.

Later, when we made it back to the boat, I took the reverend aside. "You KNEW we wanted a non-denominational service! We agreed to pray with you privately beforehand. You KNEW Eileen and her parents are Jewish! Why did you do that?!" And just like out of a scene from *The Exorcist*, Reverend Kalama looked me in the eye and proclaimed, "The power of Christ compelled me."

The nine of us partied for several days after that.

Eileen and I renewed our wedding vows ten years later without a guest appearance from Jesus.

THE SENSITIVE AND GORGEOUS EILEEN JOY DAVIS MUMY.

WE CLEAN UP FAIRLY WELL SOMETIMES.

42. BE MY GUEST

Speaking of guest appearances, we had an incredible array of guest stars on *Lost in Space*. Most all of our eighty-three episodes included guest appearances from outside talent and because our show changed from drama to campy comedy and back, we were fortunate enough to have some wonderful dramatic actors like Michael Rennie (who starred in my all-time favorite science fiction film *The Day the Earth Stood Still*), Warren Oates, and Strother Martin as well as some very gifted comedians such as Al Lewis and Hans Conried appear on *Lost in Space*.

Some of the most memorable for me personally in terms of my acting alongside them, were Albert Salmi, who played a pirate named Alonzo B. Tucker, Malachi Throne, the great "Thief of Space," and Kurt Russell who Will Robinson faced a challenge against. I had very good chemistry with those three in particular. There are many other gifted actors who appeared on the series but some of them are memorable for other things besides their acting ability.

Edy Williams worked on the show. Everyone on the 20th Century Fox lot was aware of her in those days. While the studio crew worked hard outside creating the *Hello Dolly* exterior, Edy would "entertain the troops" by flashing her boobs. The episode of *LIS* that she appeared in is called "Two Weeks in Space" and it's one of the sillier, campy shows. One day, as we wrapped about 6:30 in the evening on Stage 11, Edy Williams approached me behind the set backdrop and she stuck her tongue in my ear and gave my crotch a squeeze. Honestly, no one had done that to me before, but there was definitely something sleazy about it and I can't say I dug it. But I suppose she thought she was doing a thirteen-year-old boy a big favor. Anyway, it was memorable.

ANGE AND ME GOOFING AROUND IN OUR CIVILIAN CLOTHES WITH MICHAEL RENNIE AND JONATHAN.

ALBERT SALMI WAS GREAT AS THE SPACE PIRATE ALONZO B. TUCKER.

KURT RUSSELL AND I FIGHTING OFF AN ALIEN MONSTER WITH SPEARS. HA!

43. TROUBLE

In 1992 I was cast to play an assassin in an action-comedy film written and directed by the late John Paragon. It was not a big budget project, but it was a fun movie and every time I've seen it, I've cracked up. John Paragon is best remembered for his work with Pee Wee Herman as Jambi the Genie. He was a smart, quick-witted, funny, pleasant man to work for and with. The film stars Peter and David Paul, the twin wrestling stars. But there's a plethora of talent in supporting roles that worked on *Double Trouble*: Roddy McDowall, David Carradine, Troy Donahue, James Doohan, and my neighbor, old softball teammate and pal, Collin Bernsen, to name a few.

Being cast as an assassin was fun for me as it's not the "usual" type of role I'm offered. Bob, my character, works as an enforcer for Roddy McDowall, who is a major crime syndicate villain. Besides shooting people, Bob dealt out some nasty martial arts kicks and punches to his victims, which was exceptionally pleasurable for me, as I was studying martial arts at the time with the late Mike Vendrell.

Working closely with Roddy McDowall was quite interesting. Roddy never ever delivered his lines the same way twice. Every single take he found a fresh new way to approach his character. I was extremely impressed with his work. The first few days we filmed together, I felt he was a bit standoffish. He kept to himself and didn't seem to be interested in engaging in much conversation with me. Until... I mentioned that he and I had something quite rare and quite special in common. I reminded him that we both had been schooled on the 20th Century Fox lot by Frances Klamt for many years. Of course, there was a large gap between when he and I were in class with Frances, he being twenty-six years older than me, but as soon as I mentioned that, Roddy lit up like a Christmas tree. "Dear, dear Frances! How I adore her! What a fabulous lady!" We had a real good relationship from then on.

In *Double Trouble*, my character Bob, the assassin, gets his comeuppance a split second before he's about to assassinate the hero. Collin Bernsen's character, a somewhat bumbling good guy, shoots me with a double-barrel shotgun just before I can pull the trigger. Well, of course the special effects crew was meticulously careful in getting me "squibbed" for the scene. They padded my torso well, and had multiple baggies of fake blood wired up to detonate with gunpowder that was triggered by a wireless signal activated from offstage. The moment Collin fired the shotgun with blanks in it, the special effects guys detonated the chest squibs and two stunt men yanked me backwards and off my feet with a rope attached to me that was hidden from camera. It went fine. All safety concerns were double-checked before filming. But for those of you out there who have ever been squibbed for a torso blast from a shotgun... you'll know what I mean when I say it hurt like hell and I was bruised for a week.

Double Trouble is silly and somewhat cheesy, but I think it's silly and cheesy in a good way.

After wrapping up filming *Bless the Beasts & Children* in the fall of 1970, Frances Klamt was no longer able to have Ange and I continue our schooling on the 20th Century Fox lot. Ange spent her senior year of high school attending Providence High, an all-girls Catholic school in Burbank that was situated across the road from the Disney lot, and for my junior and senior years I matriculated to Alexander Hamilton High, a public school on Robertson and Venice Boulevards. I did not enjoy my time there at all.

Hamilton was a fairly tough school back then. A lot of teenagers were bussed in from various areas and there were plenty of gang members around. Crypts and Bloods. You definitely wanted to stay out of their way. Although the campus was only about two miles from my house in Cheviot Hills and I could walk there, the trek involved a lot of hills and took longer than I wanted it to, so I drove myself there most every day in my very first car, a beige 1969 British MGB-GT. It was a cool little car with wire wheels and a hatchback that I could open and fit two acoustic guitar cases into nicely. It had black leather seats and a four-speed manual transmission, with hand cranked windows, no air conditioning, and the legendary troublesome British electrical systems that caused more than a few problems. I named the car "Grace." I had a thing for Grace Slick in those days. A state of the art 8-track tape deck was installed under the passenger side console. Parked a block away from Hami, Grace was broken into and burgled three times in two years. By the time I was done with school, the console was so torn up it was hard to get a tape player to stay mounted.

I got mugged sneaking back INTO school one day after ditching for lunch. Two gang guys stopped me as I was about to enter through a gate on the football field and told me to give them my money. I pulled out two quarters and said, "This is all I've got on me. (Which was a lie.) It's my cigarette money." Their palms remained open, so I dropped the two quarters into one of their hands. The other dude replied, "Where's MY cigarette money?!" and punched me in my face. Hard. That is the only time in my entire life that I have been punched in the face by a basically full-grown man. The jolt to my jaw hurt. A lot. I had no desire to stick around for what could happen next, so I ran as fast as I could into school and straight to the attendance office where I got into some kind of stupid trouble for ditching.

All I wanted to do was play music with Redwood and be with Ange. The remaining academic requirements of my high school curriculum held zero interest for me. Geometry, Civics, Physiology, English, P.E., etc... I wanted nothing to do with any of it. By this point in my life, I felt like my path was set. I'd been working since the age of five in showbiz and I intended to continue doing that as both an actor and a musician. I knew I wasn't going to become an accountant, or a lawyer, or a doctor, and I just wanted to be finished with school. I managed to get through it all with mostly C's and B's and one D (in Physiology).

However, there was one elective subject that I became passionate about: photography. I studied photography for two years at Hami. Brenda Abramson taught the class, and she was terrific. Brenda was quite young, in her twenties, and she related to her students with compassion, empathy, and a liberal attitude. She was also very enthusiastic about photography and I dived in headfirst and have never discarded my appreciation for capturing the world around me through a camera lens. Within a few weeks of my first semester, I had built a darkroom in the gardener's shed in our backyard. We always called it the Bomb Shelter as it was made of thick concrete. I purchased a Bessler 23-C enlarger with a Nikkor lens, a printer, and trays to hold the funky chemicals used to produce images. I got a Canon 35mm camera and I would develop my own negatives and then spend countless hours down in the darkroom. I brought a stereo record player and a blacklight and rock & roll posters down there and fastened the blacklight on the wall so it became a cool place to just hang out in, as well as a functioning facility. Within a year, I switched from the Canon to a black Nikon FTN. I loved that camera and brought it all over the world with me. While filming *Papillon* in Jamaica I bought several different lenses with some of my per diem money: a wide angle 28mm, a portrait 105mm, and a telephoto zoom 200mm. I still have that camera, but honestly, since the world went digital, I haven't used it much.

Photography remains a passion of mine.

In 1966 I had a lime green, small frame, Schwinn Varsity ten-speed bike. Since the age of five, my folks had gotten me new bikes regularly. They were all Schwinns and they all came from Wheel World on Sepulveda Boulevard in nearby Culver City. In those days, when you bought a new bike, you got a license tag to go with it and it was placed as a decal on the bike.

One day, Scott and I rode to May Company at Overland and Pico. We both locked our bikes at the bike stand and goofed around for a while. Scott also had a ten-speed. His was a Schwinn Continental and it was gold in color. When we returned to get our bikes and pedal back home, my bike was gone. Despite being locked, it had been stolen.

Bummer.

Well, I couldn't be without a bike for long. My dad and I returned to Wheel World shortly after my Varsity had been pinched and I got a purple Schwinn Stingray Deluxe. (I still have it.) Although, it didn't have the gears like the ten-speed Varsity had, I loved the Stingray. I must've logged thousands of miles on that bike.

Jump ahead in time several months from when the lime green Varsity was stolen. My dad was shopping at the Culver City Center, which was one of the earliest malls in West Los Angeles. It had a JC Penney, a Grants department store, a great bakery, a Hardy's shoe store where I bought many pairs of fabulous dark brown suede zip-up boots that I wish I could duplicate today, a Thrifty drug store, and several other businesses. While shopping, my father's eye caught sight of a small frame, lime green, Schwinn Varsity ten-speed bike parked against the wall near Thrifty Drugs. He walked over to the bike and then opened his wallet. In his wallet was the license number of my stolen bike. Yep. This was indeed my bike. So, once he was positive about it, my dad simply stole it back.

When I got home from filming *Lost in Space* that evening, my dad told me to go out to the garage and check something out. There, next to my purple Stingray, was my lime green Varsity. For a while, I had two bikes.

I also thought my dad was super cool for that.

TODAY MY STINGRAY RESTS UP ON OUR GAZEBO.
IF BIKES COULD TALK... WOW!

44. The Nelsons

The Adventures of Ozzie & Harriet ran on network television for an astonishing fourteen seasons and 435 episodes. From 1952 through 1966, the country grew up alongside Rick, David, Harriet, and Ozzie Nelson. How unbelievably cool is that? To work alongside your brother and parents, and eventually even your wife, playing yourself, bringing joy to everyone in America, entertaining with humor, wit, and positive values packed into every twenty-five minute episode. There was nothing like it before it existed, and there's never been anything similar that approached the quality and uniqueness of *The Adventures of Ozzie & Harriet*.

I loved working as a guest-cast member on three episodes of the long-running series. It really was a different vibe from any other series I ever worked on. Ozzie was a genius. He wrote and directed the entire series. It was Ozzie's show to run, and he ran it beautifully. *The Adventures of Ozzie & Harriet* had been a successful radio show before transitioning to the new medium of television. Ozzie secured an incredible ten-season guarantee from ABC before a single episode had aired. That's a remarkable deal. Nowadays a creator is lucky to be guaranteed that six episodes will air.

The three episodes I appeared in (as Billy) were titled "Freedom of the Press," "The Pennies," and "The Ballerina." They all originally aired in 1964 and I think they hold up really well. I watched them not long ago and laughed at all the jokes and realized the beats were timed perfectly. Without a doubt, they were encouraging stories with surprising twists and all around goodness in them.

The majority of my scenes were with Ozzie, and he was as cool and as friendly to work with as he was to watch on TV. He never got upset or angry and his comedic acting was understated, warm, and pleasurable.

I filmed several scenes with Rick, and I really dug that. I've been a fan of Rick Nelson's music for as long as I can remember. I loved his rockabilly records of the late 1950s and early 1960s. What a band he had! Rick, with his singular, deep, articulate vocals played rhythm acoustic guitar alongside the amazing James Burton playing mind-boggling riffs and solos on a Fender Telecaster. James Burton's contributions to Rick Nelson's catalogue can't be overstated. On drums was the steady grooving Richie Frost. James Kirkland played bass and pianist Gene Garf completed the original rocking group. With the Jordanaires on background vocals, Rick Nelson scored thirty Top 40 hits between 1957 and 1962. After *The Adventures of Ozzie and Harriet* wrapped up, James Burton went on to join Elvis Presley's band.

Years after working on *The Adventures of Ozzie & Harriet*, I went to see Rick perform live a few times. He always had a great band and his voice was so special. I saw him at the Troubadour with his Stone Canyon Band and in 1984, Eileen and I went to see him rock at the Palomino Club. His death at the age of 45 in a plane accident with his band on their way to a New Year's Eve gig, December 31, 1985, was tragic and so very sad. Since his passing, I have performed several of Rick's songs at tribute events dedicated to him.

While filming my episodes of *The Adventures of Ozzie & Harriet*, one of my biggest thrills was watching Rick and the band perform. Sure, they were only lip-syncing to pre-recorded tracks, but the playback was loud and watching them made a big impression on me. I started taking guitar lessons a few months after working on *Ozzie & Harriet*. James Burton sent me a cool birthday greeting video for a recent birthday of mine and that meant a lot to me. He remains a major guitar hero and big influence on my playing.

The memory that has stuck with me more than any other regarding that special show really is a stellar example of how unique a family production it was. I remember when we broke for lunch one day, there were several TV sets on the stage and Ozzie turned on a football game. I don't remember who was playing, or if it was a college game or what, but I clearly recall that Ozzie and the crew really got into watching it passionately. When lunch was over and the bell on the soundstage rang signaling everyone that it was time to get back to work filming the television show, Ozzie waved it off and we didn't go back to filming for quite a while, not until the football game had ended.

OZZIE NELSON WAS ONE OF THE MOST TALENTED
AND EASYGOING GUYS I EVER WORKED WITH.

45. Idols and More

I've had the interesting experiences of working with many teen idols. Rick Nelson definitely made the best music of them all in my opinion. He was also very laid back and easy to work with. Fabian co-starred in *Dear Brigitte*. I never became familiar with his music at all, he did have a couple of pop hits that I've still never really heard, but he was nice and easygoing. As an actor, he was very natural, although his character in the movie didn't require much dramatic stretching.

I guest-starred in an episode of *Here Come the Brides* alongside Bobby Sherman and he was terrific. When I worked with him, he was selling millions of records and was constantly plastered on the cover of all the teen magazines. We got along very well, and he rolled with the showbiz punches and eventually gave up the entertainment scene to become an emergency medical technician (EMT). David Soul was also doing double duty as an actor and a singer on that series, and he too was totally cool.

Davy Jones of the Monkees was not someone I knew well, but I did perform onstage with him twice. I played guitar while he sang "Daydream Believer" at a couple of tribute concerts dedicated to John Stewart. I sang along on the choruses. Davy seemed at his best onstage in front of an audience.

David Cassidy and I recorded together and made several appearances at charity events together and we hung out quite a lot in the 1970s. David was probably the biggest teen star of them all, but I can't say he was easy going. Shaun Cassidy is one of my best friends and watching his half-brother David go through the teen idol experience, Shaun was very much prepared for it psychologically from the beginning. He surfed that huge wave well. Besides me having been the rhythm guitar player in his touring band, he and I have collaborated on songs and miscellaneous projects.

BOBBY SHERMAN WAS A HUGE TEEN IDOL, BUT HE WAS REALLY EASY TO GET ALONG WITH. A TOTAL PRO.

I shot a few rounds of pool with Sajid Khan and Dino, Desi & Billy at the Daisy Club back in the 1960s too. Teen actor-singer and eventual big band orchestra leader Johnny Crawford and I worked on *Overload* together. Johnny was very talented and had a unique interesting vibe. I admired his sensitive but tough acting as Mark McCain on *The Rifleman*. Johnny had a very intense work ethic, and he always delivered the goods. I've never worked with Paul Peterson, but we know each other.

Most all the folks who were child actors during the 1950s, 1960s, and 1970s seem to have met up at one time or another and there is an unspoken fraternal-type bond that unites us. It's a weird club. The teen magazines that flourished in the 1960s and 1970s like *16*, *16 Spec*, *Fave*, *Tiger Beat*, and others often featured articles on me and all my showbiz peers. They usually seasoned fantasy with a decent amount of truth that created an odd melding. Although I certainly participated willingly, allowing photographers and writers into my personal space several times, I always kept my guard up with that type of publicity and promotion. I never really wanted a shiny, cuddly, white-washed, squeaky-clean image. From an early age (around eleven or so) I thought of myself, and preferred to present myself, as a serious musician who happened to be a working actor. The teen magazine photographers always worked hard to get you to do something stupid like jump in your pool with clothes on, or make silly funny faces. Sometimes they'd take hundreds of photos and after reluctantly acquiescing and allowing myself to do something inane for a frame or two... those would inevitably be used in the magazines. I put my "stupid radar" guard up early.

THE CHILD STAR CLUB... 2012. YEAH, IT'S A THING...
JEANNIE RUSSELL, ME, BARRY LIVINGSTON, PAUL PETERSON, TONY DOW,
STANLEY LIVINGSTON, BILLY GRAY, AND JON PROVOST.
PHOTO BY EILEEN.

《》

"**W**eird Al" Yankovic is a buddy of mine and even though he became a really big star, fame never changed him. Despite being an extrovert and a comedian on stage, Al is basically a fairly shy guy. After "Fish Heads" became a pretty big hit, especially on the Dr. Demento globally-syndicated weekly radio show, "Weird Al" was hanging out with Barnes & Barnes quite a lot and we appeared together in character on Dr. Demento's radio show often. Robert, my partner in Barnes & Barnes, likes to think he guru'd Al in many ways, but I'm not sure that's true. What I do know to be true, is that Al was always a great musician, a witty guy, somewhat introverted (comedians often are), and very easygoing. Al played accordion on several Barnes & Barnes tracks and on some of my solo projects. His terrific band, that has remained the same since the beginning, backed up Barnes & Barnes for a television gig honoring Dr. Demento, and Al has always been humble and approachable.

He carved out a singular showbiz niche for himself and it's proved to be a huge success. When I was working on *Babylon 5* in the 1990s, I fixed Al up with a friend of mine who was the hairdresser on *B5*. Kim Ferry is sweet, talented, and gorgeous. Kim and Al used to babysit for Eileen and me when Seth and Liliana were very little. They didn't end up having a love connection, but that didn't stop my matchmaking when it came to Al Yankovic.

**"WEIRD AL"
BABYSITTING SETH.**

Suzanne Krajewski worked at Fox Studios promoting syndicated shows, like *Lost in Space*, and I met her in 1989. Originally from Texas, Suzanne came out to Hollywood, and she was incredibly impressive not only in her work, but in her everything. Quick as a flash, cute as can be, super smart and outgoing; I have to admit, if I wasn't happily married to Eileen when I met her (which I was), I'd have pursued Suzanne. We worked on several *Lost in Space*-related projects together and became friends. She had no problem getting dates and being pursued by notable people. One day however, in the late 1990s, she called me up and told me she was frustrated and tired of dating the type of people she'd been going out with, and she asked me if I knew a "nice guy" that might be interested in her. Well, anyone with a pulse would be interested in her, but the truly "nice" part wasn't that easy.

My mind instantly went to Al. And I told her. "You mean, "Weird Al"? THE "Weird Al"?" she asked. I confirmed that I did indeed mean THE "Weird Al." "Wow. Let me think about that one." Our conversation ended and a little while later, Suzanne rang me up again. "Do you think your friend Al would still want to go out with me?" I told her I was sure that would be an affirmative. She agreed. I helped them set up a first date and they've been happily married since 2001. They have a fabulous daughter, Nina, who attended a school Eileen and I recommended where Seth had thrived, and that worked out truly great. Al is still the same legit nice guy he was when I first met him. Now, whenever I need a great accordion player... I get him for free. Just call me Matchmaker Mumy.

"WEIRD AL" AND ME WITH DR. DEMENTO AT THE RADIO STATION GUESTING ON HIS SHOW.

46. Happiest Place on Earth

*I*n the summer of 1969, Walt Disney's *Rascal* had recently been released and it did good business. Although I surely could have received a free pass to Disneyland, no one in my world ever thought of asking for that sort of perk. Perhaps that attitude kept me more grounded emotionally than some other child actors. Anyway, as was my annual summer tradition, I brought a friend to Disneyland for two days. This time it was Paul. At the time, he and I were working hard writing and arranging Gully songs, as our rock & roll band Energy had recently broken up. My dad drove us to the Magic Kingdom in the morning and then said, "I'll see you back at the hotel by midnight." We had our own room, and he had a room. We were fifteen and on our own.

There's a certain invisible "civilian" attitude that I always had and that, along with a pair of sunglasses and a hat, kept me from being recognized much in crowded places like Disneyland back in those years when I was pretty famous.

Somehow, because of *Rascal* and my Disney past projects, like *Sammy, the Way-Out Seal* and *For the Love of Willadean,* Paul and I found ourselves under the park visiting with the musical group The New Establishment that played a set of music every half-hour or so at the Tomorrowland Terrace. The dressing room was underground. I honestly can't recall what the catalyst was for us being there, but we were hanging with the band and talking about music gear and songs. The New Establishment's instruments were set up on their stage and the conversation turned to a song by the Buffalo Springfield "Go and Say Goodbye." The Stephen Stills tune has two very intricate and somewhat impressive guitar parts that Stills and

Neil Young played on the record. Paul and I shared the fact that we knew those parts perfectly. The guitar players in The New Establishment were impressed by that. Paul and I picked up their guitars, turned on their amps and started playing "Go and Say Goodbye."

Hello! The stage suddenly rose. Someone on the crew obviously thought the group was starting their next set a little early and before we could get to the chorus of the song, the crowd at the Tomorrowland Terrace was curiously staring at Gully, Paul Gordon and Bill Mumy, two fifteen-year-olds in patched jeans, laughing as we ripped through the Buffalo Springfield song.

Within a few seconds, the stage lowered, and the amps were turned off and Paul and I cracked up and headed off to Tom Sawyer's Island.

《》

When I first went back to public school in 1968 after *Lost in Space* was cancelled, I tended to reconnect with the kids that I'd gone to Canfield Elementary School with several years earlier. Even though my entire experience at Canfield was one of constant coming and going, I had friends there who had known me since kindergarten that understood my acting work and didn't judge me or have preconceptions about me. Still, *Lost in Space* had been a pretty big deal and I felt unsure about certain old friends really still being my friend or just playing me in a way because of me being "Will Robinson."

For a while, I guess you could say I had a girlfriend. Janice Bundy was a petite, pixie-like, perky, pretty girl I'd known since the first grade. She lived with her mom and her older brother in a modest upstairs apartment just off of Robertson Boulevard. It was about two miles from my house in Cheviot Hills and sometimes I'd ride my purple Schwinn Stingray bike to her apartment, but the trek back home was all uphill, so most of the time I'd just walk. Janice and I never officially "went steady," but I did give her an I.D. bracelet with my name on it.

In those days, a few friends from school would gather in the evening at Janice's apartment, put on records, turn out the lights, and we'd make out. That's all Janice and I ever did. We'd lie on a couch or sometimes her bed and make out for hours. Sometimes the group would play games like Truth or Dare and Spin the Bottle and even Twister, but we never did anything but make out. It was silly young teenage hormonal fun.

The first time I ever really got stoned was at Janice's. I'd smoked weed with Paul several times, but it was always really shitty weed and maybe I'd get the giggles or something, but I'd never been seriously stoned off of it. One night at Janice's, we were playing the Rolling Stones album *Their Satanic Majesties Request*, which is a very trippy record to begin with, and Janice's older brother, Michael, had some "Acapulco Gold" weed. We smoked some of that and listened to that album and… whoa… I got really stoned for the first time. It kinda freaked me out. So Janice and I made out until the high settled down and then I walked back home uphill in the dark.

To this day, I can't listen to that Stones album without remembering that first serious buzz.

I don't really know what became of Janice. She sure was cute and I hope she's had a good life.

47. LOST INSIDE SPACE

*I*n 1992 NBC/Universal launched a brand new cable network. It was called The Sci-Fi Channel and its focus was on… science fiction. The network ran the old episodes of *Star Trek*, *Lost in Space*, *The Twilight Zone*, and lots of other vintage "space" shows. They also produced several new specials that were mostly clip shows looking at the history of those old 1960s projects, and I was cast to host a couple of them. To fill out the broadcasting hours, the new network created a fairly low-budget, in-house-produced, weekly half-hour educational talk show called *Inside Space*. For the first season of thirteen episodes, it was hosted by Nichelle Nichols of *Star Trek* fame. For the second season, I hosted *Inside Space*.

Inside Space was a multi-camera videotaped show that was shot out of an office building soundstage in New York. The format was totally consistent for the thirteen episodes that I hosted. The sparse set resembled the view from a deck inside a space station. A large telescope was placed center stage and pointed out at an impressive star cluster. Depending on the segment, a couple of chairs would be there. Wearing a suit, but never a tie, I would greet the viewers on camera each episode and explain what we'd be introducing over the next half-hour and then I'd narrate specific segments that would cut away to pre-taped video short bits, usually quite technical. Similar to the way *Sesame Street* does it, only I wasn't as cute as Elmo. I never had a problem reading the cue cards that scrolled across the camera monitors and the small crew I worked alongside were always friendly, easygoing, and knew what they were doing. The CGI effects were admittedly pretty cheesy, but the information shared was always interesting and well researched.

I was fortunate to interview several very impressive individuals during my time hosting the series, such as nuclear physicist and UFOlogist Stanton Friedman. But by far, the favorite interview I conducted was with American astronomer, planetary scientist, cosmologist, astrophysicist, astrobiologist, author, and science communicator Carl Sagan. He and his lovely wife, Ann Druyan, arrived right on time, and they were easygoing and a pleasure to hang out with. We chattted while the set was being lit for our interview and the subject turned to basketball. I love watching basketball and I'm a lifelong Los Angeles Lakers fan. Carl and Ann were enthusiastic New York Knicks fans and their only concern regarding the interview and taping was that it wrap up on time because they had tickets to the Knicks game that evening and they absolutely didn't want to be late.

We sat down to begin the interview, and Carl reached into his pocket for his tie, but he didn't have it on him. Ann looked through her purse. No tie. They'd left it at home. Carl felt he should wear a tie for the interview (unlike me) and so two crew members dashed up the street to a nearby Gap store and bought several ties for him. Returning, they laid them out for him to choose. He couldn't have cared less which tie he wore. Ann made the call, and we taped our interview while three video cameras recorded it from different angles. My questions were pre-written, and I read them off the scrolling cue cards in the monitor, but having been a fan of Carl's brilliant *Cosmos* series and generally interested in his thoughts on extraterrestrial life, I ad-libbed and we "jammed" on the subject a bit. He was so composed and articulate and passionate and knowledgeable. I enjoyed that experience very much.

What I didn't enjoy all that much was flying to New York and back to Los Angeles every three weeks. *Inside Space* would tape three episodes each time I was there. Those were long days. Things were very different in 1992-93 compared to the way airplane travel is now. After the terrible attacks on 9/11, restrictions and security changed totally. Back then, it was much more relaxed and easy, but I'd had several very scary and unpleasant experiences on flights in the past and I'm not a very comfortable airplane traveler. The Sci-Fi Channel, now known simply as SyFy, flew me first class on TWA 747 nonstop flights and put me up at a very nice hotel near Times Square. It was usually the W. I enjoyed hosting *Inside Space* and it was nice to be back on television every week, even though the cable watching audience of *Inside Space* was minuscule compared to the audience of forty million weekly watchers of *Lost in Space* back in the 1960s. I had accepted the gig for little money. Now that my first season was wrapped up and in the can, my deal needed to be renegotiated. Surprisingly, the network seemed to really like me and wanted me to continue as the host. They were willing to double my salary. That would have worked for me, but they were insisting I sign an exclusive contract that placed them with precedence over anything else I might want to work on.

In the end, that turned out to be a deal breaker. Yes, I really enjoyed the gig. The flying was a drag but it was manageable. I didn't accept the offer to continue because there really wasn't any actual acting involved in my work on the show. Since I was four years old, I've liked the actual acting part of showbiz much more than any other part of it. When the soundstage bell goes on, and everything gets settled and quiet and the camera is pointed at you and the director calls "Action" and you ACT… that's the best part. Always has been. I just couldn't allow myself to be hosting a half-hour videotaped educational talk show if the offer to act dramatically on a film or a television project presented itself, and I contractually wouldn't be able to do it. So, with good vibes to and from all, I parted company with *Inside Space*.

And within a few months, I was signed to a five-year contract acting on *Babylon 5*.

<«»>

In the 1980s Barnes & Barnes were guest DJs on LA's alternative radio station KROQ a few times. We had also been regular radio performers on the Dr. Demento Show. In the 1990s, after being a guest on the syndicated *Mark & Brian* radio show broadcast from KLOS in Los Angeles, I guest hosted their show for the entire week with Miguel Ferrer while Mark and Brian went on holiday. We brought our pals David Jolliffe and Steve Lukather (of Toto fame) into the studio, and along with producer Nicole Sandler, had a blast being morning DJs in LA from 6 to 10 a.m. Radio was a lot of fun. So, impulsive guy that I am, when I got the offer to produce, write, and host a weekly radio show of my own, I quickly accepted.

Thus was born *The Real Good Radio Hour*. From 2010 thru 2014, I produced 136 hour-long radio segments. My intent was to showcase good music that may have slipped through the cracks of public awareness, and tell stories of their creation and share some hopefully interesting history regarding the composers and the artists who performed this music. As the show progressed, it also included "The Poetry Parlor," which meant I read a poem and sometimes, I wrote one as well. I took the gig seriously and enjoyed the process immensely. There were no guests or interviews on the series. *The Real Good Radio Hour* was all about sharing the art. It was not a money-making gig by any means, but often I am not motivated by the lure of profit. I do things for the creative experience and the opportunity to play in new arenas.

The Real Good Radio Hour aired on KSAV.org and as of this writing, all episodes can still be heard in its archives.

48. Fun and Games

I honestly never felt like I missed any goofing around or playing sports time with my friends, because I never really did. I always found time on the weekends, or during a hiatus, or even in the summer evenings after work, to meet up with pals and toss a Frisbee or swim, play ping-pong or tennis, shoot hoops at the park, fly kites, go to the beach, body surf, skin dive, scuba dive, go horseback riding, ride bikes, go roller skating, ride skateboards and later motorcycles, play racquetball, and softball.

One thing that may or may not be revealing about me is I've kept my true friends close all my life. My best friends have been in my life for most all of it. Maybe because I never had any siblings of my own, my connections with good pals have remained tight ones. Another reason may be because although I've travelled a lot, I haven't lived in many places and they've all been within ten miles of my very first address.

Sometimes when reflecting on my recreational life fifty-some years ago, it seems almost unbelievable to me now because the world has become such a sadder and much more dangerous place. For instance, in 1967, when I was thirteen years old and was very recognizable from starring in *Lost in Space*, my regular routine during the summer, if I wasn't working, or on weekends when I was, would be to walk by myself from our house in Cheviot Hills on Forrester Drive, up Motor Avenue past Rancho Park to Pico Blvd where the 20th Century Fox Studios lot was and get on the Number 7 bus by myself and ride it to the end of the line which was the

Santa Monica beach. I would get off the bus, walk across the street to an A&W Root Beer stand and get a beverage and maybe a burger and then stroll down to the sand, past Synanon, where drug addicts were being treated, and then meet up with a bunch of my friends from the neighborhood or from school days. I'd spread my towel down on the hot sand close to kids I knew. Lots of transistor radios would all be tuned to the same AM radio station, usually 93 KHJ, and I'd lay out in the sun for a few minutes, close my eyes and listen to the pop music of the day and then I'd dash out into the water wearing cutoff blue jeans and spend literally the next four or five hours body surfing waves in the ocean at Santa Monica. I'd check my divers watch once in a while and when it got to be around 5:30 or 6 p.m., I'd pick up my towel, shake it off, put my t-shirt back on, and walk back up the hill where I'd catch the eastbound Number 7 bus back home. I'd make the walk from Pico and Motor back to my house before it got dark. Once home, I'd jump in our warm swimming pool for a few minutes to wash off the salt and sand and then sit at the round table in our den with my parents and grandmother for dinner where my mom and I would usually argue about something.

There were no cell phones in those days and there was no need to find a pay phone and let my parents know I'd gotten to the beach okay or was heading back home soon, etc. It was a completely different world. The thought of my kids when they were thirteen doing that causes my soul to shudder. Sad, but true.

As mentioned previously, from 1975 through 1978 I played softball in the newly formed West Hollywood Celebrity League. There were several teams that competed on the weekends and among them were The Hollywood Vampires that included my close friend and bandmate David Jolliffe, along with Alice Cooper, Micky Dolenz, Peter Tork, Davy Jones, Albert Brooks, Mark Volman, and others.

Happy Days had a team with Henry Winkler, Garry Marshall, Donny Most, Anson Williams, and Ron Howard. My team, for the first two years, was called Showbiz Kids (a name I always hated even though it was chosen because of the Steely Dan song of the same title) and it included Shaun Cassidy, Miguel Ferrer, Ben Weiss (who went on to direct *Friends*), Keith Farrell (whose grandmother created Fatburger), Joey and Jess Hamilton (Carol Burnett's stepsons who sadly both died very young from drug overdoses), Scott Ehrlich, my best friend and roommate who was working on *Welcome Back Kotter* then, and me. A handful of other friends rotated in and out of the team. Of course there were other teams in the league and other players who came and went, but that was our core group.

DANGER! DANGER! SHOWBIZ KIDS!
BACK: BLAISE BELLEW, SHAUN CASSIDY, ME, MIGUEL FERRER, JIMMY HAYMER
FRONT: SCOTT EHRLICH, BEN WEISS, BOBBY GRAHAM.
SOFTBALL WAS NEVER THE SAME.

I played short center field and center field and occasionally was drafted to play catcher, but I was never comfortable playing catcher. I hated those bats swinging so close to my face. Shaun played left field. Miguel was at second base. Although we did practice, we were pretty much consistently the worst team in the league. Rarely did we win a game. Once, and only once, we beat the Vampires and the victory party at Carol Burnett's house was insanely wild. I mean, straight out of *Caligula*. After two losing seasons stuck with that name, Paul Gordon (who had just joined the team) and I convinced the other guys to change the name. We dumped Showbiz Kids and became The Boss Team. We still lost just about every game.

MORE TROUBLE... SHOWBIZ KIDS.
ME, BLAISE, JOEY HAMILTON, BOBBY, CHERYL, SCOTT, MIGUEL, KEITH FERREL,
LISA, LORI, BEN, AND SHAUN. GADZOOKS!

《〉》

Everybody knows George Clooney now, but back in the early 1980s George was just Miguel's cousin who was living at Rosemary's house. Moving from Kentucky to see if he could make it in Hollywood showbiz, it only made sense for him to move into that huge house at 1019 Roxbury Drive. Rosie and Miguel gave George a hard time when he first arrived. She put him to work running a lot of errands and helping to fix up the place, which was always in serious need of fixing up. By this time, Miguel's acting career was on the upswing and he guru'd George and introduced him to some casting directors. George has always been charming, self-effacing, fun, and easy to hang with. He's seven years younger than me and we definitely shared several years of good times together. Most all of my "Beverly Hills" friends had motorcycles and there were usually a few extra bikes in someone's garage. I've never been too enthusiastic about motorcycles, but I've borrowed several and came close to buying a Harley in the 1980s, but Eileen passionately requested I didn't, so I didn't. Happy wife, happy life.

Here's a fond remembrance. I'd say this happened around 1982 or '83. It was definitely before George was on *ER*. A bunch of us were hanging out at Rosie's, as usual, and we were certainly a scrappy looking group. Long hair, beards, ripped up T-shirts and jeans, and funky boots, that was the uniform of the day. Rosie's house was less than a mile away from a very nice flat park next to a Beverly Hills fire station on Coldwater Canyon. Six or seven Harley motorcycles were kicked into idling almost in unison with a heavy metal roar. Miguel grabbed a hefty wooden box that looked almost like a small coffin and strapped it to the back of his 1940s Knucklehead Harley with a suicide clutch and a metal skull for a shifter. He led the pack out of his long driveway and onto Lexington Avenue. This "gang" of bikers shortly reached their destination at the park next to the fire station. Pulling up in tandem and shutting off the thunderous Harleys, we made quite a scene. People watched cautiously as Miguel extracted the large box that looked like it could have held machine guns and we all walked into the center of the verdant park.

Miguel, George, Benny, Shaun, Jolliffe, Jimbo, and I helped Miguel remove the contents of the box... Croquet mallets and wickets and wooden balls.

Yep. For a while, we were into croquet. This motley crew of "Showbiz Kids" proceeded to play a few rounds of croquet before firing up the Harleys and heading back to Rosemary Clooney's mansion. We did that a few times.

SHAUN, JOLLIFFE, MIGUEL, AND ME... MUSIC AND MAYHEM MAKERS.

49. Rockin' the Big Screen

In 1983 I worked on a feature film for close to two months. *Hard to Hold* was a starring vehicle for Rick Springfield who is a very nice, multi-talented, cool guy. But, *Hard to Hold* is honestly hard to watch. It's the story of a fictional rock star. Larry Pierce, the director, cast me as Rick's keyboard player, Toner. I was cast simply for the reason that he wanted an experienced actor who was a legitimate musician to be a part of the band, to help wrangle the acting performances of the other guys who were cast as band members, because they were not actors but serious session musicians. Mike Baird, great drummer, Pops Popwell, amazing bass player, and Tony Sales, mighty fine guitarist, made up the band with me on keyboards. Honestly, there was no need for me to assist with any acting suggestions regarding the guys. They were all natural and comfortable on camera and the dialogue we had to say was contrived and pretty lame.

But we did really play the instruments. It was cool jamming and performing with those cats. As the keyboard player, I mostly just played some pads to thicken out the chords and sweeten the songs a bit. Rick wrote the songs we played in the film and he of course sang them and played guitar and some keyboards. We filmed a "concert" at the Los Angeles Sports Arena where it was full of Rick's fans making up the audience. We played each of the songs from the movie several times and that was a blast.

Patti Hansen co-starred in the film. It was shortly before she married Keith Richards. Keith visited the set. That was cool. I have an autographed photo of him that reads, "To Bill, So am I!! Keith Richards." It took me quite a while to understand the inscription. "I'm lost in space, too! Haaaaa Haaaa!"

JAMMING WITH THE MULTI-TALENTED, NICE, AND GENEROUS RICK SPRINGFIELD WHILE WORKING ON HARD TO HOLD. 1983.

Rick knew I was into vintage guitars and he and I discussed our mutual affection for old Gretschs. We arranged a day when he would bring in his Gretschs and I'd bring in mine. Rick brought in a very cool mid-1950s (probably a '56) big orange 6120 Chet Atkins and a modern solid body Gretsch. I brought in a 1958 6120 of mine along with a '67 Tennessean and a '67 Country Gentleman. It got just a little strange when Rick said he'd buy my guitars. I didn't want to part with them, and I never expected that by bringing them in I would be asked to sell them to him. I simply passed on the offer as nicely as I could, but I think it bugged him a little.

When we wrapped up shooting the film, Rick had his assistant bring me the solid body Gretsch he'd shown me a few weeks before. It was the guitar he had been featured playing in his "Jesse's Girl" video. "Rick wants you to have this." "Oh man, thanks. He doesn't need to give this to me. That's cool." "Rick wants you to have this." "Wow. Okay, great. Thank him for me." So, I accepted the gift and brought the guitar home.

Barnes & Barnes had a record deal on Columbia Records at the time and we were cutting some tracks at the Village Recorder in West LA. We brought Mike Baird in to play drums. I recorded two tracks using the Gretsch that Rick had gifted me, but I just couldn't connect with that guitar at all. It was neck heavy. It had strange humbucking pickups, not the twangy Filtertrons or Dynasonics of other Gretschs, and it didn't have a Bigsby vibrato tailpiece, which I use on all my Gretschs. I ended up keeping one track that I used that guitar on and went back to my usual Gretschs. Shortly after, I was in Voltage Guitars in Hollywood and fell in love with a stripped 1965 Fender Telecaster. I traded the Gretsch Rick had gifted me for the Tele. I still have the Tele and have used it ever since. Well, Rick found out that I'd traded his gifted Gretsch away and it pissed him off. I certainly didn't mean to be ungrateful or hurt his feelings in any way. But I didn't want that guitar in the first place. I tried my best to use it and connect with it, but it just wasn't right for me. I hope it went to someone who really dug it and enjoyed making music on it. I haven't seen Rick in over thirty years now. He's a hard-working, talented, nice man.

Hard to Hold put a swimming pool in my backyard. In fact, my earnings after commission and taxes came to almost exactly the cost of the pool. Laurel Canyon has some challenging hillside topography and soil. My pool is only four feet deep, and it has no deep end or shallow end. It's just... four feet deep. Over the many years, it has proven to be a nice pool for children to learn how to swim in, and it certainly helps to beat the heat. But perhaps the grooviest thing about my pool is it's the one and only Splooge Ball Court in the world.

What is Splooge Ball you ask?

Splooge Ball is a game invented by me, Miguel, Ben Weiss, Jay Gruska, George Clooney, and Brandon Lee. Two players stand in the pool while one player is out of the pool in a reclining lounge chair. It is played with a single blue rubber racquetball. The player "at bat" must keep one of his shoulder blades attached to the lounge chair at all times and he must bounce the ball only ONCE on the deck or off the walls behind and around the pool and land the ball in the water without one of the two players in the pool catching it on the fly or touching it, before it makes contact with the water. If the player at bat fails to successfully bounce the ball once into the water or doesn't manage to achieve a bounce at all before the ball enters the water, it is an out. If a player in the pool catches the ball on the fly, it's an out. If a player in the pool touches the ball but doesn't catch it before it hits the water, it's a single for the at-bat player. If the pitched ball makes it into the pool on one bounce without being touched at all by a player in the water, it's a double for the at-bat player. Like baseball, there are three outs per inning and the players rotate from pool to lounge chair until the nine-inning game ends and the player with the most points wins.

Let me share this simple truth with you: we literally spent YEARS playing Splooge Ball. We had T-shirts made that were designed by Joan Farber and distributed to the players. Over time, the group of people who played Splooge Ball grew by a lot. My backyard was the place to be and Splooge Ball was the game to play. It's legendary within our little society of friends. We had two annual Splooge Ball Championship Tournaments. Ben Weiss, a leftie, won them both. Eventually, we all got back to actually working and playing Splooge Ball faded into the background.

50. Brandon & Miggy

*T*his isn't really about me, per se, but I'm the only one still standing who can share a few treasured memories I had with Brandon Lee and Miguel Ferrer. Brandon was a very bold and spiritual young man. He, Miguel, David Jolliffe, Ben Weiss, and I all trained in martial arts with Mike Vendrell. Miguel met Mike on a film where Mike was hired as stunt director and soon we were all close friends and studying under Mike. That's how we connected with Brandon.

Brandon and I shared the same birthday, February 1st, and he enjoyed my remembrances of hanging with his late father, Bruce Lee, back when I was filming *Lost in Space* and Bruce was playing Kato on *The Green Hornet*. His dad had passed away in 1973 when Brandon was only eight years old so any stories that could connect him to his father, he appreciated. Brandon was a huge fan (bordering on obsessed) of Jim Morrison and although my personal experience being with The Lizard King was very brief, Brandon would ask me to tell him about it over and over, and he really dug the photographs of Morrison and the Doors that I had taken at the Aquarius Theater back in 1969.

In 1987, Miguel and I were writing a graphic novel for Marvel Comics called *The Dreamwalker*. It was a pulp-inspired "James Bond meets The Shadow" type of project illustrated by the late great Gray Morrow. Miggy and I were hard at work scripting one day at Miguel's rented house in Studio City when Brandon arrived on his motorcycle. I clearly recall he and I talking about Tom Waits for a few minutes and then Brandon declared, "I want some chili. You guys wanna go get some chili?" I reminded Brandon that I don't eat meat and would definitely pass on that, and Miguel said that he and I really needed to get several pages scripted so he'd get chili another time.

With that, Brandon fired up his bike and split to get some chili.

In Texas.

He rode straight to Texas on his motorcycle to get some chili and then rode back. That truly happened and it tells you a lot about who Brandon was.

The next year, 1988, Miguel and I were performing at the WonderCon comic book convention up in Oakland, California with our band, Seduction of the Innocent. The group consisted of Miguel on drums and vocals, comic book artist Steve Leialoha on bass, comic book writer Max Allan Collins on vocals and keyboards, Chris Christensen on percussion, guitar and harmonica, and me on guitar and vocals. We played mostly 1960s garage band rock & roll and a handful of original songs we'd written that were lyrically themed around comic books. The band had debuted the year before at the San Diego Comic Con and proved to be a huge crowd pleaser. So, for a few years we played a bunch of comic book conventions and had a lot of sloppy fun doing it. Shaun Cassidy joined us for a gig at the Santa Monica pier celebrating Golden Apple comics and he belted out an impressive Jim Morrison-type vocal on "Light My Fire."

Anyway, we flew up to Oakland to play the big party at the con but when we got there, Miggy realized he had left his drum cymbals at his house. Drummers are finicky about their personal cymbals and he really wanted to play this gig with his. So, Miguel called Brandon and said, "Brandon, we've bought a plane ticket for you. Go to my house, you know where I keep the key, look for the cymbals and get up here as soon as you can!" Brandon, always up for an adventure, agreed.

An hour-and-a-half later, we got a phone call from Brandon. "Miggy, I'm in your house. I'm looking for the symbols. Are they Ankhs? Crosses? Yin and Yang? Star of David? I can't find 'em, Bro." We laughed for years. "Brandon, they're my drum CYMBALS. They're in the leather bag next to the front door." "OH! Right! I see 'em! Cool! See ya soon."

Brandon grabbed the cymbals bag and flew up to the gig in Oakland and we partied pretty hard that weekend. As Max Allan Collins used to say, "Rock & Roll happened."

I'm smiling right now remembering Brandon's boldness and his sweetness. Losing him so senselessly (he was shot by a defective prop gun while filming *The Crow*), losing Mike Vendrell so suddenly (he died in his sleep), and losing Miguel to cancer was tough. Remembering the good times and adventures we shared together makes it a little easier.

MIGGY, ME AND ... BRANDON. YOU ARE MISSED, BOYZ.

51. Curse of the Mumy

It's not my intention to say negative things about anyone, but I will say that the absolute worst professional experience I ever had was working with Crispin Glover. Barnes & Barnes produced his one and only album and it was a nightmare undertaking. As I said earlier, my partner in Barnes & Barnes, Robert Haimer, is a huge Doors fan and he came up with the idea of us producing a spoken word album for Crispin. Robert's vision was inspired by the Doors *American Prayer* project where the surviving Doors musicians wrote and recorded music to place behind Jim Morrison's spoken poetry. We had met Crispin through our friend Mark Mothersbaugh of Devo. Crispin was a fan of the two Wild Man Fischer albums that Barnes & Barnes had produced, 1981's *Pronounced Normal* and 1984's *Nothing Scary*. I'm a fan of those projects as well. Wild Man Fischer was a primitive but very soulful and unique artist. Preserving his music was worth the troubles. He was also a manic-depressive paranoid schizophrenic.

Robert was impressed by Crispin's acting in films such as *Back to the Future*, *River's Edge* and *What's Eating Gilbert Grape?* I too, acknowledged his powerful performances in those movies. I had worked with Crispin's father, Bruce Glover, on *Bless the Beasts & Children*. Bruce was a nice guy and he and I are both members of the Academy of Motion Pictures Arts and Sciences and I used to see him at Academy screenings often.

Mark Mothersbaugh suggested Barnes & Barnes could work with Crispin, and Robert had a strong drive to do so. We met with Crispin at his Hollywood apartment to discuss the possibility in late

1987. Crispin's apartment was a testimony to weird. He had painted the walls black but painted the ceiling blood red and the scarlet paint dripped randomly down his walls. Hanging from his ceiling were balloons covered in tar. He explained to us that various animal fetuses were inside the balloons, and he thought of them as planets. He had a diseased eyeball collection. Robert thought it was very artistic. I wasn't digging it. But we were on a path and I went along with it.

Crispin claimed to be a writer, but I don't think that's an appropriate title for what he did. He bought really old books that were in the public domain, and he randomly blacked out sections, so the book would read in a helter-skelter, nonsensical but I suppose somewhat artsy way. I was not at all impressed, but Robert was. Robert laid out what he thought would be a cool project… Crispin would come into our studio (meaning my house) and record sections of his "books" and then Barnes & Barnes would score those sections to create an album. Crispin enthusiastically embraced and agreed to that. I thought it just might turn out to be somewhat cool.

But it turned out to be something else completely. In the beginning, Crispin did what Robert wanted. He recited bits and left. Then Robert and I wrote and recorded music to accompany his spoken vocals. But after a few sessions, Crispin's ambition grew, and he wanted to make a different type of album. The big problem was, he was totally incapable of describing what his vision was. The other big problem was Robert kissed his ass and acquiesced to all his flip-floppy thoughts.

My wife Eileen was pregnant during the time Crispin was here recording and he brought some negative energy into our house that was totally unacceptable to me. As the recording sessions went on and on, and changed from the original concept to him demanding to cut a rap song, to him wanting to cut a cover of a punk rock tune, and then a cover version of "These Boots Are Made For Walkin'," it went on and on and on.

I can't say Crispin was mean-spirited in any way. He wasn't on drugs at all and he was kindhearted. But he was completely undisciplined and spoiled and could not communicate whatever he was thinking, and he acted like a child throwing tantrums when he didn't get his way. He smashed his fist against my wall and nearly broke his hand once. But the bottom line, what pushed me too far, was when he insisted on recording a Charles Manson song. I put my foot down. I absolutely refused to allow that to happen in my house and on a project I was involved with. I knew quite a lot about the Manson family and the murders they committed. I knew how important music was to Charlie, especially his own music. There was no way Manson music was going to be recorded here and included on any album I produced.

But it was and it is. Robert capitulated once again to Crispin's ego and desire and when I wasn't home one day, he and Crispin cut the Manson song "I'll Never Say Never to Always" in my studio in my house, against my clearly stated firm opposition. That was the end for me. I refused to participate in the completion of the album and my ire towards both of them reached an extreme level. I've never spoken to Crispin since and I have no desire to. Robert, my friend since I was twelve, my professional partner in Barnes & Barnes, pissed me off so much that I didn't talk to him for a year and a half. To this day, he shrugs it off and acts like I was overreacting. He doesn't get it and he never will. The deep wound may have healed, but the scar remains.

The Crispin Glover album, *The Big Problem Does Not Equal the Solution. The Solution Equals Let It Be* was released on Restless Records in 1989. I've never listened to the whole thing. Whether it has a valid artistic soul or not, I'm not going to ever give that another minute of my time. Without any shadow of a doubt, that was the most unpleasant project I have ever been involved with.

<<>>

Security expert Gavin de Becker lived at Stan Freberg's and at Rosemary Clooney's houses in the 1970s and we were close for many years. Gavin is a brilliant man with a rapier wit, which in his youth could be used to reduce those around him to babbling idiots quite frequently. But he remains someone I trust implicitly and have turned to for security advice more than once over the years. Gavin once told me that for any celebrity of any level at all, there will be at least one mentally ill person who fixates on them. And as history has proven, that can be fatal.

In the mid-1980s, before I became a parent, I flew to many science fiction and comic book conventions around the world and those personal appearances were usually booked months in advance.

In my home, I have always had a personal phone number and a business phone number. I recall the business line ringing on a specific afternoon while I was home alone. I answered and a male voice said he was a reporter for *Starlog* magazine. I had done several in-depth interviews with *Starlog* and I had no reason to doubt the validity. He explained he wanted to ask a few follow-up questions for a miscellaneous column that would be printed soon. I agreed. After a longer than expected pause, he said, "It must've been great working on *Lost in Space*." I assured him it was. Then he said, "It must've been great having a robot for a friend." My spider-sense started tingling. He continued. "I loved the way the Jupiter 2 looked." It went on like that for another minute or two and it became very clear that I was not talking to a *Starlog* magazine reporter. I politely extricated myself from the conversation and didn't think much about it. Until the business line began ringing much more frequently the next few days. I let the answering machine take the calls and I told Eileen not to answer as well. For a few days, the *Starlog* ruse continued, "I'm calling back for a few more questions for the magazine." Etc.... and then it got very disturbing. "Answer the phone, fucker!" "You're a fucking dick. You're a motherfucking dick. I'll fucking kill you. I'll kill you!"

Yep. No fun hearing that. So, I called the police. They put a trace on the line. They got his phone number. I went to my agent Gary Salt's office at the Paul Kohner Agency on Sunset Boulevard just west of Doheny and met with two Beverly Hills police officers, and we called him. He answered. I firmly explained to him that the police were with me and that his messages threatening to murder me were recorded and traced to his number. I further explained to him that threatening to kill someone on the phone from out-of-state was a federal crime and I could have him arrested for it. (Pretty weird that if you called me from around the corner from my house and said that, it wouldn't be a federal offense!) He started freaking out. He apologized profusely. He stammered and was truly afraid of the potential consequences of his actions. I then said, "Look, I'm sitting here with the police, taking up their time. If you want to ask me anything about *Lost in Space* do it right now, because I don't ever want to speak to you again. Is that clear?" He had no further questions and the conversation ended.

His phone number was traced to a residence in New York. I gave the information to Gavin, who added it to his information files. The only residual issue was that I was scheduled to make an appearance at the New York Comic Con in two weeks. Eileen suggested I cancel. A few close friends agreed with her. But, I was young and I remember saying, "I won't let fear dictate my actions." Honestly, after becoming a parent, I would definitely have cancelled, as my entire perspective on reality changed once the kids were born. But back then I felt much bolder.

It was Shaun Cassidy, one of Gavin's closest friends, and certainly a major celebrity who had dealt with this type of threat before, who drove me to a police equipment store. At Shaun's urging, I bought a bulletproof vest.

The convention was in November, so it was winter in New York. For several days while doing question-and-answer panels and signing autographs, no one realized I was wearing a bulletproof vest under my sweater. But I was.

Nothing unusual happened at the convention. I flew home and eventually gave the bulletproof vest to my neighbor's son who was a bouncer at a funky club in Hollywood.

<<>>

Many years ago, when I was on the road as rhythm guitarist in Shaun Cassidy's band, I learned not to register in hotels under my real name. Fans would frequently find out what hotels we were staying in, and they'd ring the band members rooms at all hours hoping for something that probably wasn't a good idea. So, we all registered under aliases. When I attend Science Fiction or Comic Book conventions and occasionally when acting on locations, I still follow that rule.

I'll bust myself here and share the secret identity I've most often used on the road… "Robin L. Wilson". Yep, an anagram of Will Robinson. Heh.

LIFE IMITATES ART — EILEEN AND ME ON THE COVER OF THE FIRST ISSUE OF MY COMIC *CURSE OF THE MUMY*, FROM *BLUEWATER COMICS*

52. Ramblin' Man

I doubt if anyone has a bad word to say about working with James Garner. In 1974 I was cast as a guest-star in the pilot of *The Rockford Files*, which of course went on to become a very successful series lasting six seasons. Besides the pilot, I appeared in a second episode of *The Rockford Files* that aired the following year as well.

James Garner was one of those incredibly natural actors. It came easy to him. He didn't make a big deal out of being the star of the series at all. He was very laid back and friendly with everyone on the crew and at least in my case, the guest actors. I was assigned a nice little dressing room trailer, but I spent most of my free time hanging out in Jim's big "Double Banger" dressing room. Lindsay Wagner and I relaxed and chatted with him in between filming scenes. I played Lindsay's brother, who was a young pharmacist and not the most likeable character. Our scenes went smoothly, and all performances were top notch.

JAMES GARNER MADE IT ALL LOOK SO EASY. FROM THE *ROCKFORD FILES* PILOT.

The series had a very catchy theme song written by Mike Post and Jim Garner's charm made *The Rockford Files* not only an interesting crime drama series, but it carried a hefty amount of comedy throughout its six seasons as well.

For the second episode of *The Rockford Files*, I played a hippie street artist selling impressionistic paintings on the Venice Beach boardwalk. It was not a major role, but I was working on the Universal lot co-starring in the short-lived *Sunshine* NBC series at the time and the casting director asked me if I'd do it as a favor. Actually, I was thrilled to accept the part because the episode was being directed by Jackie Cooper. He was of course, a brilliant child star and an original cast member of the *Little Rascals* shorts. I very much respected his history, and I was excited to work with him. He proved to be very impressive, friendly, and relaxed. I enjoyed acting for him. We talked a little about working conditions when he was a child and when I was a child. There was quite a bit of humor in the scenes with me and James Garner in that episode and Jackie Cooper didn't need to offer much direction in terms of our performances. It was a one-day shoot for me that I'm glad is part of my catalogue.

From my observation, *The Rockford Files* was a pretty stress-free, happy production and Jim Garner was a shining example of how to get things done quickly, correctly, and without taking the whole thing too seriously.

«<»

A friend of mine, who shall remain nameless, is a doctor, a general practitioner as well as being a professional musician. One afternoon in 2009, he called me and said, "Hey, I'm in your neighborhood. You want a flu shot?" I answered with, "Sure. Thanks. Come on over." He arrived and headed into my home recording studio. Within a few minutes, he was checking out a new acoustic guitar I'd recently added to my arsenal. The wood on the back and sides are gorgeous and for a new smaller-sized acoustic, it projected a mighty tone. He liked it a lot. I picked up another guitar and he and I jammed for about an hour. He looked at his watch and said, "Oops. I'm running late." Reaching into his doctor's satchel, he pulled out the vial of flu vaccine and gave me the shot and then dashed off into the canyon. "Thanks, Doc!"

Well, I'm the type of guy who doesn't ever like to go to doctors. So, a few days later, when I told Eileen I needed to get to a doctor as soon as possible, I was definitely feeling seriously shitty.

We were escorted into an examining room where we waited for what felt like a really long time. Finally a nurse showed up to take my blood pressure and temperature. I was running a fever of 103. My blood pressure was too high. I couldn't stop coughing and my throat was killing me. I told her, "I think I have the swine flu." She smiled and shrugged that off quickly saying, "Everyone thinks they have the H1N1 swine flu lately. You don't have the swine flu. But let's take a swab to confirm that."

Several minutes later the doctor appeared and confirmed that I indeed did have the H1N1 swine flu.

He hypothesized that the vaccine shot I was given had probably been from a bad batch, possibly because it wasn't refrigerated properly and that, most likely, was the reason I had come down with it.

I was sent home and quarantined alone in our bedroom for ten days of sweating, sleeping, taking antiviral medications, coughing, fever, chills, body aches, and high anxiety.

That was the last time I jammed with a doctor.

<<>>

But jams continued. In 2002, my friend Jeffrey Foskett, who was Brian Wilson's right-hand man, vocalist, and guitarist for many years knew that I loved the Byrds. So, when he and the late-great Andrew Gold put a Byrds tribute band together, Byrds of a Feather, featuring Andrew and Jeff on guitars and vocals, another talented pal of mine Randell Kirsch on bass and vocals, Pat Robinson on tambourine and vocals, and Stephen J. Artie on drums, I was asked to sit in and play and sing on a few songs.

I'd jammed with Andrew before. What a great player. He could play any instrument really well. He and I performed at Dewey and Penny Bunnell's wedding, and Andrew did some work with America. People seemed to think he and I looked very similar. I guess it was the red hair and the red beards. Andrew had a lot of energy and like me, he really dug the original Byrds.

The first gig was in West Los Angeles at a club called The Mint. It's a nice room with an excellent sound system and it was totally packed. Rumors floated around that David Crosby and Chris Hillman from the original Byrds might show up. They didn't. I joined the group onstage and performed Roger McGuinn's "Mr. Spaceman," a song I've played many times over many years because of its *Lost in Space-* type connection. McGuinn sent me an autographed photo many years ago that was inscribed, "Hey Bill, don't get too spaced out!"

Anyway, I played Crosby's guitar part on a vintage Gretsch Tennessean and sang McGuinn's lead vocal while Andrew sang Crosby's harmony part and played McGuinn's Rickenbacker 12-string bits.

A few months later, I joined the band again at a club in Studio City called Platinum. Andrew was impressed with my McGuinn-type vocal sound and the fact that I knew the Byrds catalogue so well. He really wanted me to officially become a member of the group and sing the McGuinn parts while he sang the Crosby parts. I had fun sitting in and jamming with the guys, but I had my own band gigging around Los Angeles at the time and so I passed on the offer, as it was tough enough to get a few hundred people to come out and hear me play my own music.

When Andrew Gold made music, he made real good music. He was the driving force behind Linda Ronstadt's hits and he wrote some great songs like "Lonely Boy" and the theme to *The Golden Girls* "Thank you for Being a Friend." I was sad when he passed away in 2011 at the young age of 59 and I was fortunate to have known him and made music alongside him.

Former First Lady Nancy Reagan had a successful career as an actress using her maiden name of Nancy Davis. She retired from acting in 1962 and her final dramatic onscreen appearance was guest-starring alongside me in an episode of the long-running western television series *Wagon Train*. We had quite a few nice long scenes together in that show. It was called "The Sam Darland Story" and featured Art Linkletter and several other child actors, although my role as Toddy was the featured character. For this gig, I wore a derby hat that resembled the hat Stymie (Max Beard) wore in classic *The Little Rascals* short films. I always dug Stymie and the Rascals. In 1962, *Wagon Train* was the most popular show on TV. We filmed it at Revue Studios, on the Universal lot.

What I recall the most from filming that episode is one of the older kid actors, I'm pretty sure his name was Blake, gifted me the 45 rpm single of "Purple People Eater" by Sheb Wooley, and I loved that record. I still have it in a box somewhere. The other thing I remember was being impressed working alongside fellow child actor Rusty Stevens, who had played Larry Mondello on *Leave it to Beaver*.

For about a year in the late 1980s, I was a co-owner/investor in a Malibu Grand Prix go-cart racing and video game arcade in Texas. I shared the same business manager as Mick Fleetwood and Gary Busey and several other celebrities, and that's where some of our investment money went. We spent a fortune at the party celebrating the opening. Shortly after it was open for business, there was a big storm in the area and then construction on the freeway closed the exit ramp to the track, and it lingered a while and then shut down for good. We sold the property and ended up losing money, but not too much.

The party was worth it.

《》

In 1966, Kurt Russell and I were honored at the annual Spotlighters Teen Awards. Here we are with some cool folks and a cake... Veronica Cartwright, Kurt, Hal Baylor (Spotlighters' President), Bob Denver, Jay North, and me.

53. Overloaded

*T*here aren't a lot of people around who once were child stars. It's a small group. I've found that even if you never worked with each other or if there's a decade or more separating the projects you were famous for, when you encounter another ex-child star, it's a very familial feeling. You instantly feel connected to them. For better and for worse, you know you've shared a rare experience and are part of a pretty unique club.

I, like countless millions of other kids, grew up watching the half hour family television shows of the 1950s and 1960s. Programs like *Father Knows Best*, *The Danny Thomas Show*, *The Donna Reed Show*, and *Leave it to Beaver*. Norman Tokar, a director I loved working for on the Disney films *Sammy, the Way-Out Seal* and *Rascal* directed close to a hundred episodes of *Leave it to Beaver*, so when Tony Dow, Wally Cleaver from *Beaver*, joined the *Babylon 5* series as a special effects director, we very quickly became good friends.

I had "met" Tony at some charity events back in the 1960s, but being eight years younger than him, I never really knew him before our work together on *Babylon 5* in the mid-1990s. Tony went on to direct many *B5* episodes and through Tony, I connected (and re-connected) with other iconic ex-child stars like Billy Gray, Johnny Crawford, Don Grady, Stanley and Barry Livingston, Jeannie Russell, Paul Peterson, and others.

Personally, Billy Gray was a big hero of mine. His character of Bud Anderson on *Father Knows Best* was the coolest of the cool and his work in *The Day the Earth Stood Still* was brilliant. Billy was a close friend and neighbor with Tony, and Eileen and I began hanging out at Tony's magnificent home in Topanga Canyon. Tony, Billy, and I would play ping-pong for hours and laugh and share our "TV Boys War Stories." Pretty soon, Veronica and Angela Cartwright started joining in gatherings at Tony and Lauren Dow's and... I became motivated.

I wanted to create a film, a dramatic science fiction story, that would star Billy Gray and several other of us grown-up child actors to showcase our still worthy talents and make a cool project for all of us to return to the screen in. Thus was born: *Overload*.

Overload was a drama set in deep space that dealt with survival, spirituality, and man's hubris in the face of certain doom. Peter David co-wrote the screenplay with me, and Tony would direct it. The cast included Billy Gray, Johnny Crawford, Angela and Veronica Cartwright, Don Grady, George Takei, Melissa Gilbert, Miguel Ferrer, Tony, and me.

PROMOTIONAL PHOTO SHOOT FOR OVERLOAD WITH VERONICA CARTWRIGHT, DON GRADY, BILLY GRAY, TONY DOW, ANGE, ME, AND JOHNNY CRAWFORD.

The score was composed by Don. The script was sold to Galaxy Pictures and a deal was made. Sets were built. The crew was hired. Wardrobe, special effects, miniatures, CGI, etc. all went into production. When filming began in February of 2000, Veronica was committed to another project, so she was replaced by Claudia Christian from *Babylon 5*.

We shot for a week and all was going great. Then, all went not great. Galaxy ran into trouble and out of money and production ended. An impressive *Overload* trailer was edited, and it can be found if one searches for it hard enough.

Tony never lost his cool. He was exceptionally exceptional. He and Lauren and Eileen and I remained very close friends until the day he passed away after a tough battle with cancer. Tony was one of the very best men I've ever encountered. I am a better person for knowing him.

"WALLY + WILL" OR "TONY + BILL". TONY WAS ONE OF THE BEST HUMANS I'VE EVER ENCOUNTERED.

54. Once a Comic Geek...

When I wasn't filming, going to school, at lunch, or goofing around in general, I was huddled on the stage writing and drawing superhero comic books that were based on the cast of *Lost in Space*.

The first one I made featured Guy and June. In reality, Guy was obsessed with his hair. He was constantly checking it before the camera rolled, so I nicknamed him "The Comb" and created a superhero who uses various types of combs as weapons. The Comb (and his crime-busting beauty Cara Mia) was a one issue special edition Mumy comic. Then I did a whole series starring Mark and me as *Captain Panther and Fox*. The Comb and Cara Mia returned in a few of those stories. All of the villains were based on various *Lost in Space* cast and crew members. The comic books are crude, sloppy, and very silly, but I had fun making them.

In the 1990s I wrote the *Lost in Space* comic book for real. I have always had a lot of restless creative energy. I wrote the *Lost in Space* comic book series published by Innovation Comics for two years, 1991-1993. The books were successful and critically very well-received. I really enjoyed writing those stories and revisiting characters I honestly felt I knew better than almost anyone else. I was fortunate to work with many talented artists telling those tales.

SOMETIMES THE COMIC BOOK CHARACTERS ARE MORE REAL THAN THIS WACKY GROUP. ANGE, MARTA, BOBBY, ME, JONATHAN, AND JUNE AFTER A REUNION LUNCH ON THE FOX LOT.

Voyage to the Bottom of the Soul became a 360 page ambitious *Lost in Space* graphic novel that really moved the arc of the classic characters in a big way. I felt real good about that one. Stan Lee generously wrote the foreword to it. It's been out-of-print for quite awhile now, and I'm hoping to republish it soon.

SETH AND ME WITH THE LEGENDARY STAN LEE.

Story originally printed in *Lost (and Found) in Space 2: Blast Off into the Expanded Edition,* © *2021* Synthesis Entertainment. Used with permission.

55. Change

I've never favored change very much. I find that interesting as I was constantly shifting from one project to another, moving on from one cast and crew to another, traveling to locations, etc. But in my personal world, I've always held on tight to my comfort zone, and nothing defines comfort zone more than your home.

I was basically born on Lockford Street and I'm not exaggerating when I say it was idyllic. Good friends all around me, friends I trusted and who knew me since before I entered showbiz, there was safety and adventures around every corner. When my parents decided to move up to Cheviot Hills (which admittedly was a bike ride or a decent walk away), I was against it. I actually ran away from home in protest. But I didn't get very far. After about half a mile I realized it was stupid so I returned and resigned myself to my fate. I promised all the Lockford gang (Jeff, Gary, Steve, David, Michelle, Don, Joe, Leenie, etc.) that I would return every single weekend. That nothing would change.

Of course it all changed very quickly. The house my parents built on Forrester Drive was very impressive and quite big. It was over 4,000 square feet with a view of all of downtown Los Angeles. Forrester Drive is arguably the nicest street in Cheviot Hills and Cheviot Hills is a nicer neighborhood than Beverlywood.

Although I filmed the pilot for *Lost in Space* while living on Lockford, I filmed the series while living on Forrester. I was very busy working and I loved my work.

Within a few weeks, I met Scott Ehrlich, his brother Craig, and neighbor Scott Shaw, and we bonded quickly. Although I did love my Lockford group, admittedly, they soon faded into the background of my world. Never forgotten though, and I still talk with Jeff quite often and thanks to social media have reconnected a bit with Gary, Steve, Paul, and David.

Like I said, making changes in the entertainment business is a necessary thing to accept. But, I've been living in the same house for forty-six years now. I guess that tells you something.

SCOTT EHRLICH (WHO CHANGED HIS NAME TO SCOTT BEN-YASHAR 46 YEARS AGO) AND I HAVE BEEN BEST FRIENDS SINCE I WAS TEN. WE'VE REALLY EXPERIENCED A WHOLE LOT OF LIFE TOGETHER HERE WE ARE BACK IN 1965 AND IN 2020. ONWARD.

PART 4

VERY HAPPY WITH ANGE IN ARIZONA FILMING
BLESS THE BEASTS & CHILDREN, 1970.

56. It's a Beautiful Day

1970 was a game-changing year for me in every way. I got my driver's license on February 1st, and within a week of that, Angela and I were "officially" a couple. We were deeply in love and basking in all the pleasures that accompany young, first passion. It was wonderful while it lasted. Over the years our relationship has shifted many times and we've been in a fine, platonic, artistically collaborative space for many years now. Angela will always remain my first true love and very important to me. In 1970, we were hot and heavy.

Gully, my musical partnership with Paul, became Redwood. Gary David joined us and the duo became a trio. Gary sang the really high parts, played guitar, violin, and mandolin and he wrote a few tunes we added to our repertoire. Redwood practiced constantly and got very good, very fast. Soon we were gigging all over southern California and quickly gathering a loyal local following. John Stewart, formerly of the Kingston Trio, took us under his wing and helped us become a tight professional unit. We became John's supporting opening act. He took us into the recording studio Sunset Sound, with Russ Kunkel on drums, Bryan Garafalo on bass, and John's brother Michael Stewart on 12-string, and John produced a demo for us. Angela was always with me. Redwood was fresh and harmonizing, gigging, and recording. My new 1969 MGB-GT was a groovy little car and Ange and I found ourselves in some pretty contorted positions at the Pickwick Drive-In, steaming up the windows in that British ride of mine. Life was great.

And it was about to get greater.

Howard Rubin, my beloved trusted agent of many years, called me and said he'd set up a meeting for me with Stanley Kramer at his office on the Columbia Pictures lot on Gower Avenue just off Sunset. It was to discuss me potentially starring in a new feature film Stanley was producing and directing that was set to start production in June. The movie was *Bless the Beasts & Children*, based on a very popular novel of the same name written by Glendon Swarthout. There had been a recent bidding war for the film rights and Stanley emerged as the victor.

There were no other people in my initial meeting with Stanley. Just the two of us. Stanley knew my acting history, and he explained that he wanted to make a strong anti-gun statement with this film. He wanted to show that outsiders were as important as popular kids and he wanted to alert the audience to some heinous acts of violence perpetrated against animals. He wanted to wake people up and make things better. I loved Stanley. He was about my height, five feet eight inches. He wore tennis shirts, and his silver hair was cut in a short crew cut. Born in Hell's Kitchen, New York, he spoke with a gruffness, like a tough guy, but there was always the flicker of a smile in his eyes. Stanley had produced many classic films addressing important social issues, such as *Judgment at Nuremburg, Guess Who's Coming To Dinner, The Defiant Ones, On The Beach, Inherit The Wind,* as well as the classic comedy *It's A Mad, Mad, Mad, Mad World*.

I really wanted to work with Stanley. I agreed to take a 67% cut in my salary to star in *Bless the Beasts & Children*. I wanted it that badly.

I worked on the film for thirteen weeks, starting in mid-June. The majority of the project was filmed in and around the towns of Prescott, Jerome, and Sedona, Arizona. We also spent several weeks filming on Catalina Island, twenty-six miles off the California coast. The buffalo stampede and animal pen scenes were all shot there. For flashback and various interiors, we worked on a few different soundstages on the Columbia lot in Hollywood. Beyond myself, the core cast included Miles Chapin, Marc Vahanian, Darrel Glaser, Bobby Kramer (no relation to Stanley), and Barry Robbins. It was an interesting and eclectic group of teenagers, with the singular exception of Barry, who was twenty-six years old at the time. Personally, I always felt Barry was miscast as Cotton and he never really chose to bond with or connect with the rest of us while making the film. He stayed to himself.

Anyone under the age of eighteen has to have a guardian with them at all times when working on a film or television project. It's the law, and there's no way around that. But I certainly found one. Scott Ehrlich, my very best friend, who lived four houses up the street from me on Forrester Drive, turned eighteen on June 2nd. I had the court appoint Scott as my legal guardian. BOOM!

The only cast member who had a parent with him was Darrel. His mom was there. Miles, Bobby, and Marc somehow had the unit manager and the assistant director appointed as their guardians. That was very unusual, and it meant that for the most part, this group of teenagers, playing a group of teenagers who didn't fit in with the cool crowd and were taking on a dangerous covert rescue mission all on their own, were pretty much all on our own.

In the summer of 1970, Prescott was a fairly small cowboy town. There were gun racks hanging in the back window of most every pickup truck and there were absolutely no long-haired hippies around. We, the cast members, were a handful of long-haired hippies. The seven of us, including Scott, all were staying in the Prescott Lodge motel. We each had our own room. As usual, I brought my guitar and a portable stereo record player and a bunch of albums with me. Music is something I need every day. I need to listen to it, and I need to play it. That hasn't changed since I was ten years old.

Stanley, the crew, and production staff all stayed in different hotels scattered around Prescott. When I think back on it now, they obviously wanted us kids to be isolated together. It worked because we became quite close. Bobby Kramer was a film buff, and he had a nice 16mm camera with him and he documented quite a lot of the behind-the-scenes making of the movie. Marc Vahanian, though only fourteen at the time, was a bold, adventurous, fearless, funny, jump-into-the-thick-of-it, likeable kid. We got along great. Miles Chapin was terrific. He was really smart and came from an impressive Massachusetts family. Steinway pianos were directly related to him on his mother's side of the family. Miles was mature for his age and he and I liked all the same music. Miles and I were also the only two who were smokers. I smoked Marlboros back then. I smoked from the age of fourteen until I was twenty-five. I'm very glad I finally stopped that nasty habit. Miles rolled his own cigarettes. He was great at it. We'd be sitting on horses waiting to film a scene, and with one hand, Miles would tap out a perfect amount of tobacco and quickly roll up a great-looking ciggy. I was very impressed by that. I could never roll anything worthy of smoking. Darrel Glaser was slightly teased by us a bit, because he seemed young for his age. He was an unusually quiet, reserved, nervous, nice, little kid. Darrel didn't hang out with us when we weren't working. Neither did Barry Robbins. Barry had an attitude I wasn't particularly fond of. He acted like he was the only serious actor on the film and he brooded and kept to himself. I recall one night Barry saying to me, "I don't think you're taking this seriously enough." I just looked at him and said, "Watch the movie when it comes out and then tell me that."

I took my work and performance very seriously. I knew exactly what I was doing, and I knew exactly how I was playing Teft. I also knew how to shut my working brain off at the end of a day's filming and have fun. Barry had done some impressive live musical theater before *Bless the Beasts* and he had played piano in some cocktail

STANLEY KRAMER WAS WONDERFUL. HE WAS TOUGH, BUT HE WAS SWEET AND HE COMMUNICATED WELL WHAT HE WANTED AS A DIRECTOR.

I BORROWED A MOTORCYCLE FROM ONE OF THE LOCAL KIDS AND HAD SOME FUN FOR A WHILE.

lounges. Honestly, I thought his performance was way over-the-top. After we wrapped up the movie, I never saw him again. Sadly, he died of complications from AIDS in 1986, at the young age of forty-one.

THE "DINGS" MISFITS ALL... BOBBY, MILES, MARC, BARRY, ME, AND DARREL.

Not only was Scott my guardian on the film, but he also auditioned for Stanley and was cast in a nice supporting role. About a week before leaving LA to begin shooting the movie in Arizona, Scott and I drove up to Big Sur and went camping for a few days. Big Sur is one of the most gorgeous locations I've ever known, and in 1970, it was a "Hippie Haven." We camped out in Pfeiffer Big Sur Campground, one thousand acres of natural beauty. We hiked the trails and followed the little stream a few miles until we came to "the Gorge." The stream opened up to a large, natural pool surrounded by high rocks where naked hippies relaxed in the sunshine. We stripped off our clothes and dove into the crystalline water and frolicked with strangers who for a few hours became friends. It was nice. Nothing sexual, just a new generation of young people feeling free and loving nature.

One night, while Scott and I were sitting around our small campfire and I was playing my acoustic guitar, two young ladies approached and joined us. Their names were Sherry and Crystal. Sherry said they lived in San Francisco, and she worked as a housekeeper for Jefferson Airplane. Crystal produced a fat joint that we all shared under the starry night sky. We sang a few songs together and Scott and I told them we were heading to Prescott, Arizona to work on a film, and we'd be there for over a month. Again, nothing sexual went down. We just hung out for a while, and they went on their way.

About two weeks into production, guess who shows up in Prescott? Sherry and Crystal. They assumed they'd be welcome to crash with us. That wasn't going to be the case with me. I had no one on my mind but Angela, and she was going to be coming up to stay with me soon. If memory serves me well, Crystal stayed with Scott. I'm positive that Sherry stayed with fourteen-year-old Marc Vahanian, because she pleasantly took his virginity, and he couldn't have been happier about it. Sherry and Crystal were true flower-power hippies and free love was something they enjoyed sharing with others. Unfortunately, another thing they enjoyed sharing was a tab of LSD with Miles.

It turned into a nightmare bad trip for him and although we all tried to talk him down and keep him mellow, Miles freaked out badly and we had to call production in the middle of the night. Miles was brought to an emergency room where he was sedated. The next day he was fine, and no one talked about it very much afterward.

Crystal and Sherry were given some cash from production and firmly asked to move on. They did.

When a major Hollywood production makes camp in a small town during summer, it attracts a lot of attention from the community. And since this film starred several teenagers, the local teenagers were drawn like moths to the flame. The film dealt with a boys' summer camp, and dozens of local boys were cast as extras. That meant dozens of local girls were hanging around. And that meant dozens of local cowboys who dated those local girls, but were too old to be cast as boy camper extras, were somewhat jealous and cranky about those local girls fawning over the actors. We started to notice cowboys in pickup trucks giving us very scary looks. It happened enough to not be a coincidence or something we imagined.

There was a Shakey's Pizza Parlor across the road, walking distance from the motel we were staying in and several times a week, Scott and I, often with Miles and Marc and Bobby, would get our dinners there. One night, after dark, Scott and I were walking to Shakey's when we observed a couple of pickup trucks driven by young cowboys take notice of us, and they slowly turned the trucks around. It didn't feel right.

We entered the restaurant and sat in a back booth. Looking out the window, we watched several guys in the parking lot get out of their trucks, huddle together, and point towards us. Scott and I had no doubt that these guys intended to kick the living shit out of us for no other reason than that was what these guys did for fun. We were really scared. And... we were right.

A group of them entered the restaurant and looked around in search of us. Scott and I were sneaking out the back door when one of them said, "There they are!" and another said, "Get 'em!"

Sometimes you just have to leap without looking, and that's exactly what we did. There was a cinderblock wall at the back of the parking lot and Scott and I vaulted over it as fast as we could. But what we didn't know was, the other side of it was not level with the ground of the parking lot. The earth below lay a good ten feet beneath the wall. The two of us dropped and tumbled to the hard ground. We were out of breath and bruised from the fall. It was pitch dark and took a while for our vision to adjust. Then we realized where we were. We had landed in a small old graveyard. The tombstones around us had dates of over a century ago. It was creepy. Scott and I huddled behind two headstones and held our breath as we listened to the bully cowboys above in the parking lot. We hardly breathed, we were so quiet. I can't honestly say how long we were there until we felt safe enough to maneuver ourselves out and run back to the Prescott Lodge, but it felt like quite a while. In the end, we managed to avoid getting pummeled by angry punk cowboys that night. So that was a good thing.

Ange was due to arrive the next day. She was taking the bus up with her friend, Jennifer. I couldn't wait to have her join me. It was going to be great to have her stay with me for a few days without us having to sneak around. I wanted to do something nice for her arrival and I asked Stanley Kramer's wife Karen, a gorgeous, smart, friendly lady, and a talented actress who came and went during the production, if she could arrange for flowers to decorate my room so it would be romantic when Ange arrived. Karen outdid herself, and my little motel room was filled with bouquets of multi-colored flowers. Ange came and we had a very romantic and enjoyable time together. Everyone on the film fell in love with her. She was, after all, an iconic actress who had literally grown up on television as Linda Williams on *The Danny Thomas Show* and Penny Robinson on *Lost in Space*. Angela was a stunningly beautiful young woman. During the day, she hung out watching us film. During the night we stayed together in my room. And believe it or not, Jennifer,

Angela's companion, ended up staying with Marc. What a little Casanova he turned out to be.

Teft was a major role for me. The rebellious character truly bridged the gap from being a kid and becoming a man. In the film, Teft steals a truck, which I drove with abandon, crazily entrusted with the lives of five other actors. He wielded a rifle and he used it. If anyone has ever doubted my horsemanship, watch the riding scenes in *Bless the Beasts*, no one doubled me in any of those scenes.

Production finally wrapped in Arizona, and we said goodbye to Prescott and relocated to the island of Catalina. I'd grown up cruising to Catalina quite often on my dad's yacht "The Char-Mur." I was very familiar with the town of Avalon where we stayed.

YES, THEY REALLY TRUSTED ME TO DRIVE THAT JEEP ALL OVER THE WINDING MOUNTAIN ROADS WITH THE ENTIRE CASTS' LIVES IN MY HANDS...AND FEET.

However, filming was done on the other side of the island. Herds of buffalo ran free there, and we needed those buffalo in the film. We worked really hard there.

Angela came to visit, crossing the twenty-six miles from Long Beach on a huge boat. As always, it was sweet to be reunited and we had a few romantic days together.

ANGE AND THE BOYS.

The school semester started up again, and Scott left to return to his studies at UCLA. Because we were filming on location with horses and buffalo every day, my dad took Scott's place as my guardian for the final weeks of work. He really enjoyed being out there a lot. I convinced him to grow a mustache while away from my mom. He'd never grown a mustache before. It looked good and he kept it for a couple of years.

Bless the Beasts & Children was one big adventure for me after another. The movie was impressively scored by Barry De Vorzon and Perry Botkin Jr. They also wrote the theme song which was performed by The Carpenters. Soulfully sung by Karen Carpenter, the single reached number two on the *Billboard* Hot 100. De Vorzon and Botkin Jr. received an Academy Award nomination for Best Original Song as well as a Grammy nomination for Best Original Score. The movie also included a short acapella chorus of a song that Paul and I wrote called "It's a Beautiful Day."

The film made its original debut as the United States entry into the Berlin Film Festival in June 1971. When released domestically that August, it didn't do very well at the box office. Shortly afterward, it was packaged with another counter-culture film called *Billy Jack* as a double feature and it made some money. It's achieved a cult status over the years.

I can't be objective about it.

Bless the Beasts & Children will always remain an important chapter in my professional and personal life.

<<>>

*I*n 1975, Shirley Jones, my first true love, and the multi-talented Johnny Crawford both sponsored me for membership into the Actors branch of the Academy of Motion Picture Arts and Sciences. I was quickly accepted into the prestigious club and have appreciated that fact ever since. I have attended the Oscar ceremonies, but I didn't really enjoy that much. It felt like being in the audience of a tense and long talk show taping to me.

I've also voted for the awards every year, but I must admit that competition, something being deemed "best of" regarding art of any kind, has never resonated that well with me. Being rewarded for the "best" at athletic competitions makes perfect sense. If you run the fastest, jump the farthest, etc., then obviously you win. You're the best at that time. But when it comes to filmmaking or music, awards declaring "best of" have always been somewhat silly to my mind.

SHIRLEY JONES... MY FIRST TRUE LOVE. STILL A CLOSE PAL.

57. QUAGMIRE

After twenty years, my marriage was in a major crisis. I take full responsibility for it, and I wear the blame. Imagine you are a body surfer and have been out far from shore in a calm ocean for a very long time. All of a sudden, a wave from outside appears and you are drawn out to it. You're quickly in deep water over your head and you don't have the strength to swim to shore. You are pulled to the wave, and you have to make a decision that can cost you your life. Do you attempt to dive underneath the wave and surface safely behind it? Do you attempt to swim into the wave and make it to the other side before it breaks? Or do you attempt to catch and ride what appears to be the wave of a lifetime? I chose to ride it and found myself wiped out, tumbling under crashing whitewater not knowing which way was up and which way was down and hoping only to make it to the surface and gulp fresh air once again before drowning. And ultimately, I did, but the wave itself crashed and was destroyed and the sandy beach it throttled was shredded and reduced to rocks.

Eileen chose to salvage our marriage and keep our family together and after a short separation, therapy and counseling, and much trauma, we got through it. But like an invisible tattoo, seen only to those with special lenses, it remains a permanent scar, that despite my best intentions, I cannot ever fully heal.

<<>>

*I*t is 1959. I am taking tap dancing lessons at the Beverly Hills Academy for Children on Doheny and Wilshire. I am five years old. I don't know why I'm doing this. I don't like it much. This isn't what I meant at all when I told my parents I wanted to get inside the television like Zorro and Superman. I learn a two-step. I stop taking tap dancing lessons at the Beverly Hills Academy for Children on Doheny and Wilshire. Where's my cape?

WHEN EVERYTHING WAS EASY. SUPER JIGGS AND ME.

58. Looking Good

Johnny Chambers was an iconic makeup artist who is perhaps best remembered for his astonishing transformations on the 1968, Franklin Schaffner directed, 20th Century Fox film *Planet of the Apes*. A little-known fact regarding that movie is that chimpanzee "Debbie, the Bloop" from *Lost in Space* was used as a model for the face masks and applications on the film.

During the third and final season of *LIS*, in the episode titled "The Space Destructors," Dr. Smith and Will discover a machine that turns Will into a duplicate of Dr. Smith. The makeup process involved for that episode was created by Johnny Chambers and one of our regular makeup crew, Frank Griffin. The result was astonishing. After making a lifecast of my face and Jonathan Harris' face, they scaled down some rubber appliances, added a wig, eyebrows, and several hours of plain old makeup skills, and I was truly transformed into an almost perfect duplicate of Jonathan. The process wasn't pleasant, as having a life cast of your face done requires your entire face to be covered in a mud-like clay that hardens while on you; and to me it felt like being buried alive. Two small straws were inserted in my nostrils while the goop did its thing. But the final results were truly impressive.

I remember after coming out of the makeup room after several hours undergoing that unpleasant process, my mother and I drove home, less than five minutes away, and I scared the shit out of my grandmother who wasn't expecting to see me looking like that!

Of course, almost thirty years later, I endured face lifecasting again and many hours of makeup on a daily basis working on *Babylon 5* as Lennier from the planet Minbar.

You just can't take the space thing out of me.

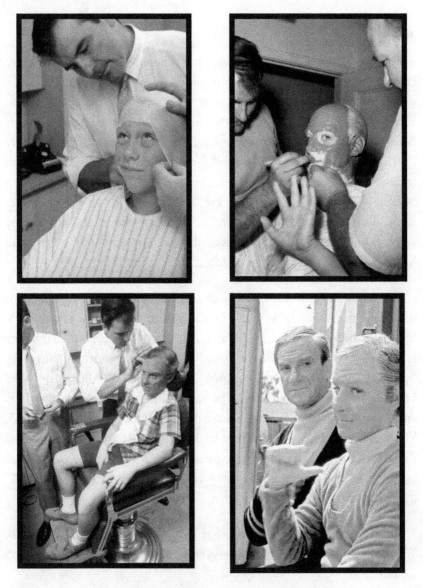

NOBODY SAID IT WOULD BE EASY.

59. Through the Looking Glass

Mark Mothersbaugh, front man and co-leader of Devo, called me up in late 1991. I'd known Mark for ten years by then. Barnes & Barnes had been in the novelty, punk rock, art rock, "outsider" film scene since "Fish Heads," and our paths had crossed many times. When Robert and I produced two albums for the legendary, manic depressive, paranoid schizophrenic, acapella singer-songwriter, Larry "Wild Man" Fischer (*Pronounced Normal* and *Nothing Scary*), both released on Rhino Records and well worth experiencing, Mark became peripherally involved. He also appeared as his character Booji Boy in Barnes & Barnes' 1987 *Zabagabee* mockumentary video. Devo wasn't gigging or recording extensively at this time and Mark had begun scoring the children's television series *Rugrats*.

"Mumy, I've got a gig for you, and I know you'd be perfect for it." "Tell me more." "I'm doing the music for a new Disney TV series. It's based on the Lewis Carroll *Alice in Wonderland* characters. It's a live-action half-hour show and each episode contains four one-minute songs sung by the various characters, like Alice, The Mad Hatter, The Red Queen, etc. I'm assembling a team of songwriters and I want you on the team. You can work out of your home studio. You write and record the songs, make me a mix with a demo vocal the actors can follow, and a track-only mix, and then the cast comes into my studio and records their vocals. What do you think?" "I think it sounds totally boss. I'm in. Thanks, Mark."

Well, little did I know that my work on *Adventures in Wonderland* would last for two years, 100 episodes, include 105 songs that I wrote, and earn me an Emmy nomination for Outstanding Achievement in Music Direction and Composition.

The best part of the gig was my son Seth was a toddler, three and four years old at the time, and besides being able to stay home and spend quality time with him at such a young and impressionable age, *Adventures in Wonderland* was a terrific program for him to watch. It was aimed at little kids and each episode included educational learning and positive stories. It was, in many ways, although not necessarily financially, a dream gig for me.

I'm a songwriter. I have good friends who score television shows and films and make a huge amount of money doing that. In 1988, I worked in that arena when I guest-starred in an episode of an Emmy-winning PBS series called *The Universe and I*. It was shot in Kentucky and the producers and crew were professional and nice. They were aware of my work in music beyond my work as an actor, and they offered me the opportunity to score the episode I starred in. I collaborated with Gerry Beckley on that, and we ended up scoring that show and two other episodes of *The Universe and I*. I could have continued working in that field. Mark Mothersbaugh offered me a shot at basically scoring an animated series he was music producer on, but I had learned from experience that scoring television wasn't the right gig for me. I found that scoring a show kind of sucked the muse out of me to create a twenty-second cue or a three-minute cue, etc. Although I appreciated and enjoyed the three shows Gerry and I scored together, it simply wasn't a career I wanted to explore further.

The *Wonderland* show was very different. I'd drive up Lookout Mountain and halfway down Sunset Plaza Drive to Mark's house several times a week and pick up a script. We lived a couple of miles from each other. The scripts were pre-marked where each song would be placed. It would read something akin to: "Alice breaks into a jaunty song here about being a cowgirl at the rodeo." At

Mark's house, I'd quickly look through the scripts and request which songs I'd like to compose. For some episodes, I would write one song and for other episodes, I would write all four. 105 Mumy songs made it onto the air. After a few months working on the series, I recommended Robert, my Barnes & Barnes partner, as a songwriter to Mark. Robert and I hadn't really been communicating much after the Crispin Glover debacle. Mark was happy to hire Robert and like me, Robert worked from his own home studio, and he ended up contributing about thirty songs to the series. He and I rekindled our friendship and partnership while working together for Mark on *Wonderland*.

The show was filmed just down the hill at the CBS Radford lot in Studio City, and I used to bring Seth to the set once in a while to watch them film. Alice was played beautifully by Elizabeth Harnois. She was twelve and thirteen when filming the series and she was a doll. She used to carry Seth around in her arms and call him her boyfriend. He loved that.

The series originally aired from 1992 through 1994 and was very successful. The executive producer and show runner, Andi Copley, was terrific to work for. Sure, once in a while I'd get notes to try a different approach with a song, maybe they wanted something a little faster, etc., that was no problem. By far, I wrote more songs than anyone else on Mark's team for the series.

I had a real good time.

60. Band Together

All I've ever really wanted to do besides "get inside the television like Zorro and Superman" was be in a band. Let's take a lingering look back at every musical configuration I've been a part of over the course of my life so far.

In 1962, Jeff Kalmick and Gary Marshank, two of my best pals who lived on Lockford Street with me, got guitars. I had a pair of bongos. That summer the Chantays had a hit instrumental surf song on the charts called "Pipeline." I remember Gary and Jeff struggling to pick out those notes and chords while I attempted to slap out a groove on the bongos. We called ourselves The Neon Tetras and we performed for our parents and a couple other Lockford kids maybe twice. I wonder where my old bongos are today.

1965 was my professional music performance debut at the Hollywood Bowl wearing a silver spacesuit and playing a nylon-strung classical Goya acoustic guitar. I entertained the audience by singing "The Tijuana Jail" by the Kingston Trio. Over the next four years I would perform many solo concerts around the country at personal appearances and on national and regional radio and television programs. But it wasn't a band.

THE YOUNG TROUBADOUR GIGGING AROUND THE COUNTRY.

In 1967, my best friend Scott and I wore matching outfits and played one gig in Westwood in an empty grocery store that was for some reason a showcase scene for a while. We played a full set of folk songs, mostly from the Kingston Trio catalogue mixed with two or three original Mumy songs, such as "I Hear the Train." We wore yellow shirts, matching gray pants with built-in belts (that we bought at a store in Beverly Hills called Burdsall's), and matching penny loafer shoes we bought at another Beverly Hills store called Rudnick's. Scott and I each played acoustic guitars. I had just traded in my classical Goya for a steel-string Gibson B-25N and Scott played my bongos on a couple of songs. We were billed as Scott & Bill: The Group Two. Scott's mother Norma Ehrlich, a tan, pretty, and quick-witted young lady at the time, suggested the name. We only played that one gig.

THE GROUP TWO, SCOTT AND I. DRESSED EXACTLY THE SAME. IT WASN'T EXACTLY THE HOLLYWOOD BOWL.

After that, things started to become more real. As noted previously, in 1968 while in the ninth grade, I formed my first serious rock & roll band Energy. Phase One of that group included Robert Haimer on organ and vocals, Glenn Hime on guitar, Steve Kessler on drums, and myself on lead vocals and guitar. Energy played several school events and some private parties and got written up in the teen magazines. Within less than six months, the original lineup changed to me, Robert, Paul Gordon on guitar and vocals and songwriting, and Ronny Solomon on drums. This much-improved version of Energy continued to play school parties and events and private parties like bar mitzvah's and birthdays where we were paid.

Energy auditioned to perform at 20ᵗʰ Century Fox on the weekends for the buses of tourists who paid to cruise around the studio when there wasn't much going on there. We were told we had the gig, but before we even started, the studio decided against it. Showbiz.

ENERGY (VERSION ONE) IN MY BACKYARD. 1968.

《〉》

Energy broke up in 1969 and Paul and I became the acoustic duo, Gully. Mostly, we practiced together, wrote a whole lot of songs, worked on arrangements, played them for friends, and went into a professional recording studio and cut demos. No booked gigs for Gully.

《〉》

In early 1970, Robert Haimer and I jammed and recorded some original novelty songs that quickly combusted out of us. That was the beginning of Barnes & Barnes, a musical partnership that has continued, although with some very lengthy hiatuses, for over fifty years now. From the late 1970s through 2005, Barnes & Barnes played select gigs, but our focus was never on live performances. In November of 2021, Barnes & Barnes released a new studio album *Pancake Dream*. It's a very dramatic, theatrical, dark, and unique concept album and there is nothing similar to "Fish Heads" on it.

《〉》

Also in early 1970, Gary David joined Paul and I and Gully became Redwood. Redwood performed and recorded nonstop for the next five years. In 1971 alone we played over 100 gigs. Without any shadow of a doubt, Redwood was the tightest, and in my opinion, the best group I've ever been a part of.

REDWOOD 1970. PHOTO BY HENRY DILTZ.

<<>>

Although we weren't a "real band," the music that Cliff de Young, Corey Fischer, and I sang and played together on the many *Sunshine* film and television projects was legit. It was us and it resulted in a hit record. We never gigged as a trio, but Cliff and I played a few charity shows for the Special Olympics together. So in a way, I will classify the Sunshine Trio as a band.

<<>>

On January 1, 1976, Gary retired from the music business and became an accountant, quitting Redwood, and sending Paul and I back into Gully mode. For the next two years we struggled to rediscover what we really were and what we really wanted to be. We tried too hard and I look back on those years with both fondness and confusion. Why did we attempt to write and perform in so many odd musical styles? I guess Paul was evolving and prepping for his eventual segue into writing Broadway musicals, and the songs I was writing back then were somewhat wimpy, although a few of them are pretty good. Instead of returning to Gully for our name, we called ourselves The Mumy-Gordon Band. Gadzooks.

For the next two years, we gigged and recorded at Record Plant and Todd Fisher's remote recording truck, but it never quite jelled together because we never quite understood what we were trying to be. Jay Gruska and David Jolliffe joined the Mumy-Gordon Band, singing and writing and playing keyboard, percussion, and guitar, and that only made us even more diverse. The camaraderie was fun, and we performed and recorded with some excellent players like Steve Lukather, Carlos Vega, Mike Porcaro, Dean Cortez, Ian Hoffman, Gerry Beckley, Willie Leacox, David Cassidy, "Papa" Elpidio Cobian, and others. The Mumy-Gordon Band showcased live for several record companies and came close to getting a deal, but in the end, we weren't signed. Jay Gruska joined Three Dog Night and then he got a solo record deal and that left me, Paul, and David Jolliffe as the remaining Mumy-Gordon Band core members. Paul didn't have the energy to start over again and deal with what songs would be on our setlist, so he went out as a solo artist with a series of excellent backing musicians.

Not long after that, Jolliffe, Jay, and I joined Shaun Cassidy's band and toured the country together playing to sold out sports arenas with screaming girls going crazy every night. The Mumy-Gordon band moved to the Cornfield.

«»

Returning from Shaun's tour, I wanted to continue gigging. Of course, I knew I wouldn't be headlining any sports arenas, but the New Wave music scene in Los Angeles was very much happening and there were an abundance of decent clubs to play at. My friend, Peter Leinheiser who had been the lead guitarist for The Hudson Brothers and musical director for Andy Gibb, put together a new gigging band with me. Peter named it the Igloos (because we were just so cool). He brought in bassist Neil Roberts, drummer and singer and songwriter extraordinaire Billy Thomas, percussionist and fabulous singer Randy Foote, and I drafted George Englund to play sax, flute, and keyboard. Peter and I handled the guitars. For two years, Bill Mumy and the Igloos played all the clubs in town and we were a very enjoyable, fun, tight band. The Igloos never recorded in a proper studio, but a few of our live gigs were preserved on a stereo cassette unit with two condenser mics.

When I occasionally revisit those tapes, I'm pleasantly surprised at how good we were. Peter, Billy, Foote, and I all composed songs that the Igloos played and the lead vocals were shared by me, Billy, and Foote. Like I said, all I ever really wanted to do was be in a good band. The Igloos were just having fun and that in itself was rewarding. We gigged a lot. After only a year into it, Billy Thomas, who was very special and integral to the band, left to join Rick Nelson's band. Can't blame him for that! He went on to relocate in Nashville and for the past forty years has been in Vince Gill's band. The Igloos were a side project for Foote, who fronted his own band at the same time. They were called ComboNation. They were great and they got a record deal on Warner Bros. So the Igloos were whittled down to me, Peter, Neil, and sometimes George, as he had come and gone somewhat from the beginning. Peter found a new drummer and a new keyboard player, but it didn't have the same energy and vibe. It was still a good little band, but once Billy and Foote were gone, The Igloos soon melted.

《〉》

Around this time, I had been sitting in at many America gigs. Usually coming out as a guest to sing and play a guitar solo on "Horse With No Name" at the end of their shows, but my relationship with Dewey and Gerry was shifting into more of a collaborative one once Dan Peek left the band in 1977. Soon, although I was never an "official" member of America, I was writing songs with both Dewey and Gerry that were featured on America albums, I was joining them in the recording studio as a guitar player, bass player, programmer, and co-producer. I began making stage appearances with the band more often. I was offered a position in the touring band, but once I was under contract to *Babylon 5*, that was off the table for me. It's always been a pleasure to make music with Dewey and Gerry. They both contributed to many Barnes & Barnes tracks, and we returned the favor with their solo projects as well as with America releases. Most of the 1980s, my musical energy was connected to Barnes & Barnes and America.

ONSTAGE AT THE UNIVERSAL AMPHITHEATER WITH AMERICA AND JIMMY WEBB. PHOTO BY HENRY DILTZ.

≪‹›≫

While attending the San Diego Comic Con in 1987, Miguel and I, along with Max Allan Collins and Steve Leialoha, were having a few drinks and listening to a terrible lounge act-type band the con had booked as entertainment. It was pure schmaltz. We made the comment that we could put together a real rock & roll band that would kick ass better than these guys any day. Jackie Estrada, who was on the board of Comic Con, and was standing with us, said, "Would you guys really do that? It would be so great!" We said, "Hell yeah." And the next year, Seduction of the Innocent made its debut at the Comic Con. Miguel on drums and vocals, Max on vocals and keyboards, Steve on Bass, and me on vocals and guitar.

SEDUCTION OF THE INNOCENT. MIGUEL FERRER, ME, ALAN COLLINS, AND STEVE LEIALOHA. MAN, WE HAD FUN PLAYING GARAGE ROCK AT COMIC BOOK CONVENTIONS FOR A FEW YEARS!

We became Comic Con faves and we really did rock hard and sloppy. We were a loud, somewhat decent garage rock band whose purpose was to get everybody dancing and to party. For several years, Seduction of the Innocent (soon augmented by utility musician Chris Christensen on drums, guitar, harmonica, and percussion) were rocking Sci-Fi and Comic cons around the country. We had a blast. Serious fun. Seduction recorded an album of original songs that were thematically comic book-related, as well as a live album recorded at the San Diego Comic Con. We played a few gigs without Miguel, but it wasn't the same. He was the soul of Seduction. He named the group and without Miggy, there is no Seduction of the Innocent as far as I'm concerned.

«<>»

Sometimes bands just fall into place out of almost nowhere and that was the case with the Jenerators. In 1989, Frank Stallone was a partner in a new club and restaurant about to open on the Sunset Strip called Blak and Bloo and I was asked if I wanted to play there with a band one night a week. Well, that sounded like a fun thing to do. And fun was all the Jenerators were really about in the big picture. So, I quickly assembled a rock & roll band that included friends. Miguel on drums was a no brainer. We'd been playing in Seduction of the Innocent together for a couple years. It was always fun with Miguel. David Jolliffe on guitar, percussion, and vocals. I brought in Gary Stockdale, who I'd known since 1971, on bass and vocals. Tom Hebenstreit, a new friend I'd met tweaking my recording studio, played great slide guitar and he also played some keyboards. Alfons Kettner, who managed Voltage Guitars in Hollywood, right across the street from Blak and Bloo, played lead guitar, and I played guitar and sang. We rehearsed for a few weeks as the club was being built and readied. The Jenerators mixed original songs with a hefty side of cover tunes and lead vocals were divided between me, Gary, Jolliffe, and Miguel. We played Blak and Bloo for over a year. We got tight. We became a "thing" for the showbiz crowd. Miggy's cousin George Clooney would come every week, Shaun Cassidy would get up and jam with us, Steve Lukather jammed with us almost every week and that certainly helped draw crowds in. We had a minor radio hit with a novelty song that I wrote with Jolliffe and Miguel called "Pussy Whipped." It was always the final song of the night and it kicked ass and people loved it. "Pussy Whipped" is an absolutely true story about Jolliffe's first marriage.

THE JENERATORS AT THE BEGINNING... MIGUEL FERRER, TOM HEBENSTREIT, DAVID JOLLIFFE, ME, GARY STOCKDALE, AND ALFONS KETTNER. WE GIGGED A LOT.

The Jenerators released three albums: *The Jenerators*, *Hitting the Silk*, and *Pony Up*. Frank Wolf recorded and mixed all three of them and we worked in great studios like the Village Recorder, the old Motown Hollywood studio, and Conway. The albums were cut very quickly, mostly live. For a while, I took the Jenerators seriously, but maybe with the exception of Tom, no one else in the band really ever did. For Miguel, who was always working on television shows and feature films, the band was just a bit of fun for him. An opportunity to play the drums and sing a few tunes and get wasted after the show on martinis with his friends. When he was on location, we had two good drummers fill in for him, Chris Ross and John "Chris" Christensen. Gary Stockdale was busy scoring Penn and Teller's shows and films and he never took being in the Jenerators seriously at all. Gary's such a truly great musician that he also never particularly wanted to practice much and that frustrated me to no end, because the rest of us definitely needed to practice and tighten up. Jolliffe was going through a divorce and was dealing with some demons that resulted in him leaving the band and then returning to the band and then leaving the band and then returning to the band. He wasn't in any shape to step up and take it too seriously. Alphons only stayed in the band for a year. He accepted a good-paying gig being Woody Harrelson's music director and we parted company on good terms. He passed away a few years later after a sorrowful battle with cancer.

THE JENERATORS PLAYED A GIG EVERY MONTH ON THE BEAUTIFUL SANTA MONICA PIER AT A COOL CLUB NAMED RUSTY'S SURF RANCH FOR MANY YEARS. HERE WE ARE ON THE PATIO AFTER A GIG. DAVE, MIGUEL, GARY, ME, AND TOM. GIRLS ALWAYS DANCED.

For reasons I don't fully understand, the Jenerators continued to gig for about twenty years. We played with some very cool acts like Mick Taylor, Spirit, Cherie Currie, Jack Mack & the Heart Attack, and we did a short tour opening for my pals Gerry and Dewey's band, America. That was a really good time.

Miggy died from throat cancer, January 19, 2017. The Jenerators reunited that July 7th to play a memorial gig where we honored our fallen friend and raised a decent amount of money for Miguel's sons. I don't foresee a Jenerators reunion in the future, without Miguel the spirit of the band is missing a key factor.

Most every Christmas season, Eileen and I go to a few holiday parties. Peter Leinheiser, from the Igloos, has a yearly Winter Solstice party and Angela Cartwright, who lives three houses away from Peter with her husband Steve Gullion, hosts an annual Christmas party and they often are on the same night. In 2013, Eileen and I went to Peter's party first. There we quickly found ourselves chatting with John Cowsill and his wife, Vicki Peterson. John and I have been aware of each other since we were kids. John of course was in his family's band, The Cowsills, and they had several hit records back in the 1960s. *The Partridge Family* television series was based on the real-life Cowsills. John and I had jammed with his brother Bob's band at a pub in Studio City a few times, but mostly I knew John through the Beach Boys. I had been hanging out with Brian Wilson and his band quite a bit and John had been the drummer and a vocalist in Mike Love's touring version of The Beach Boys since the year 2000. In 2012, Brian's band and Mike's band were combined for a 50th Anniversary Beach Boys tour that I attended. Backstage at the Hollywood Bowl, John and I hung out for quite a while sharing old memories and talking about how we'd like to make some music together if we could find the time someday. John said he dug my solo albums and would love to add some drums and harmonies. I knew Vicki, but not well, from meeting her at Bangles gigs. I was friends with Susannah Hoffs for a while and Vicki and I had chatted at a somewhat recent House of Blues Bangles gig. The four of us connected and clicked instantly at Peter's party, and we huddled together for over an hour. Then, I explained that we were leaving to go a few houses up the street to Angela's party that by now was in full swing. "Angela Cartwright?!?" John asked, like it was a holy something or other. "Yeah." "Penny Robinson?" Vicki smiled and added, "I wanted to be Penny Robinson when I was a kid!" I said, "Come on. Join us. It'll be fun." "Oh no, we couldn't just crash her party!" Vicki stated. "Of course you can! You're with us. Come on." So, Eileen and I brought John and Vicki to Ange's party. Well, it was probably about 10:00 p.m. when we arrived, and we stayed there until after two in the morning. After making introductions and having a couple cups of cheer, Vicki, John, and I spent several hours at Steve and Ange's upright piano playing classic Beatles, Beach Boys, and Dylan songs. It seemed like we knew every word and every chord and when our voices joined together in three-part harmony that we naturally fell into, it was a sound and a blend that took us by surprise. It was special. By the time the night ended, the three of us enthusiastically agreed to get together again and see how we might sound working on some new original material.

A week after the party I was at a gig with America, and I got into a conversation backstage with Rick "the bass player" Rosas. Rick was an excellent musician and a super nice guy. He'd played with Joe Walsh, Neil Young, Crosby, Stills, Nash & Young, Buffalo Spring-field, and many other heroes of mine. Rick asked what I was currently working on, and I mentioned that John, Vicki, and I were thinking about putting a band together, at least going into the studio and seeing what might happen. "You guys have a bass player yet?" He asked. I told him we didn't. "You do now. Can I join?" Wow! It happened that easy and he meant it. Rick was so cool and so mellow and so much fun to make music with. I started writing a batch of new songs, and Vicki wrote, and she and John polished up some of my new ideas and before you knew it, the four of us were recording an album at ReadyMix Music in North Hollywood. ReadyMix is a very cool retro-vibe studio with modern and vintage gear. In the 1970s it was Jackson Browne's and Little Feat's space. The studio is owned now by my friends, Paul Horabin, who is the house engineer, and his wife Sarah Taylor, who manages the business. Over the course of six recording sessions that began early in 2014, Vicki, John, Rick, and I finished an album. It was great cutting the basic tracks live together in one room, looking at each other and playing together as a unit. I loved it.

The band needed a name. John and I were jamming on names, half-kidding and half-serious. He said, "I like the name Action Figures." I said, "I like the name Peace Skulls." So we said, "let's be Action Skulls."

JOHN COWSILL, VICKI PETERSON, AND ME... ACTION SKULLS AFTER FINISHING UP OUR FIRST ALBUM. PHOTO BY EILEEN.

Vicki thought we were kidding, but after a few weeks, it just stuck. I made everyone sterling silver skull rings, and the first Action Skulls album was pretty much in the can.

Then we got the terrible and sudden news that Rick passed away on November 6, 2014, just after wrapping up work on the Meryl Streep film *Ricki and the Flash*. He and I had been texting each other regularly and I had been sending him the Action Skulls tracks as we continued to record the vocals and some sweetening bits. Rick was a cheerleader for the project, and he was pleased with the way it was coming together. But he told me he was very burnt out. He'd been drafted at the last minute to join Neil Young as bassist in Crazy Horse for a European tour that Rick said was grueling. He went straight from that tour on to the film and then he went home, and he simply died. Eileen was with Vicki when we got the news. I called John who was on the road with Mike Love's Beach Boys, and we cried over the loss of Rick. No one could take his place, so I have handled the recorded bass parts since his passing by myself. Action Skulls played a few gigs with old friend Robby Scharf on bass, and we have recorded two more albums. Between losing Rick and the COVID global pandemic, making progress with the band has been a slow process.

In 2020, to celebrate the 50th anniversary of Redwood, I proposed that Paul, Gary, and I record three new songs together to see if the old spark could be reignited. Paul and I produced songs, but Gary wasn't able to. Gary came into my studio, and we laid some tracks down and I felt it was going to come together nicely. Paul did as well. But it wasn't working for Gary, so he bailed on the Redwood reunion. That left Paul and I pretty much back where we were in 1969. We decided to make a Gully album! And what a unique album it is. When we were young teenagers, we wrote many, many songs together: some that became Redwood songs and some that just never were really finished, that resided in limbo for half a century. Paul and I began re-exploring those unfinished songs and completing them. I found it extremely inspiring going back to tunes that originated from fertile, young, unsophisticated, and uncompromised perspectives and completing them after fifty years of composing, recording, and gigging. The Gully songs stand as a truly unique melding of innocence and maturity, and I absolutely love the Gully album. Writing and recording with Paul Gordon has remained a blessing throughout my life as a musician and I very much respect and appreciate the partnership we've maintained.

But don't expect a Neon Tetras reunion.

PAUL GORDON AND ME, GULLY (AKA THE MUMY-GORDON BAND) BACKSTAGE AT THE ICE HOUSE WHERE WE PLAYED FOURTEEN SETS A WEEK BACK IN 1975.

61. Collector Mentality

I've been a collector since I was a very young boy. My first collection was buying 45 rpm singles, and then I added Duncan Imperial yo-yos, Pez dispensers, and comic books to my quest for stuff. I had started getting autographs quite early in my acting career. I suppose that was my mom's idea. When I'd wrap up a show, I'd walk around and request signatures from cast members and directors. I still have a couple of those autograph books somewhere. There's some classics in those, for sure. I've continued to collect autographs and signatures over the years.

IT'S A PEZ WORLD.

I understand and respect the mindset of collectors. I see people sometimes get quite nervous when asking for my autograph and I do my best to let them know I've been in their shoes. It's always flattering and nice, except when it infringes on a meal and then it's somewhat awkward and a bit of a drag. Still, in the big picture, it's not such a bad problem to have.

Over the years, I've signed some interesting things... beyond photographs, posters, trading cards, albums, guitars, etc. I've autographed hundreds of robots, baseballs, laser guns, countless toys, board games, hats, shirts, and a few times, female breasts. ("Well, if you insist...")

While making a personal appearance with most of the cast members from *Babylon 5* in Blackpool, England, in the mid-1990s, a small group of passionate fans requested that me and several other cast members sign their arms as they were planning on having the autographs tattooed. I strongly attempted to dissuade them, but they were quite insistent. A year later, a few of us returned to England for *B5* promotion and sure enough... Some of those fans from the previous year were there and showed me that my autograph had been permanently inked on several arms. I told them I hoped they won't hate me in thirty years.

This will make you cringe. It still makes me cringe well over fifty years later. The great Jimmy Stewart and I spent a lot of time in between filming scenes on *Dear Brigitte* tossing a baseball back and forth. I was really into baseball then and it was a relaxing and bonding exercise that accentuated the "father-son" relationship we shared in the film. When the movie wrapped, Mr. Stewart gifted me a baseball that was autographed by all the Yankees who were in the World Series that year. I kept that ball on a shelf in my bedroom next to my *Hardy Boys* books.

Well, one late afternoon, me and Scott and Craig Ehrlich and Scott Shaw were playing ball in the street on Forrester Drive where we all lived, and we lost the ball we were playing with because it rolled onto Motor Avenue and dropped down into a sewer. So... you guessed it, I went home and got the baseball with all the autographs on it and yes... we batted that ball around for hours. I still have it somewhere in a box in my storage space. If you look really hard, beyond the grass stains and the scratches you can still make out Mickey Mantle and Yogi Berra.

FROM "THE OLD COWBOY"
WITH FRANCHOT TONE, A
FAVORITE OF MY MOM.

JAMES DRURY AND ME.

62. How the West Was Won

One of the finest westerns I ever worked on was *The Virginian*. Because it was a ninety-minute program, there was room to really develop characters and tell a full story without skimping on key emotional beats. The episode I guest-starred in was called "The Old Cowboy." It aired on March 31, 1965. I remember it was one of a few projects I worked on that my mother was really excited about for me. Franchot Tone starred in it as Murdoch, my grandfather, down on his luck, looking for a gig, caring for his young grandson Willy (me). Murdoch gets the opportunity to work at the Shiloh Ranch, but his age becomes his enemy, and he struggles. Willy remains his steadfast cheerleader.

The series-regular cast members included James Drury, Doug McClure, and Randy Boone. As usual, I brought my guitar with me to practice with when I wasn't filming, and Randy Boone turned out to also be a guitar player. Like me, he was a fan of the Kingston Trio's catalogue and he taught me how to play "Scotch and Soda" while I worked on *The Virginian*. It's not that easy a song to play and I really appreciated him showing it to me. I recall that quite fondly. My dad accompanied me on this project, like he usually did when we were doing exteriors and westerns. He had a good time, and he whittled a lot while I worked.

Being barely eleven years old when we shot "The Old Cowboy," I wasn't aware of Franchot Tone's resume. But my mom really loved his catalogue. She swooned over the fact that I was working with him. I found the Oscar-nominated actor to be truly great and I think we delivered fine performances as family.

63. ALL-STARR

*T*hursday, June 30, 2016, I got a phone call from my close pal, Steve Lukather. "Mumy! What are ya doing, Saturday night?" "Nothing." "Come play the Greek Theater with Ringo and the cats! You're approved!" "WHAT?!" "Yeah, man! We were flying back from Chicago and Bissonette suggested it and I said, "He'd love that!" and Ringo said, "Why not?" So learn 'With A Little Help From My Friends.' We're doing it in the same key as 'Sgt Pepper.' You can play my 12-string and sing with me on it. Then we'll go into 'Give Peace a Chance.'" "Seriously, Luke?!" "Absolutely, bro. I'll call ya when I get home."

People often ask me if I was nervous working alongside iconic movie stars and I never really was. Mainly, because I was just a kid and I wasn't familiar with their catalogues. But, joining Ringo, a Beatle, onstage to play guitar and sing... That amazing opportunity, did indeed make me nervous. So, I picked up a guitar and made sure I knew how to play "With A Little Help From My Friends" right. Really right. Then I went on the internet to YouTube and studied a very recent post of Ringo and the All-Starr Band, so that I could learn the little "kicks" and accents they were currently arranging the song with. Then, I probably played along to that post fifty times!

The night of the gig, Eileen and I took a limo to the Greek Theater. I'd played the Greek a few times before with America and with Shaun Cassidy, but honestly, this was different. My adrenalin was pumping. I knew my way around the backstage areas and Eileen and I were quickly escorted into the band dressing room. There were certainly a lot of extremely talented musicians in Ringo's 12th edition

STEVE LUKATHER, HIS DAUGHTER LILY, ME, RINGO, AND EILEEN
BACKSTAGE. WHAT A FAB NIGHT! BELOW: JOINING RINGO AND HIS ALL-
STARR BAND ONSTAGE AT THE GREEK THEATRE!

of his All-Starr Band and they were all really nice to me. Gregg Bissonette, drummer extraordinaire, was the first to greet me and he was super excited to talk with me. Gregg was a big fan of *Lost in Space*, he'd just made an album called *Danger, Will Robinson* and it had been his suggestion to Ringo, along with Luke's, for me to be a guest at this gig, which was the final night of their 2016 tour. Gregg really made me feel like a celebrity when I was feeling like a fanboy. I'd met Todd Rundgren before, with Shaun, and he was friendly and we chatted for a while. Todd seemed to be well aware of my Barnes & Barnes catalogue and he told me the band had some spontaneous sing-alongs to "Fish Heads" and other more eclectic B&B songs during this tour. I told Todd that I'd been listening to his second album, *The Ballad of Todd Rundgren,* a lot lately and that his harmonies sounded like the illegitimate child of Brian Wilson and David Crosby. He laughed at that compliment. I exchanged howdys with Greg Rolie, Richard Page, Warren Hamm, and several of their wives and ladies and then Lukather came and said, "Come on, I want you to meet the boss." He brought me and Eileen to another room that was Ringo's private dressing room.

Now, I had prepared myself for a chat with Ringo. I have several friends who have worked with him on film, television, and other music projects and I'd planned on breaking the ice by bringing them up. Eileen had seen the Beatles play live in her hometown of Detroit when she was a kid and that was a huge event for her. She had planned to share the memory with Ringo, but I swear, when Luke brought Ringo over to meet Eileen and me, we both just got instantly stupid. I was in the presence of Fab and everything I'd intended to say just went straight to the Cornfield. Ringo was sweet and kind. He took a few photos with Eileen and me. "So, you're joining us tonight, is that right?" "Indeed it is." "Do you know the song?" "Who doesn't? Yeah. I know the song." "Do you know the words?" "I do." "Ahh, but... do... you... know... the CHORDS?" "I do." Ringo nodded at me and said, "You'll do." And he went off to greet the many Hollywood famous faces that were quickly filling up the room.

As you might expect, Ringo's security was amazingly impressive. Eileen and I were given excellent seats near the front of the stage and I was told the setlist, and instructed to head to the backstage door during "Photograph." I did and literally the second I got there, the road manager showed up to meet me and brought me to the wings of the stage, where he handed me Luke's 12-string Yamaha. It was perfectly in tune of course. He asked if I needed a pick and I told him I had my own picks, and as the band onstage completed a rockabilly classic, Buck Owens' "Act Naturally," I was walked onstage, the roadie plugged my guitar in and Ringo announced, "Well, well, who do we have here? It's Billy Mumy!" The packed sold-out crowd cheered, which really felt great, and the band kicked in to "With A Little Help From My Friends." I was very happy that I'd practiced. I shared a microphone with Luke and we sang the background "Do you NEED anybody" vocals together. What a blast!

The song ended and Ringo dashed offstage, and the band segued into John Lennon's "Give Peace A Chance." Again, I'd learned the arrangement and it just felt magical to be a part of the band performing it to a loving crowd. Ringo returned to add his vocal and peace and love. The gig ended. I joined the band for the final bow and after-show celebration. I have to say, that was one of the best nights ever. I'm blessed in so many ways. Having my beautiful, supportive wife Eileen there with me, seeing her huge smile, made me feel like the luckiest guy in the world.

64. Bag of Memories

*T*he day after I played the Greek Theater with Ringo and his All-Starr Band was the 4th of July. My family had planned a very small barbecue at Mumy Manor. I called Steve Lukather and asked what he was doing and invited him and his daughter Lily to join us. The Ringo tour had ended the night before and I knew he might not have plans. Luke had gone out of his way to bring me up for the Ringo gig and he's been a great pal for over forty years now. Luke and his young daughter Lily were happy to join us.

My daughter Liliana had been in a relationship with Andrew Burkle for three years and Andrew's father, Ron Burkle, was co-owner of the Pittsburgh Penguins hockey team. The Penguins had just won the Stanley Cup. Ron was planning on joining us but called to say he had unexpected business calls he needed to make and wouldn't be able to attend, then he added, "But I can send the Cup over if you want." I laughed and said, "Hell yeah. Send the Cup!"

I didn't tell Luke, and about an hour and a half later… the doorbell rings, and sure enough…There was "The Keeper of the Cup" with a huge anvil case. I welcomed him in and you should've seen Luke's eyes pop out of his head! What a fun surprise for him and Lily. I was so glad I could do a little something special as a way of thanking Luke for inviting me to play with him and Ringo.

My family (Eileen, Liliana and Andrew, Seth and Alexa) were all in on it and we gathered in the living room as the Stanley Cup was placed on a table. We enjoyed hearing stories of the Cup and its long history. The "Keeper's" sole gig is to travel with the Cup around the world and to take care of it and share its glorious history. He's a super nice guy who's name eludes me now. He assured us the Cup was cleaned constantly and said we were free to drink champagne out if it if we wanted to. We did, and we did! It tasted like victory.

THAT TIME THE STANLEY CUP CAME OVER TO MUMY MANOR FOR A VISIT.

《〈〉》

I have had the pleasure and the privilege of performing live and or recording with some of the greatest rock drummers of all time... including: Ringo Starr, Jeff Porcaro, Russ Kunkel, Carlos Vega, Steve Ferrone, Mike Baird, David Kemper, Billy Thomas, John Cowsill, and Doane Perry... not bad for a kid from Beverlywood.

《〈〉》

I'm thinking about the smokey voice of Glynnis Johns; her British accent and her understated, natural acting skills. Often when I've been asked about filming *Dear Brigitte*, after reminiscing about Jimmy Stewart and Brigitte Bardot, I move on to another subject. Glynnis was one of my favorite "moms." Honestly, everything about working on that film was positive. Cindy Carroll, who played my sister, Pandora, was really fun and easy to hang with. Although I never listened to Fabian's music, working opposite him as an actor I thought that he was unaffected and professional. I liked him in *Ride the Wild Surf*, too.

When I let my memory float to the three months I spent working on *Dear Brigitte*, I remember a good time for me and for my family. My dad and mom both accompanied me to France and to Sausalito on locations for the film. I saw *West Side Story* in a theater on the Champs Elysees and ate some seriously good French food there. We took in quite a lot of French sights while there. Having Jimmy Stewart starring in the movie opened up a lot of doors. I can't stress enough how wonderful a guy he was to work with and the huge impression he left on me about how to behave on a production, both as an actor and as a human being.

*I*t's the summer of 1966. I am onstage at the Coco Palms Resort in Kauai. I am playing a just-acquired Kamaka ukulele and singing "Pearly Shells" with Irene Ryan (Granny Clampett from *The Beverly Hillbillies*) to a packed room full of happy people who are absolutely thrilled to see the two of us. I don't even know Irene Ryan. Sometimes my life is weird. "…when I see them, my heart tells me that I love you more than all those pretty pearly shells."

65. THE EIGHTIES

The decade of the 1980s held little on-camera acting work for me. I worked on two feature films, *Twilight Zone: The Movie* and *Hard to Hold*. Television gigs included a nice guest-starring role on *Matlock* as Andy Griffith's nephew Doctor Irwin Bruckner, who is framed for a murder. Andy Griffith impressed me with his eye for detail while working on *Matlock*. The first day of filming, I went to my dressing room trailer and got into the wardrobe they had laid out for me and then went to the set. After meet and greets, Andy looked at my wardrobe and shook his head and declared, "Oh no. He wouldn't wear that." And so, we waited a while until the wardrobe person brought in a change that Andy approved. I respected that.

I also did a cameo in the *Alfred Hitchcock Presents* remake of "Bang! You're Dead" and guest-starred on a short-lived, but cool series starring James Earl Jones, Holland Taylor, and Lisa Eilbacher called *Me and Mom*. It was a detective/comedy/drama that ran for only six episodes on the ABC network. I played a Stephen Spielberg-type film director.

Speaking of Spielberg, he came to the set of *Twilight Zone: The Movie* when I was working and introduced himself to me. He was carrying a puppy at the time. I think it was a Cavalier King Charles Spaniel. He told me I'd been a big influence on him as a child and thanked me for doing a small role in the film. He was quite nice. I accepted the cameo because Carol Serling, Rod Serling's widow, and Buck Houghton, who had produced the original *Twilight Zone* series, called me at home personally and asked me to do it as a favor. Soon after working on the *Twilight Zone* movie, Spielberg would be

I DID A CAMEO IN THE TWILIGHT ZONE MOVIE. 1983.

suing Barnes & Barnes for our novelty song "I Had Sex With E.T." It's a very funny record that was getting a lot of airplay and press immediately upon its release. *Playboy*, *People*, and *Rolling Stone magazines*, as well as KROQ and other New Wave radio stations were jumping on it. I still think it's hysterical but trust me, Spielberg and Universal squashed it like a bug. I'm not really supposed to even talk about it. Whatever. Let's just say I don't expect to be in any other Spielberg films.

Besides making four albums and several short films with Barnes & Barnes in the 1980s, we produced two unique albums for Wild Man Fischer. These are really special projects and I absolutely stand by their artistic credibility. They are not for everyone, but they are very emotional and honest and trippy. I also worked with America throughout the decade in the studio and as a co-writer.

Shaun Cassidy came to Barnes & Barnes in 1984 and we produced and co-wrote a four-song demo for him. Shaun was inspired and in strong voice. All four songs came out really good. Shaun has never released them though. They were recorded in my home studio, Lumania, on analog eight-track. At the time, Shaun ultimately decided not to toss his hat back into the pop music scene, because he felt it might compete with his career as a television writer and producer. Hopefully someday he'll want to share those tracks with the world.

For a few years in the mid-1980s, I became a composer for the NBC soap opera *Santa Barbara*. Eileen had become friendly with several people on the production after she had appeared on the show for several episodes as a labor coach, which was something she was doing for real at the time, besides teaching and running the Pregnancy and Recovery exercise program at Jane Fonda's Workout studio in Beverly Hills and Encino. Dominic Messinger was the music supervisor on *Santa Barbara* and within a short amount of time after he met with Eileen, I was writing songs for the series. They became themes for various characters and sometimes they would just be background music. It turned out to be a nice little side project and fairly lucrative.

I was also travelling quite a lot and doing personal appearances and solo acoustic gigs at science fiction and comic book conventions all over the country. At a show in Chicago in 1985, Miguel Ferrer was with me, I was chatting with Jim Shooter, who was at that time editor-in-chief of Marvel Comics. Jim asked what I'd been doing lately besides music. I told him Miguel and I had just written a script for the new *Twilight Zone* project. He immediately replied, "Why don't you write for Marvel?" Well, my passion for superhero comic books has never really diminished since I was five years old. The idea of writing for Marvel was too good to be true. I assured him that we'd be sending him a proposal sometime within the next week. And we did. And Marvel dug it. And we created and wrote a six-issue comic book series titled *The Comet Man*. Illustrated by Kelley Jones with covers supplied by Bill Sienkiewicz, *The Comet Man* sold half a million copies. Miguel and I included The Hulk, the

Fantastic Four, Nick Fury, and S.H.I.E.L.D. in the initial six issues. I loved writing comic books and I went on to write many Marvel stories by myself after that, including another *Comet Man* saga, *Spider-Man*, *Iron Man*, *She-Hulk*, *Wonder Man*, and a few other stories Marvel bought that never were published. In 1987, Miguel and I wrote a graphic novel for Marvel titled *The Dreamwalker*, which was something of a melding of James Bond and Zorro. I went on to work for DC comics as well, co-writing with Peter David. I scripted stories featuring Aquaman, the Flash, Green Lantern, The Spectre, and a trio of "Classic" *Star Trek* issues. *Trypto, the Acid Dog* was another creation of Miguel's and mine, fabulously illustrated by our Seduction of the Innocent bandmate, Steve Leialoha, that was published by Dark Horse Comics, Renegade Comics, and by Britain's A-1 Comics. For Epic Comics, Marvel's darker publishing line, Miggy and I wrote a creepy story for an issue of *Clive Barker's Hellraiser*.

IN THE 1980s I DID A LOT OF COMIC BOOK WRITING. HERE I AM AT GOLDEN APPLE COMICS WITH MIGUEL, JACK KIRBY, AND FRANK MILLER. WE WERE SALUTING THE RELEASE OF A NEW BOOK FEATURING JACK'S WORK.

66. WAY OUT

During the 1990s, my manager at the time, Suzie Dietz, had connections at Nickelodeon and found out that they were looking for new live-action half-hour television shows for their Saturday night programming that was called SNICK. At the time, I was frequently collaborating with Peter David on comic books and some spec projects. Peter and I came up with an idea that seemed perfect coming from "Billy Mumy." We created a series about an academy in space where a class of misfit kids from all over the galaxy sneak aboard an alien spacecraft that appears out of nowhere. The ship suddenly bonds with the kids and identifies them as the crew and slips through a spatial rift that deposits them on the other side of the solar system along with their teacher, vice principal, and an android. Meaning, they are not lost in space... but it's going to take them about five years to get back to their sector, assuming they can figure out how to run the ship, called the *Christa*. We named it after the schoolteacher, Sharon "Christa" McAuliffe, who perished when the Challenger space shuttle exploded shortly after takeoff on January 28, 1986.

We pitched the project to the head of Nickelodeon, and he loved it. Originally, the title was *Way Out*, but it was quickly changed to *Space Cases*. Nickelodeon partnered with a Canadian film company, Cinar, that had produced *Are You Afraid Of The Dark?* for them, and so *Space Cases* became a Canadian production that was filmed in Montreal. The series debuted on Nickelodeon, March 2, 1996, and ran for two seasons and a total of twenty-seven episodes. It aired in fifty-seven countries. Peter went to Montreal for the shoot, and I was there for the pilot and then again for about a month. The coldest weather I'd ever experienced! Man, that was rough. I had a little apartment that was a few hundred yards away from a grocery store. Just walking there for a few bags of groceries was crazy. My entire face would freeze. And I wore a hat, scarf, glasses, heavy coat, etc. I don't know how people can live like that. It was tough. Peter and I wrote almost every episode and that was fun. We sat in a conference room every day from about nine in the morning until about eight at night. We had already written the loglines out for the entire season, and they had been approved by the network. So, we'd assign each other acts in a script to write. Peter would write the first act of an episode and then I'd write the second act and we tag-teamed writing like that. Then, we'd polish the final shooting scripts together after receiving notes from the network. Once in a while, the network notes would be so stupid we'd go crazy. For instance, we wrote a scene that involved a spacewalk to repair something on the exterior of the *Christa*. The network didn't want the character to wear a spacesuit as it would make it harder for the audience to recognize them. We explained that you can't exit a spaceship in deep space without wearing a protective spacesuit. They replied, "Why not?" We explained there was no oxygen in space, and they'd freeze and wouldn't be able to breathe. They replied, "But the kids watching won't know that." We insisted on the spacesuit and eventually got our way. Dealing with notes like that from network assistants was very frustrating. Yes, it was a series intended for a young audience, but we didn't want to present false science.

Suzie Dietz, my manager, became an executive producer on *Space Cases*. She, Peter, and I had a lot of say in terms of casting the series. We auditioned young actors in Canada, New York, and Los Angeles and because of Canadian content rules, we had to balance things delicately. Since Peter and I were Americans and were writing the series, we needed to hire Canadian directors. The cast was largely Canadian, but we had a few Americans as well. Our core cast consisted of Walter Emanuel Jones as Harlan Band. Walter had recently starred in the popular kids series, *Mighty Morphin Power Rangers,* as The Black Ranger. Casting Walter was great for me personally because my son Seth, who was seven at the time, was a huge *Power Rangers* freak. He absolutely loved that show and having a Ranger star in *Space Cases* really upped my dad cred! Jewel Staite played Catalina, and Jewel quickly impressed everyone with her acting. She was really great and went on to star in the sci-fi series *Firefly* years later. Kristian Ayre was cast as Radu, and Kristian had to deal with pretty tough alien makeup every morning. I was still working on *Babylon 5* during *Space Cases*, and if anyone could relate to the process of transforming into an alien every day for work, it was me. Kristian was a total pro and a good sport, and he turned in excellent, sensitive performances. Rahi Azizi played Bova, who was pretty much based on Eeyore from *Winnie the Pooh*, but Rahi was so spunky and funny that we tweaked his character a bit to match his true personality. Next to join the series was Paige Christina who was cast as Rosie. Rosie was red and that makeup was a bit of a drag for Paige, but she survived it and was a trouper. Thelma, the android (or techno-human emulating machine), was brilliantly played by Anik Matern. Her timing and delivery was always perfect. Anik was fantastic. We got lucky casting Cary Lawrence as the uptight, by-the-book, vice principal T.J. Davenport. She had to endure being the butt of many jokes and stunts and was always a joy to work with. Finally, Captain Seth Goddard (I wonder where that name came from?) was played by Paul Boretski. Paul was terrific and everyone loved working with him.

For the second season, Rebecca Herbst joined the cast as Suzie, who had been Catalina's invisible friend during the first season. She turned in fine performances. We really were lucky with our *Space Cases* cast.

I called in some favors for guest-starring roles and we featured a variety of celebrity guest stars throughout the two-season run, including George Takei, Michelle Trachtenberg, Katey Sagal, Danny Tamberelli, Robin Leach, and my good pal, Mark Hamill.

ON THE SET OF SPACE CASES WITH JEWEL STAITE (ABOVE), WALTER EMMANUEL JONES AND PAIGE CHRISTINA (LEFT), AND MARK HAMILL (BELOW)

Peter and I brought the wise, talented, and acerbic Harlan Ellison on board as a creative consultant. For the initial run of the first season, Harlan wrote and narrated the opening of every show. I had hired Gary Stockdale, my bandmate in the Jenerators, to compose an orchestral opening theme. Paul Gordon and I wrote the closing theme song music and lyrics, and Nickelodeon chose to re-edit the first season and use that as the opening. The lyric was tweaked for the arc of the second season with Walter Emanuel Jones doing vocals. It's always nice to keep things in the family.

Creating, writing, producing, composing, and acting on *Space Cases* was a great experience and it was also a lot of hard work. I was co-starring on *Babylon 5* throughout shooting *Space Cases*, which meant I'd get up at about four in the morning, go in to *B5* for the Lennier makeup, work a full day, come home to Eileen and the kids (Seth was seven and Liliana was three), enjoy some family time, and then pop in a VHS video of the *Space Cases* dailies from Montreal that was FedEx'd to me every day and give my notes on what takes I preferred and what I especially liked or didn't like. Then, Eileen would go over the next day's *Babylon 5* scenes I needed to memorize, and then I'd address any script changes for *Space Cases* that Peter, up in Montreal, would alert me to. Finally, I'd have a gin and tonic and try to turn my brain off, which has never been an easy thing for me to do.

I could never have accomplished any of these things without the constant support and love of my amazing wife Eileen, who has always had the energy to be my rock. I would have loved to have seen *Space Cases* last more than two seasons, but I am grateful we got to do it and survived!

《》

Once in a while a television show will want to "stunt cast" an episode. That means a certain theme runs throughout a script and the producers want to cast all the ancillary parts with actors who are well known for their previous work in the particular genre that fits the theme. Such was the case when I guested on an episode of *Diagnosis Murder* in 1998. The script was titled "Alienated" and the subject was conspiracy theories having to do with science fiction. Besides myself, the guest cast included *Star Trek* alumni George Takei, Walter Koenig, Majel Barrett, Wil Wheaton, and Grace Lee Whitney. I only worked on the episode one day, but it was fun, and they treated us all very nicely. Dick Van Dyke is a classy, generous, good-natured man and I was happy to work with him again. We had done charity projects together in the mid-1960s. In "Alienated," after a quick dramatic scene, my character was murdered and the final scene I filmed was as a corpse on the autopsy table with Dick examining my body. They did a real good makeup job on it. I looked damn dead.

STUNT GUEST CASTING ON *DIAGNOSIS MURDER*... WITH GEORGE TAKEI, CHARLIE SCHLATTER, THE MIGHTY DICK VAN DYKE, ME, AND WALTER KOENIG.

67. INSIDE THE TV

Some of the shows I worked on I remember clearly, but some I can barely recall anything about. For instance, I had a very good guest-starring role in an episode of *Perry Mason* "The Case of the Shifty Shoe Box," that originally aired in October 1963. I was nine years old when we shot it. It was filmed at CBS Studio on Radford in Studio City, on Stage 4 at 20th Century Fox, and we shot a part of it in downtown Los Angeles at the courthouse. I had a lot to do in this crime drama but all I honestly can clearly remember is shooting a scene on the porch of a house outside on the Radford lot with Raymond Burr. I was barefoot, wearing pajamas and a robe and I clearly recall stubbing my toe on a wooden "T" mark on the ground for me to hit, and there was a nail in the mark, and it really hurt! Not a big deal, no blood or crying or anything like that… but that's my only crystal-clear memory about actually working on that one.

RAYMOND BURR ADJUSTS MY WARDROBE ON *PERRY MASON.*

<<>>

The fantastic Cloris Leachman played my mother for the third time in 1962 in an episode of *Going My Way*, starring Gene Kelly, Leo G. Carroll, and Dick York. The episode was titled "Keep an Eye on Santa Claus" and we shot it at Revue, which was on the Universal lot.

THE THIRD TIME CLORIS LEACHMAN PLAYED MY MOM.

I did a lot of work at Revue and I was very comfortable on that lot. I clearly remember the little shop next to the commissary where people went to buy magazines and cigarettes and candy. I went there for comic books. The shop was run by a lady named Lorraine. She was super nice to me for several years. There were several times that Mary Badham and I ran around the Universal lot together going from one stage to another checking things out. Mary was filming the classic film *To Kill a Mockingbird* and I was coming and going guest-starring on multiple shows like *Going My Way*, *Wagon Train*, *The Jack Benny Program*, *Alfred Hitchcock Presents,* and others. My goal was to check out the candy machines in the lobbies of every sound stage because I was hunting for Pez dispensers. Back then, different dispensers with various character heads could be found in the machines all over the Universal lot. For a quarter, I'd add a Casper, or a Bullwinkle, a Popeye, an Astronaut, or one of my very favorites: a "Regular." Regulars are the original Pez dispensers with no character on the top. They look somewhat like lighters. Anyway, I did find brown and powder blue Regulars on the stages at Universal. Mary used to like me and she was up for a good scavenger hunt as my partner when we both had a little free time. Usually, we'd finish our lunches early and then run wild until we were due back on our separate stages. She was great.

Of course I was comfortable working with Cloris again and I remember her being somewhat "bawdy" on the set. My mother was quite impressed that I was working alongside Gene Kelly, but I wasn't familiar with his work. I was impressed to be working with Leo G. Carroll because I was a big fan of the *Topper* television series, and he of course had played Cosmo Topper in that.

WITH THE LEGENDARY GENE KELLY.

The only clear memory I have of *Going My Way* is filming a scene where my character Mark is auditioning for the choir, and it turns out that he's totally tone deaf. I had to sing "Jingle Bells" and sing it way off-key. I remember that it wasn't the easiest thing I ever had to do, because reflexively, I wanted to sing it in tune. I remember the director, Joseph Pevney "showing me" how to sing it in a flat monotone kind of way. Other than that... Nothing else is very clear about it in my memory banks. It aired in December of 1962. I was eight.

<<>>

In 1960, one of my earlier gigs was on the *National Velvet* series filmed at MGM, which was pretty close to our house so travel time was short. The series was based on the classic 1944 film that Elizabeth Taylor starred in. I played Willy in an episode called "Donald's Friend" (I was his friend). Donald was played by an actor my age named Joey Scott. Literally the only thing I can remember about this show was going to the MGM cafeteria and having to wait a long time with my mom to get a table. I was six.

I worked with Joey Scott again in 1963. I guest-starred on an episode of *The Eleventh Hour* called "Sunday Father." It was the second time I worked alongside Red Buttons who played my dad. In 1962, we worked together on *A Ticklish Affair*, starring Shirley Jones, Gig Young, Red, Carolyn Jones, and Edgar Buchanan. We filmed that at MGM too. I was insanely in love with Shirley, and we laugh about it to this day. I called her on her birthday recently and we had a great chat. I'm still in love with her. Anyway, *The Eleventh Hour* was a dramatic series starring Ralph Bellamy. It was an hour-long drama and again, we filmed it at MGM in Culver City.

Red Buttons was a very pleasant, easy-going man and we had a fine time playing father and son. I remember we got our scenes together done quite quickly. I also recall that while working on this show, I went to school at the "official" studio school for a few days instead of being taught in a trailer outside the stage. If memory serves me well, I went to the schoolroom to get all three hours of the mandatory time done at the start of the days, 9:00 a.m.-noon then lunch from 12-1:00 p.m. and then filming until 6:00 p.m. I recall being in the classroom with the Osmond Brothers. They were regulars on the *Andy Williams Show* and for a few days we were in the same school. But they had their own teacher and I had mine. They sang great barbershop-style harmony and seemed like real nice guys to me. And as was my usual routine, I indeed combed the candy machines at MGM in search of new Pez dispensers. I still have a great Pez collection. I was nine when we filmed "Sunday Father."

I LIKED RED BUTTONS AND HE LIKED ME. WE WORKED TOGETHER TWICE.

I was on the Radford lot in Studio City in late 1961 working on "Obituary for Mister X," a first-season episode of *The Dick Powell Theater*. I remember working with Dina Merrill and a dog, but I had more to do than that. Nancy Reagan (billed as Nancy Davis) was in this episode and she and I worked closely together the next year guest-starring in a *Wagon Train*. Other than the dog being super cool and Dina being gorgeous, I'm pretty much blank on this one for details. I was seven when we filmed it. It doesn't seem to be running anywhere and I probably haven't ever seen it. I think *The Dick Powell Theater* aired after my bedtime.

<>

I wasn't really familiar with Jackie Gleason, "the Great One," when I worked with him because I wasn't old enough to stay up late enough to watch his show. But I was a little nervous because taping a live television broadcast makes you nervous. It's different than filming a show where you can cut and start all over again. But my appearance on *The Jackie Gleason Show* went fine. I walked onstage and over to him and had a very brief chat about playing baseball. I remember one of my lines was, "I wouldn't have struck out if my pants hadn't fallen down." I was six years old.

*I*n 1964 I appeared in the fifteenth episode of the first season of *The Fugitive*. I always thought that was a very impressive and well-done series. "Home is the Hunted" is the episode title and I played David Taft, Dr. Richard Kimble's nephew. In the episode, I almost got him busted when I discovered his hair dye. Clint Howard, Ron's younger brother, played my younger brother, and the very talented Jacqueline Scott played our mother. Jacqueline played my mother more than once. We worked on a very good episode of *Wide Country* together before filming *The Fugitive* episode. Barry Morse and David Janssen gave excellent, intense, and subtle performances and it was a joy to work with Andrew Prine, who I had also worked previously with on a western series called *Empire*.

I had the chance to spend a few minutes chatting with Jacqueline at a personal appearance shortly before she passed away in 2020. She was sharp as a tack and it was a pleasure to reconnect and reminisce with her about the projects we worked on together.

I thought because I was cast as Kimble's nephew, there might be more *Fugitive* episodes for me to work on. But 'twas not to be. By the time they did do another episode that included his nephew, I was quite busy working on *Lost in Space* and couldn't do it.

Along with many millions of television viewers, I keenly recall watching the final episode of *The Fugitive* when it aired in 1967.

THE FUGITIVE WAS CLASSIC TV. GLAD I WAS A PART OF IT. HERE I AM WITH JACQUELINE SCOTT'S BACK, BARRY MORSE, AND CLINT HOWARD FROM THE "HOME IS THE HUNTED" EPISODE.

68. Seventies Rock

In 1970, when Angela and I were a young teenage couple, she was filming *Make Room for Granddaddy*, a one-season series sequel to *Make Room for Daddy* which ran for seven seasons when she was a little girl. It was a return to *The Danny Thomas Show* with the original cast. I visited her on the set a few times and Danny Thomas gave me the side-eye every time. My hair was really long, and it was obvious he didn't approve of my look.

There was a pretty actress on the series named Jana Taylor. She and Ange became very close friends and Jana came to several Redwood gigs and dug the band. I wrote a song for her that Redwood performed for a year or so called "Jana, the Lonely Loving Lady." At the time, Jana was dating one of my biggest musical heroes, Phil Everly. The Everly Brothers were just amazing. Don Everly and I were born on the same day, February 1st, I also share that birthdate with Bob Shane of the Kingston Trio; both were huge musical inspirations to me. Don Everly's songwriting, guitar playing, and his lead vocals with Phil harmonizing so perfectly will never go out of style. It's a heavenly sound.

The four of us, Ange, me, Jana, and Phil spent Christmas Eve of 1970 together. We went out to dinner and then back to Phil's. It was a legitimate thrill for me to have played Phil's guitar that night. His iconic, black Gibson Everly Brothers Model J-180 had a magnificent tone. I was honored to hold it and play the song I wrote for Jana on it. I now have two gorgeous Gibson Custom Shop Everly Brothers models of my own and they have a wonderful sound and great character and when I play them, I sometimes recall that Christmas Eve long ago and think how lucky I was that night. I have appropriately named my two Everly guitars, "Phillip" and "Donald."

<<>>

Speaking of rock & roll... In 1972, the Who's rock opera *Tommy* opened as a theatrical production for a run at the Aquarius Theater on the Sunset Strip. The Who hosted a party for the event, and I received an invitation and went by myself. Keith Moon, the legendary drummer and wild man, was the only member of the Who there and he was the master of ceremonies. It wasn't a huge event, but it was very cool. The Kinks played the party. I remember watching their set very closely, and loving their looseness. Ray Davies was elegantly wasted. He was definitely pretty buzzed, but he still sang and played great.

AT THE AQUARIUS THEATER ON THE SUNSET STRIP ATTENDING THE PARTY FOR THE WHO'S *TOMMY* STAGE PRODUCTION. 1972. DIG THAT HAIR.

I mingled with my friend Stephanie Steele, who at that time was co-starring in a television series called *Arnie* starring Herschel Bernardi and another pal of mine, Del Russell. Del and I had worked together as kids in the feature film *Tammy, Tell Me True*. A few of the cast members from *The Brady Bunch* were also at this Who party. We all were enjoying being entertained by Keith, who was very gregarious and quite toasted.

Memory escapes me about the details of how we got there, but I ended up at the Troubadour drinking brandy with Keith Moon and Maureen McCormick in the front booth of the club. Bizarre. When exiting the Troub, quite late that night and certainly a bit buzzed myself, some paparazzi snapped photos of me and Maureen coming out of the nightclub together. Sure enough, the next month, there we were in some teen magazines, Mumy and McCormick, the hot new couple! Ha. I never dated Maureen and actually, I don't think I've really ever had a conversation with her since, beyond a "Hello there."

ME, STEPHANIE STEELE, KEITH MOON, CHRISTOPHER KNIGHT, BARRY WILLIAMS, AND MAUREEN MCCORMICK

Redwood did sing background vocals on a song that ended up on Keith Moon's one and only solo album "Two Sides of the Moon." We were recording at Record Plant and were asked to pause our session to help out on a session for Keith. He wasn't even there when we sang, but it's another fun memory of those wild 1970s.

I do still enjoy a snifter of brandy... or two.

REDWOOD WORKING ON A TRACK AT RECORD PLANT.
PICTURE BY ANGE.

69. Getting Lost

No one loved *Lost in Space* more than I did. The late great Jonathan "Dr. Smith" Harris came in a close second, though. Will Robinson was everything I had ever wanted to be as a character. To me, he was a superhero like Zorro and Superman, the two iconic television characters that truly inspired me to become an actor at the ripe old age of four. And not only did it manifest into reality with the character of Will, but Guy "Zorro" Williams played my father! And in a way, Zorro was my acting "father" as he gave birth to my drive to get inside the television and be like that.

I was ten when *Lost in Space* began, and I was fourteen when it ended. There's a whole lot of life experienced in those years. Along with Angela Cartwright, I have already co-authored a book on my years working on the series, which we recently updated as *Lost (and Found) in Space 2: Blast Off into the Expanded Edition,* so a part of me feels like that's been covered well already, but there are endless memories and thoughts that continue to spring to mind.

Once in a while, the casting of a series is perfect. You can give credit to the executive producer, or the director of the pilot, or the casting director of course, but really there's an X factor involved that can't be formulated. It either happens or it doesn't and when it does, it is something very rare and something that stands the test of time. I absolutely believe *Lost in Space* was perfectly cast. Guy Williams, June Lockhart, Mark Goddard, Marta Kristen, Angela Cartwright, and I bonded like a legitimate family while filming the pilot, directed by creator and producer Irwin Allen himself.

Irwin was a strong-willed, old-timey, Golden Age of Hollywood character. He demanded, and received, a lot of "Yes" responses. Like many creative types, Irwin poured himself into the smallest details of his projects and made sure they looked as grandiose as he had envisioned them. He raised and spent big money on his shows. But then, like many creative types, once his projects were launched and on the air, his personal energy quickly moved on to the next big and bold concept and his desire to tighten the budgets was in full swing. In some ways, to me, Irwin Allen was just a big kid who wanted to play with dinosaurs and go on adventures deep under the ocean and far out into unknown space and travel through time and meet bizarre, strange beings and have wild adventures. He loved explosions and monsters and bright colors.

Irwin's original concept for *Lost in Space* was a dark and a serious one. A pioneer family on a deep space mission that goes awry find themselves lost on an alien world and encounter unpredictable danger at every turn. The budget for the pilot was the most expensive ever made at the time. Irwin spared no expense in making sure his sets and props and wardrobe and effects were absolutely top-notch. He personally directed the pilot with a megaphone in his hands, and a bravado that was both truly impressive and somewhat comical.

The theme music was brilliantly composed by John Williams and the power it brought to the series cannot be underestimated. The black and white cinematography was excellent, and the shadows enforced the drama. The cast quickly proved they clicked perfectly and the show was bought by CBS.

When the series debuted on September 15, 1965, it was a big hit. But things changed quickly and Irwin Allen's strong vision for the tone of his space show did not last long.

Two characters were added to the series in between wrapping up filming of the pilot and the beginning of filming the series: a robot, which was a brilliant idea, and a saboteur, another very smart move. Our robot, "Model B9," was designed by Robert Kinoshita, who had previously created the famous robot, Robby, from the classic sci-fi feature film *Forbidden Planet*. A fabulous design of function and art. Bobby May, a young performer with vaudevillian roots was cast to be inside that claustrophobic and dangerous prop and he brought it to life for three years. What a trouper Bobby was! The role of Dr. Smith, the saboteur, went to veteran character actor of stage and screen, Jonathan Harris.

Television history was about to be made.

Midway through the first thirty episodes of the series, the tone of *Lost in Space* changed dramatically. It switched from a serious, ensemble, adventurous science fiction show into something much lighter and campier. There's a lot of speculation about why the series changed and as the saying goes, "where there's smoke there's fire." Jonathan always said that he knew the snarling, murderous, pure evil character of Smith, as originally written, would not have staying power. He began shifting the character to more of a selfish, cowardly, campy troublemaker that you love to hate. Jonathan slowly was given free reign to rewrite his own dialogue and he certainly made the most of it. However, the single biggest reason for the change in tone did not come from Jonathan's sense of self-preservation. It came as a mandate from CBS. The network aired *Lost in Space* at 7:30-8:30 p.m. on Wednesday nights. That time slot was designated as the network's "Family Hour." CBS received a lot of mail from parents saying that *Lost in Space* was too scary for their little children. So, the network demanded it be toned down into something less dramatic and lighter. There's a well-known anecdote that Jonathan often shared, that one day Irwin Allen called him up to his office on the Fox lot, where he proceeded to poke his finger at Jonathan and said, "I know what you're doing!... Do MORE." So, he did. I ended up playing straight man to both Jonathan's over-the-top campy comedy and the Robot's ridiculousness as the series progressed.

The 1960s was such an amazing decade and *Lost in Space* holds a permanent place in pop culture history.

In a short amount of time, *Lost in Space* pretty much stopped focusing on the entire ensemble and started concentrating on the trio of Dr. Smith, the Robot, and Will. The bulk of the eighty-three hours that were produced pretty much prove that. Now, for me, being thrust into a leading role on the series was great. I was used to being a lead and I absolutely loved playing Will and I was never insecure about my abilities to know my lines, hit my marks, and deliver the goods believably. But the truth is, it also made me uncomfortable because of everyone else's work being greatly reduced.

As I said, the cast really bonded tightly when we shot the pilot and of course, there was no Smith or Robot in the pilot. Adding them was smart and probably was a big reason for the series' success, but I often felt guilty in a way that I had so much to do while my "family" had little to do.

Lost in Space was never an unprofessional or unpleasant set or atmosphere. We all got along really very well. Some of us were closer than others, but there was no hostility. Of course Guy Williams became unhappy. He was cast to be the star. The lead. He ended up doing much less than he'd expected to do. But, and trust me, I was there, Guy's attitude was most always easygoing. I know for a fact that he was fine making the same amount of money if he had ten lines in a show or if he had fifty lines in a show. If he had to work three days instead of six days, it made his personal life that much easier. He and Jonathan didn't go to lunch together, but they didn't argue or have negative energy either. Jonathan told me that once, and only once, he'd had a private chat with Guy and had expressed his empathy to him regarding the shift in the show and Jonathan's regret at having that happen. Guy was a very proud, smart, impressive, capable man. I was just happy that Zorro in a spacesuit taught me how to fence!

I modeled Will Robinson on the Jack Kirby-Joe Simon Golden Age comic book character, Bucky Barnes. Captain America's sidekick Bucky was no "Robin, the Boy Wonder." He carried a rifle and he shot Nazis. He was as tough as tough can be, yet he was also a kid and he had a boy's sense of wonder about everything. Bucky also was a redhead. At the time we were filming the series, Jack Kirby and Stan Lee were creating Captain America and Bucky stories in the monthly Marvel comic *Tales of Suspense* and those were some of my very favorite comic books.

Interestingly enough, in 2018, when I returned to *Lost in Space*, this time as "The Real Dr. Smith" on the Netflix series, I became good friends with Maxwell Jenkins who played Will Robinson in the new, very impressive show. Max's Will is very different from mine, and we talked a lot about how we saw them. Max, like me, is a guitar player and has a band and he's also a comic book geek. Turns out that Captain America is his favorite character. When I told him I had modeled my Will on Bucky, it blew his mind. While on location in Vancouver, I remembered a cool comic book store that I'd frequented years before when filming "It's Still a Good Life" for *The Twilight Zone*. I took a long walk, found the store was still there, and bought Max the collected reprint of those Jack Kirby-Stan Lee mid-1960s *Captain America and Bucky* stories. I also got him the *Winter Soldier* collection, which may be my favorite comic book run of all time. Beautifully written by Ed Brubaker and illustrated to perfection by Steve Epting, the *Winter Soldier* is the resurrection of Bucky, who for fifty years had been the one "dead" comic book character Marvel could never successfully bring back into continuity. But Brubaker found the right buttons and made it happen brilliantly and with believability. I wrote him a fan letter after reading it. It was printed in *Captain America* #14.

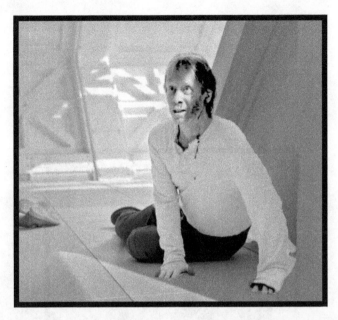

PLAYING THE "REAL DR. SMITH" ON NETFLIX'S *LOST IN SPACE* REBOOT
WAS PERFECT CASTING IF I DO SAY SO MYSELF.

KEVIN BURNS WITH TWO WILL ROBINSONS, ME AND MAX JENKINS,
WHILE FILMING SCENES I WROTE AS BONUS BITS FOR THE NETFLIX *LOST
IN SPACE* FIRST SEASON DVD RELEASE. WHAT A HOOT!

PART 5

BEING A FATHER IS THE BEST ROLE I'VE EVER BEEN CAST IN.

70. Simply The Best

October 25, 1989 and April 16, 1994 are the two best days of my life. Those are the birthdates of my son, Seth Davis Mumy, and my daughter, Liliana Berry Davis Mumy. Yes, I've played many different types of roles over the years in my career, but none of them were as important as the role of father. I tried my best to get it right. Sometimes I fell short of the mark, I suppose. There are no "take twos" in reality. We print everything in life.

Eileen and I often talk late at night in bed together, about how our favorite memories of all time are when the kids were little. There are four and a half years separating Seth and Liliana. Sadly, Eileen had a miscarriage in between them. We both caught terrible flu viruses, and I was hospitalized briefly and she lost the baby.

When Seth was four years old, he prayed for a baby sister. He was delighted to learn a sibling was coming. "What if it's a boy and you'll have a brother?" "I'll throw it out the window. I want a sister." He got his wish. You couldn't have asked for a more loving, patient, enthusiastic big brother. Seth was protective and very involved with baby Liliana. She came into this world with a full head of bright red hair. She was so red that Seth insisted her name be "Berry" because she looked like a berry. We did indeed incorporate that officially into her name.

We live walking distance from the Wonderland Avenue Elementary School in Laurel Canyon. Life was truly ideal when Seth was in the fifth grade and Liliana was in the first grade. In the mornings when the "final bell" would ring, meaning children had two minutes to get to their classes, we'd walk them into the school. Eileen was part of the school's Arts Cadre and very involved in all aspects of the school.

I was perfectly content to be working mostly only as a voice-over artist during those years. The kids would go to school and I'd drive down to Hollywood and narrate an episode of *Biography* or record some animation or commercials and often be back before the school day ended. I really wanted to be with Eileen and the kids as much as possible and fortunately, I was able to.

HAPPY MUMYS. PHOTO BY ANGELA CARTWRIGHT.

I often traveled on weekends to do appearances at comic book and science fiction and autograph conventions around the world. I also invested into upgrading my home recording studio and was producing a solo album almost annually.

Many of our friends are in the arts. One evening, film director Martha Coolidge, at the time best known for the features *Valley Girl, Rambling Rose,* and *Angie,* was having dinner at our house. She was casting her next film, a period fantasy family film called *Three Wishes.* Martha had already locked Patrick Swayze as the lead, but she said she was having a difficult time casting the role of the young son, Gunny. Without missing a beat, Seth, not quite five years old at the time (who was goofing around with Martha's son, Preston) said, "I'll audition for you, Martha." Those were his exact words. Yes, because of my history as a child star, I'm sure you could say that made Martha take him a bit more seriously than if I hadn't been. But I wasn't the kid who memorized the scenes and walked into Martha's office with her and a casting director and an assistant and a producer and performed and got the gig. It was all Seth. Martha treated him wonderfully and he had a fabulous time and I think he turned in a real good performance. Martha drafted me to play a small role in *Three Wishes* too. Seth went on to make two more features: *Dear God,* directed by Garry Marshall, and *Paulie.*

PROUD DAD WALKING THE RED CARPET AT THE PREMIERE OF THREE WISHES CO-STARRING SETH MUMY!

Seth worked with several people that I had worked with when I was a kid, including Gena Rowlands and Jack Klugman. He did a few television episodes, including a *Babylon 5* as an alien, and some voice-overs as well. *SpongeBob SquarePants* was his favorite voice-over gig and he still gets residual checks from it. After about three years, Seth decided he'd rather play basketball than audition for acting gigs. The last thing I would ever do is push him against his will. So, by the time he was nine, Seth had retired from the thespian life.

But Liliana is a different story. Her natural talent couldn't be contained. Not only was she visually stunning, but acting seemed to be in her DNA (duh). She wanted in to the family business. Hollywood quickly embraced her, and she booked impressive jobs one after another. After co-starring in Fox's remake of *Cheaper by the*

PROUD DAD WITH MOVIE STAR LILIANA MUMY AT THE
PREMIERE OF *THE SANTA CLAUSE 3: THE ESCAPE CLAUSE*.
LILIANA WAS BRILLIANT IN THAT MOVIE!

Dozen and the sequel, and Disney's *Santa Clause 2 & 3* films, Liliana was a recurring character on the hit television series *My Wife and Kids.* She went on to appear in dozens of other guest roles on television and commercials and really found her calling in animation. Ever since Liliana started talking, she's had a smoky little voice that the microphone loves. Disney cast her as Mertle in their *Lilo & Stitch* animated series and she's always had an animated series since. Liliana has done hundreds of animation projects, both for feature films and for television. I've been blessed to have worked alongside her several times in animation on projects like *Holly Hobbie, The Loud House,* and I played her father for several seasons on *Bravest Warriors.* Her talent is beyond impressive. But perhaps the single greatest acting experience of my entire career came in 2003 when I worked with Liliana on *The Twilight Zone: "It's Still a Good Life.* "

RETURNING TO ANTHONY FREMONT AND *THE TWILIGHT ZONE* WITH THE FABULOUS LILIANA MUMY AS ANTHONY'S DAUGHTER AUDREY FREMONT, WHO IS EVEN MORE POWERFUL THAN HER FATHER. "IT'S STILL A GOOD LIFE" IS TRULY THE CHERRY ON TOP OF MY ACTING CAREER SUNDAE.

71. STILL A GOOD LIFE

*I*t's fair to say that besides Will Robinson on *Lost in Space*, I'm best known for the role of Anthony Fremont in *The Twilight Zone's* 1961 episode "It's a Good Life." In 2002, the UPN network announced that they were re-launching *The Twilight Zone* as a new series. My good friend and neighbor, Ira Steven Behr, was offered the job of executive producer and showrunner. He and I discussed it. Ira felt like it was a losing proposition. No one could ever replace Rod Serling. I agreed. But I encouraged him to take the gig, because as I passionately told him, he could protect the franchise. Ira is a great writer and a very good producer, and his integrity is unquestionable. He took the job. But he was somewhat correct in his initial instinct regarding it. UPN wanted to bring a "hip hop sensibility" to *The Twilight Zone*. Ira was frustrated and did his best to keep the anthology show on the right track. Forest Whitaker was brought in to host the episodes. One evening as the new *Twilight Zone* was still in pre-production and Ira and I were chatting over a cocktail here in my living room, while our wives were gardening and our kids were playing making-movies with the video camera they bought by selling lemonade together, I said, "It would be cool to see what Anthony Fremont was up to forty years later." Ira nodded his head.

About a week later Ira called and said, "They want to do it." I said, "Who wants to do what?" He replied, "The network wants to do a sequel to 'It's a Good Life.' And they want it fast." I was somewhat stunned. "Write up some ideas. I'll write up some ideas too and we'll see what we've got." So, a day or so later, Ira and I exchanged notes. Mine were very dark. Ira's included Anthony's daughter, who he clearly saw as being played by Liliana. Wow! We went with Ira's vision.

I was a little apoplectic about it. "It's a Good Life" had gone into the "classic television" category. It is truly "real good" television. Could we pull off a sequel? What if it sucked? Should we even attempt it? Ira was so great. He absolutely guaranteed me that if I didn't like his script, they wouldn't do it. He promised me that no one but me would play Anthony Fremont and that regardless of the network's notes, if I didn't think Rod Serling would have approved it, he'd send it to the Cornfield. And then he said, "And I think I can get Cloris." And he did. How great to reunite with the amazing Cloris Leachman alongside Liliana. It couldn't get any better. We shot the episode in Vancouver, and it turned out to be good. Real good. I am beyond proud of Liliana's performance. She was brilliant.

72. ODE TO CLORIS

I had the great privilege and pleasure of working closely with Cloris Leachman four times in my acting career. I played her son in all four of those projects which were starring roles for both of us. We worked on *The Loretta Young Show*, *Going My Way* (with Gene Kelly), and *The Twilight Zone* (in the classic episode, "It's a Good Life" and in "It's Still a Good Life"). I've been fortunate to work with many iconic talents over the course of my life, but NONE were better than Cloris. She was an amazing talent. Any actor who was lucky enough to work with her will immediately know what I mean when I say she truly bumped up your game. You rose to the occasion when acting alongside Cloris Leachman because she wouldn't accept anything less than the very best you had inside to bring, and she helped you find it.

Cloris was a force to be reckoned with. I can't say I ever knew anyone bolder than her. She was bawdy and brave and sassy and hysterically quick and funny, and she took no prisoners. She taught me a lot about acting when I was only a very young child. We remained friends over the decades. Her son, George, and I were in a band together. My kids went to Easter egg parties at her home when they were little. I will always appreciate her greatness and I will never forget how lucky I was to work with her multiple times. Thankfully, Cloris's immense talents were very well acknowledged, and she lived a long, uncompromising life.

I'm sorry she's gone but I am grateful she was here for so long and left us so much. Many people are not aware of the fact that Cloris was an incredibly talented pianist. I consider myself blessed to have heard her play.

A FREMONT FAMILY REUNION AT THE HOLLYWOOD SHOW.
CLORIS, ME, AND LILIANA.

CLORIS AND LILIANA ON
THE SET OF "IT'S STILL
A GOOD LIFE."

73. The Bachelor

Chuck Barris' offices on Vine Street in Hollywood were packed with eclectic, young, counterculture employees. It was different than most production companies. Between 1969 and 1972 I appeared on three episodes of *The Dating Game*. That type of entertainment never really appealed to me much, but I did the first one alongside veteran child actor and friend Barry Livingston. Barry and I were two of the "bachelors" that were questioned stupidly and were not picked to go on the date. What I enjoyed about doing it was that as a union actor, I was given the choice of being paid scale for the taping or given my choice of anything from a catalogue. I think it was a Spiegel catalogue, but I can't really be sure. I chose a nice stereo console that had a record player and AM/FM radio and decent speakers. That's what I liked about doing the show. I had that stereo in my room at my parents' house for years and they ended up keeping it for the rest of their lives.

THAT TIME BARRY LIVINGSTON AND I COMPETED FOR A DATE.

The second time I did *The Dating Game* I was the one who asked the questions and chose the date, so I was guaranteed a trip somewhere. I remember doing the pre-show interview a few days before taping and the Barris staff writing questions from what info I'd shared. It was pretty stupid. One question I remember was, "I'm a photographer. If we were in the dark room together, what would develop?" Oy. Anyway, I picked a girl named Linda and the date ended up being pretty impressive. We flew to France and attended the Le Mans Grand Prix race. I saw Steve McQueen there in the pits. It was quite a groovy little trip. I was fifteen and I think my date was thirteen. I wasn't rude to her, but I spent the few days in France flirting with the chaperone, who was about twenty-one.

My hair was well below my shoulders, and I had a goatee when I once again returned to *The Dating Game*. This time I was eighteen. They worked hard to cajole me into doing it. I protested and they persisted and although the game was not rigged in any way, they intimated I'd be on the receiving end of a very nice holiday. So, I did it. I don't remember the banter, but again, I was the one who picked from three ladies. I remember at the end of the show, when my "date" appeared, she was very pretty. They announced we'd be going to the Rose Bowl football game. My expression shifted from a smile to a confused look. While working on *Lost in Space*, I was IN the Rose Parade a few times. Riding on a float, waving to people on the street, freezing my butt off, face hurting from maintaining a smile for hours, and having to be there in the middle of the night. I am not a football fan. Haven't been since I was about nine years old and got creamed multiple times playing football with my friends who all outweighed me and were bigger than me. It's just not a sport I'm particularly interested in. I'll watch the Super Bowl with my son Seth once a year, and that's the extent of my footballing.

So, I ended up passing on the date. Which does not make me an asshole. The young lady got to pick a date of her choice and had the experience with all the perks and without a complaining Mumy by her side.

I also got a color tv out of it.

YES, I DID *THE DATING GAME.* THREE TIMES! GADZOOKS.

74. Ms. Bardot

Having the distinction of being the first American actor to receive an on-screen kiss from Brigitte Bardot is a little-known trivia fact that I have always enjoyed. Filming *Dear Brigitte* took place way back in 1964. For the scenes with Ms. Bardot, Jimmy Stewart, my parents and I, and the film crew flew to France.

The film duplicated the interior of her personal home and really got the details correct. Brigitte Bardot was the first celebrity I ever met who actually had an entourage. At that time, she was one of the most famous and iconic women in the world. I found her to be sweet, charming, professional, and very, very sexy. She smelled amazing, a citrus ginger vanilla scent. Believe me, I was very close to her.

We filmed quite a lot of her scenes the first day and then of course waited overnight for the dailies to be watched and approved. I was not privy to viewing dailies, but I recall that someone at Fox felt there was too much of her cleavage showing, so we reshot those scenes the next day with a flower-type bow pulled up on her dress.

Looking back on it, it's not a surprise that my father instead of my mother chose to escort me to the set those days. Brigitte Bardot was mesmerizing. Sounds cheeky, but I clearly remember sitting on the sofa with her arms wrapped around me and my shoulder pressed up tightly against her breast. Yes, I was only ten years old, but I definitely enjoyed that for all the right reasons.

These days, I support several charities with monthly donations and I try to help make the world a better place for those who can't speak for themselves, and animal rights groups are important to me. I've haven't eaten any meat for over forty years, although I do eat some fish, so that makes me a pescatarian.

In 2005, I learned of Brigitte Bardot's passionate multi-decades-long work for animal rights and her "Fondation Brigitte Bardot." The kind lady who ran my fan club at the time, Glennda Kountz, contacted her foundation and I had thirty-five 8x10 photographs of Ms. Bardot and me printed and shipped to her and back to me. We both signed them, with all proceeds going to her animal foundation (although I did keep one copy.) She and I exchanged letters and it was lovely to reconnect with her and help raise a few thousand dollars for the benefit of animals.

As Erasmus Leaf said in *Dear Brigitte*…. "Enchante, Mademoiselle Bardot."

75. The Important Things

Sometimes when we stop to smell the roses, we prick ourselves on thorns. Such is the nature of life. Not all my memories and life experiences have been joyful, but for the most part they have been positive. I've tried to learn from the negative and it feels like only recently have I begun to really understand there must always be a balance. I've been both a spiritual and a very materialistic person. I like stuff. I collect a lot of it. I have been a collector all my life. But a few years ago, the Santa Monica Mountains and nearby canyons were on fire, and Eileen and I got evacuated from our home. We gathered up Josie B, our dog and constant companion, some important paperwork, medicines, a small amount of jewelry, and some cash and then paused to look around. I've lived in this same house over forty-five years... books, tapes, photos, guitars, collectibles, etc... I dig it all. But at that moment, I realized it meant very little.

We were fortunate and the fires did not reach us. I would have hated to have lost it all. I know several close friends who did lose everything they owned in fires. Am I grateful and happy that our neighborhood was spared? Of course I am. Do I have great sympathy and empathy for those whose homes were lost? Of course I do. But as I loaded up our car and drove away with my wife and my dog, not knowing what we'd find when we returned... I understood how truly lucky I was and how I had everything I needed with me right then.

CH 76. LATELY

I am a very restless man. I need to constantly be in a creative state or I'm unhappy and edgy. I'd rather be in my studio working on a song or a mix or just playing guitar or piano or painting or writing. I do spend quite a lot of time listening to music though, Music recharges me and motivates me. It always has. I can't help but reflect on the fact that even as a ten-year-old, I brought my guitar to the studio and had a stereo record player in my dressing room. That was always important to me, and I went out of my way to make sure music was with me at work. I do read quite a bit, but mostly in bed at night. Although I've traveled quite a lot, I don't like leaving home much anymore. I dislike airports and airplanes and I've become quite spoiled when it comes to going out of my comfort zone. I suppose that's a reward for working so long and because my parents invested my childhood acting money well.

I enjoy writing and producing and I'm grateful that I get paid to do it. I've worked as a consulting producer on the History Channel's *Ancient Aliens* television series for several years now. My late, very good friend, Kevin Burns created the series and I've been involved with it since the beginning. It's a show that asks important questions and presents evidence to support concepts that have not been socially accepted in the past; concepts regarding the potential history of humankind being extraterrestrially guided. Working as a producer on the series is something I can do from home. I submit ideas for episodes, and I view rough cuts and add my thoughts on how to make them better as they progress before airing. It's a good gig and I take it very seriously. It's nice to still be working in television.

WORKING AS A PRODUCER ON THE HISTORY CHANNEL'S LONG-RUNNING SERIES ANCIENT ALIENS HAS BEEN A VERY COOL GIG. HERE I AM IN THE PROMETHEUS OFFICES WITH DAVID CHILDRESS, GIORGIO TSOUKALOS, AND WILLIAM HENRY.

«‹›»

I've often been asked why I haven't been on another television series "lately" or why I haven't been in many films "lately." Well, the truth is that after working for five years on *Babylon 5*, in all that alien makeup, I honestly felt burnt out regarding on-camera acting. I also was frustrated at the level of representation that I had. I've never really been interested in doing bit parts, cheesy low-budget exploitation films, or fluff nonsense. I've done some of that, but it was never satisfying. So, for the most part and definitely because I couldn't get powerful representation like I'd had when I was younger, I chose not to pursue auditions anymore. There are countless actors who would do almost anything to book a few scenes or even speak a few lines in a dumb television show. I'm not one of them. Let those hungry cats get those spoils. Should the opportunity to do some interesting acting in a quality production come my way, I will be more than happy to return to on-camera work.

I have found voice-overs, writing and producing gigs, and making a lot of music to be extremely rewarding and I do most all of it from right inside my house. I grew up and worked prolifically in an era when there was no internet, no cable or subscription television, no cell phones, and no streaming. There were only three major television networks and a few local stations until the mid-1980s. So the sheer volume of viewers who watched a lot of my work was massive compared to today's audiences with countless channels and choices. Thirty to forty million people used to watch *Lost in Space* every week when it was originally airing. A season of television was around twenty-six episodes. Nowadays, a season is six or ten episodes.

There is a part of me that understands and accepts that I'll never reach the amount of people I grew up reaching ever again and I'll admit that can be frustrating. Plus, unfortunately, the union that I have been a member of since the age of six has also been terribly whittled down over the years. I don't want to work as an actor for almost no money and under less-than-comfortable conditions. Those are the main reasons why I haven't aggressively pursued on-camera work for quite a while.

I create because the muse continues to come to me. I learned decades ago, never to ask the muse to pause, or to shrug it off and think it will still be waiting for me in the morning. If I get a lyric or a melody or an idea for a story knocking at the creative door inside my head, no matter what time it is or what I'm doing, I have disciplined myself to listen and to record it or write it down. I'm very grateful that the muse continues to visit me.

THE MUSE HAS MANY NAMES... MINE'S BUCKY...

77. Do We Have a Bidder

I understand the mindset of collectors. But I must admit, I was quite surprised to see the prices some vintage *Lost in Space* costumes recently sold for at a Heritage Auction.

Ange, Marta, and I showed up for some publicity with the impressively preserved outfits we wore for three years, well over half a century ago. It was cool to see and touch them again. Basically, there were always three sets of each outfit. One for a stunt double or stand-in, and two for the main cast. I think Ange and I may have had a couple more created since we were growing so fast, but I can't confirm that.

I've watched the prices rise steadily over the years as the wardrobe surfaced for sale. Fans bring it to my attention or the current owners bring it to personal appearances and want us to take photos with the old velours and silver spacesuits.

But in 2021, the final bid for my third season purple velour, yellow turtle dickie, and purple ski pants shocked me: $93,750! Wow. That's a lot more than I got paid to wear it!

Showbiz.

Collectors.

Indeed!

IF ONLY I HAD THOUGHT TO KEEP A COUPLE OF THESE!

«<>»

I would never part with them, but I wonder how much my autograph collection would sell for? Here's a couple of my very favorites... Jimmy Stewart and Elizabeth Montgomery.

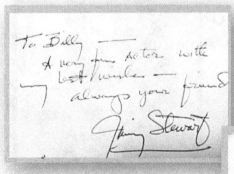

78. Music is My Life

Since the age of ten, my life has really been about music. Beyond my acting workload, which I wholeheartedly enjoyed, I took private guitar lessons at my house for a little over four years. Once a week, for one hour, a teacher would come, and we'd sit on two chairs in my upstairs bedroom and go over the lesson from the previous week and then work on a new lesson.

I went through three different teachers over those four years. My first guitar teacher was an Italian named Frank Giovanni. He was a really passionate musician and when I managed to master something tough, he'd kiss me on the cheek, which was only slightly creepy because he was the epitome of a "typical" Italian guy with a heavy accent who always "talked with his hands" and it didn't really bother me much. When I wasn't working hard enough on a piece or played something wrong, he'd whack my hand with a baton. He was quite a character. But I really learned a lot from him between the ages of ten and twelve. He taught me dozens of right-hand fingerpicking and flamenco techniques and I learned all the basic first position and bar chords from him. After two years, Frank considered me a success and said he'd taught me all he could. I don't know if that's true, but he definitely taught me a lot. I really wanted to be a good guitarist and I worked hard at it. Learning my lines for acting projects always came easy and quickly to me. I enjoyed my acting work, especially my years on *Lost in Space*, but I grew way more passionate about music than acting. I practiced a lot. Sometimes I brought my guitar to the studio and would find time to practice there after school was in the can and in between filming set ups. My parents never bugged me to practice. If anything, they'd bug me to give it a rest.

I was a major folk music freak when I was a kid. Yes, I'd been really into Jan & Dean and Chubby Checker and the Beach Boys and the Beatles, but once I became exposed to the Kingston Trio and Peter, Paul and Mary and Pete Seeger, my path for the next few years was clear to me. It was folk music. My second guitar teacher was named Pat, and I've forgotten his last name. I'd switched from a nylon strung Goya Classical guitar to a steel string Gibson B-25N. Pat taught me how to read tablature and I got quite good at it. Nowadays, I've lost that skill, but I could probably figure it out again if I tried. I'd play a record of a song I wanted to learn and Pat would figure it out and write it out for me and by the time of my next lesson, I'd have it down and we'd work on other tunes I wanted to learn.

My third and final teacher was a fine picker named Sandy Chadbourne. Scott Ehrlich found him and we both studied with Sandy, although separately, for about two years. I learned music theory from him. He's responsible for me understanding the math of music. That if a song has the chord changes of say, C to F to G… that's also 1 to 4 to 5 and that can easily be transposed to other keys… for instance, G to C to D. That was a big learn. Sandy was also an excellent fingerpicker and he taught me a lot of Lightnin' Hopkins-style playing. By the time I turned fourteen, I was in a band and learning with my friends by jamming and playing together and I stopped taking lessons.

Sandy went on to become an astrologer. He changed his name to Arthyr and for a while, decades later, he was Dr. Demento's manager. Small world. We reconnected and it was very nice.

My family was musical, but we didn't really ever play together much. My mom was a very competent pianist. She was a sight reader and you could put a piece of sheet music in front of her and she'd sit down and play it. She never played classical music to my knowledge though. She played hits from the 1930s and 1940s. She was actually good, but I hardly ever heard her play. I'd bug her once in a while and she'd sit down and play "Peg O' My Heart." I still have the piano she was gifted as a wedding present at age eighteen when she got married for the first time. It's a 1920s Brambach baby grand, made in New York. "Fish Heads" and countless other songs were written and recorded on that piano. It's in storage these days. Anyway, it's a good thing my mom's marriage to Walter Coffee only lasted from 1930 to 1935 or I wouldn't be here.

My dad had a western swing band in Bishop during the 1930s and 1940s. I have a wonderful photograph of them. But they never recorded so I don't have a memory of hearing them. They wore fancy embroidered satin cowboy shirts and Stetson hats. I still have my dad's Stetsons and I have several of his fancy cowboy shirts too, but I used to wear them at my own gigs a lot and several of them literally disintegrated over time. They were beautiful shirts. My dad played fiddle in that band and I also have his violin to this day. He also had a saxophone and an accordion which I still have as well. I've played his sax on several Barnes & Barnes tracks, but I wasn't very musical with it! I even played his accordion on a Jenerators track in the 1990s. But I never could figure out all those buttons. Nowadays if I need an accordion part, I call "Weird Al."

I asked my dad to teach me the violin when I was a teenager, but I never could get it right. A mandolin is tuned the same as a violin and that I can play, but the fretless neck of a violin and the right bow technique wasn't for me. I did teach myself how to play the 5-string banjo though. I bought a Vega Pete Seeger model, just like the Kingston Trio used and I got Pete Seeger's "How to Play the 5-string Banjo" book. (The "red" edition.) I still play some folkie banjo every now and then. I was never a bluegrass player, but old-time traditional folk songs I can handle fairly well.

MY DAD'S BAND IN THE
1930S AND 1940S IN BISHOP,
CALIFORNIA. PRETTY WELL-
DRESSED BUNCH OF GUYS.
THAT'S CHARLES MUMY ON
THE FIDDLE.

ME ONSTAGE PLAYING THE
PALAMINO CLUB WEARING MY
DAD'S OLD COWBOY SHIRT
FROM HIS VINTAGE BAND DAYS.

TWO CHARLES WILLIAM MUMYS ENJOYING A
RARE JAM ON MANDOLIN AND FIDDLE.

When I was fourteen and Paul Gordon joined Energy, he taught me how to play "Soul Kitchen" by the Doors on my piano. That's the only piano lesson I've ever had, and I can indeed play keyboards.

Because of my love of Bob Dylan, I started playing harmonica when I was about thirteen. Add that to my list of instruments I can play along with basic drums.

So, when I wasn't actually practicing or performing music... I was going to gigs. I must admit, my parents were very cool about that. The first band I saw live was Peter, Paul and Mary in 1964 and I really never stopped going to gigs after that. One of the very biggest regrets of my entire life was passing on going to see the Beatles at the Hollywood Bowl and to the meet and greet with them in 1965. Angela and I were both invited to schmooze that historic event and I remember saying, "Who wants to be in a crowd of fifteen thousand screaming girls listening to 'yeah, yeah yeah'?! I'm gonna stay home and listen to the Kingston Trio!" So, Ange went without me. She has photographs of her with the Beatles and she absolutely loved the show. I did, however, join Ringo's All-Starr Band to sing and play guitar with them at the Greek Theater in 2016. I played and sang on "With a Little Help From My Friends" and "Give Peace a Chance." That's one of the greatest musical times ever for me.

As I said, my parents were great about letting me go to gigs and before I could drive, my dad was cool about dropping me off and picking me up. I went to the Newport Pop Festival in 1968, which was the first rock festival attended by over one hundred thousand people. It was wild. In 1969, Ange and I went to Devonshire Downs, another huge festival.

Hendrix, Cream, the Doors, the Rolling Stones, the Who, Janis Joplin, the Byrds, Crosby, Stills, Nash & Young, Bob Dylan, Simon & Garfunkel, Elton John, John Sebastian, Fleetwood Mac, the

Beach Boys, Steppenwolf, Blue Cheer, Sly & the Family Stone, Jefferson Airplane, Grateful Dead, the Band, Ike & Tina Turner, Stevie Wonder, Spirit, Iron Butterfly, the Kinks, Canned Heat, the Chambers Brothers, Leon Russell, Donovan, Country Joe & the Fish, the Jackson 5, and so many, many more... I saw them all before I was old enough to vote. All of those gigs were outside or in huge arenas.

Once I got older, some of the more memorable concerts I attended included: more Rolling Stones, more Dylan, more CSN&Y, more the Who, Tom Petty and the Heartbreakers, the Pretenders, the Police, Bruce Springsteen, Devo, David Bowie, ELO, Yes, the Eagles, Fleetwood Mac, Toto, Brian Wilson, the Everly Brothers, Paul Simon, the Blues Brothers, Crosby & Nash, Stephen Stills, Neil Young, Alison Krauss & Union Station, Ray Davies, Merle Haggard, Marty Stuart, B.B. King, Santana, the Bangles, the Monkees, Emmylou Harris, Peter Green, Lucinda Williams, Norah Jones, Mark Knopfler, Paul McCartney, and many others.

The intimate, inside club shows were even better to me.

The Troubadour was the place to be. The legendary club sits at Doheny and Santa Monica Blvd. and from the 1960s through the 1980s, that stage was graced by some of the greatest talents ever. And I was there to take it all in.

The first time I played the Troubadour was with Redwood in 1970, opening for John Stewart. The sound system was amazing. The sound technicians really knew how to mic acoustic instruments and the room pulsed with magic, night after night. Redwood played the Troubadour several times as did the Igloos and the Jenerators. It was always a very special place to gig. But forget about my personal Troubadour gigs... here's a very incomplete list of some of the acts I saw at the Troubadour (many of them several times) in no particular order...

Joni Mitchell, Neil Young (solo and with Crazy Horse), Cat Stevens, Laura Nyro, James Taylor, Arlo Guthrie, Bette Midler, Poco, Billy Joel, Carly Simon (who kissed me on the mouth), Rick Nelson, Bonnie Raitt, Jim Croce, Linda Ronstadt, Jackson Browne, Tom Waits, Hoyt Axton, Leon Redbone, Randy Newman, Carole King, Barry Manilow, Manhattan Transfer, Dan Hicks & the Hot Licks... the list goes on.

Most of these gigs I went to with friends. Quite a few I went to by myself. Nothing stopped me from seeing live music. The Troubadour was located about three miles from my house in Cheviot Hills when I lived with my parents. Many times, my father would drop me and Paul or Robert off and then pick us up after the shows. Several times I walked. It was always worth it.

REDWOOD PERFORMING AT THE TROUBADOUR, 1974.

79. MUSINGS

I miss the little things much more than the big ones. I miss driving with my Dad to Hoi Ping's Chinese Restaurant on Pico near Beverly and sitting at the bar with him while he waited for our take-out order. I would watch the tropical fish dash about in the aquarium that had a pirate skeleton at the wheel of a sunken plastic ship with bubbles coming up out of it. My dad would have a Mai Tai and chat with the bartender and the owner, while I counted guppies. I looked forward to getting the little plastic sword that held the cherry in my father's cocktail. I'd bring those home and glue them to my army men figures and turn them into "other superhero guys." My dad and I did that ritual together quite a lot when I was a boy.

ABOUT TO HEAD OUT AND CRUISE TO CATALINA ON MY DAD'S BOAT.

A HAPPY MUMY FAMILY. I COULDN'T ASK FOR ANYTHING MORE.

I miss resting my head in my mother's lap and having her pet my woe away.

I miss grass stains on the knees of my jeans.

I miss the smell and sound of the puffy breath from my horse.

I miss the thrill of learning a new guitar chord.

I miss watching Liliana play Little League.

I miss watching Seth play league basketball.

Most of all, I think I miss not knowing how the world really works.

A MODELING SHOT
OF MY MOM FROM
THE 1930s.

VINTAGE SHOT OF MY MOM AND HER DOG IN THE 1920s.
MY GRANDMOTHER "LALA" IS BEHIND THE WHEEL.

80. MURIEL

My mother lived to be ninety-seven years old. She would have made it to 100 I'm sure if she hadn't broken her hip when she was ninety-five. I spoke with her on the phone every single day after my father died. She looked forward to it and it became a ritual. Sometimes we'd talk for only a couple minutes, sometimes we'd go on for an hour. Even at ninety-seven, she found reasons to argue with me most the time. Eileen, Seth, Liliana, and I went out to see her and take her to lunch most every weekend. Sometimes it would be every other weekend. I'd bring her and her current parakeet Sweetie, that Liliana picked out for her, here to our house where we had a bedroom and bathroom suite for her. She'd stay for a weekend and sometimes longer. She was loved and she loved her family, but she was not an easy person to get along with.

Muriel Mumy had an impressive amount of willpower and she was determined to speak her mind and stay around as long as she possibly could. She was playing tournament bridge and walking daily before she tripped and broke her hip. From there, it was a continual downward spiral, but she stayed in her own home until the end.

Two sisters, Monica and Lucy, tag-teamed staying with my mom and caring for her needs at her home the last year of her life. My mom was a fighter in every definition of the word. She fought to stay alive, and she fought with everyone she disagreed with. She was tough. Opinionated, judgmental, stubborn, well-read, and smart.

January of 2010 found her back in her own home under hospice care that checked on her a few times a week after being hospitalized with pneumonia twice. She was frail, but feisty as always. My mom lived forty miles away from me. Not very far, but far enough if an emergency phone call came at a heavy traffic hour, it could take a good hour and a half to get to her.

Even at ninety-seven, my mother was extremely difficult in terms of accepting help from me or relinquishing control of any kind. I had zero access to her finances. She refused to give me power of attorney even after she'd had several serious health issues after my father died. My mother had open-heart surgery to replace two valves at eighty-five. She renewed her driver's license at ninety-three. After suffering the broken hip, she spent three months in the Motion Picture Home and then was back in her home, and at first was recalcitrant about having caregivers with her, but she finally relented on that. They were kind and she grew to appreciate and care for them, but she was not an easy woman to care for.

The last day of my mother's conscious existence, she woke up, had her breakfast, played with her parakeet Sweetie, and then went to her desk and wrote checks to pay in full all her outstanding bills. "Where's the Visa bill?" she asked Monica, her caregiver. When told it hadn't come yet, my mother called the bank to inquire about the balance of her Visa bill and then wrote a check to cover it. She watched *Jeopardy* and *Wheel of Fortune* and then said out loud matter-of-factly, "My mother's here."

Those were the last words my mom spoke. She collapsed unconscious after saying that. Monica immediately called me, and I told her I would be there within an hour. She called the hospice people, and they were there before we arrived. Monica moved my mom to her bed. Eileen, Seth, Liliana, Alexa, and I made it there in forty-five minutes.

My mom was there on her bed. But I knew she was gone. Like Elvis, she had left the building. I held her hand, I whispered in her ear, I spoke loudly to see if there was any response, but there was none. I squeezed her hand and encouraged her to give me a squeeze back, but absolutely no response was her response. However, my mother had a pacemaker, and every minute or so her body would twitch from the pacemaker forcing her heart to beat. It was tough to watch.

We sat with her through the night. Doctors were called and the next afternoon her pacemaker was remotely turned off and she officially was pronounced dead. But she really died when her mother, my grandmother Lala, came to get her. And Lala waited until her favorite television shows were over.

Honestly, I couldn't feel angry or terribly sad about her death. She lived an uncompromising long life, and she left in a very extraordinary way.

THE ALMOST IMPOSSIBLY STRONG-WILLED MURIEL GERTRUDE MUMY
AND HER SON A FEW MONTHS BEFORE SHE LEFT REALITY PRIME.

81. The Child Star Club

I have never believed that show business eats its young. But I have seen way too many grown-up child actors fail as adults and die sad bitter deaths. I do understand that it can be difficult knowing that many millions of people were watching and enjoying your work regularly on television for several years, and then that can just suddenly stop. It takes a strong sense of self and an acceptance of the present to get adjusted to that shift, that lack of attention. It can definitely cause some insecurities, frustration, and depression. But that's the same for a lot of arenas and ages. Professional athletes, trial lawyers, dancers, etc. When the time comes and you find the spotlight no longer shines on you, you have to adjust your emotions and accept it. That doesn't mean you lose your self-worth. It just means you can't throw a fastball anymore or whatever.

It's my opinion that a lot of child actors simply aren't really talented good actors. So, when they outgrow being kids, or the series they were on gets cancelled, they have a hard time understanding that they should train themselves and find a new career. On the other hand, it's my opinion that the truly gifted child actors who want to stay in the business usually make that not-so-easy transition successfully and work all their lives if they choose to.

Obviously, money is a big deal. I know child actors who found out that when they became adults, there was very little money tucked away for them. Their parents had spent the majority of it. A percentage of a minor's income is placed in trust that no one can touch, but it's a small amount. So, yeah… If you worked for years as a child actor and expected a nice nest egg of money would come your way and it didn't... I understand how that can mess someone up. I've seen it happen more than a few times. But it didn't happen to me. The money I earned working as an actor when I was a kid was invested well for me, and I'm thankful to my parents for that, and I'm thankful to myself for not blowing it all when I could get my hands on it. I've never been truly wealthy compared to the big earners, but I've never been poor either.

I sometimes get depressed and when I do, I allow myself to feel that way. Often, I'll get a good song out of it.

FATHER'S DAY PROMO WITH MY FELLOW
CHILD STARS BACK IN THE 1960s.
CAN YOU NAME THEM ALL?

82. Rules to Live By

My philosophy on life is: "Do the best you can and can the best you do."

《》

I'm not one to give advice, but I will. "NEVER *ever* fool around with a Ouija Board."

《》

Some may say I've been my own worst enemy and others may say I've chosen wisely, but I will say that ever since I was eleven years old, musical integrity has been super important to me. I enjoyed playing guitar in several episodes of *Lost in Space*, and I almost always brought my guitar with me to the studios, especially during summer when I didn't have to spend three hours a day in a school trailer. While filming the Disney feature *Rascal* during the summer of 1968, the powers that be at Disney noticed and they offered me a record deal on their Buena Vista label. I was of course flattered and happy, but I was, even then, protective of my music and my image. I was writing a lot of songs by then and some of them were honestly pretty good. I wanted to know if I'd be able to record my own songs and if I'd be able to have a say in the arrangements and production. They answered, "No." They would choose the material and they would produce and arrange it as they saw fit and they were quite sure they knew how to do it. So, without testing the water further, I said thanks but no thanks.

Seven years later, I really tested how far I would go in that musical integrity mode. After filming the *Sunshine* film, and after MCA released a single and a soundtrack album where I played guitar, banjo and harmonica, and sang, Universal decided to turn *Sunshine* into a series and we started negotiating the contract. David Cassidy was a friend of mine, Peter Tork and Micky Dolenz were friends of mine, and I knew many other people who were involved with music/acting crossover projects. I was a member of the musician's union by then and I thought long and hard about it and I demanded a "no dubbing" clause in my deal. I wouldn't take their word on it, and it had to be in writing. No one could re-record or play my musical parts or sing my vocal parts on any *Sunshine* episodes or related projects unless I was physically unable to do it myself. Universal said no. They said that would set a precedent they weren't willing to set.

There's a term in contract negotiations that means exactly what it says, and I knew full well not to play that card if I didn't mean it. I told them that it was a deal-breaker for me. I was absolutely committed to my position, and I wasn't going to risk being turned into a "fake musician." I would have walked away from the project and never looked back. After a few days of complete silence between Universal and my agent, they agreed. I'm glad to say every guitar chord, every banjo riff, every harmonica note, and all my vocals on every one of the *Sunshine* projects are all mine... for better or worse.

I'm the kind of guy that honors an agreement I sign. Many times, agents or managers or advisors have said to me, "Don't worry about it. If it goes, we'll re-negotiate." But I've never accepted that advice. Sure, if something becomes a huge hit, then I agree, go back to the table and see if you can get a sweeter deal. But if you can't, or if a project continues but struggles in ratings, you'd better be okay with the original deal you made. Seems only fair to me and that's how I've tried to be with all my deals.

83. Dream Come True

*T*here are many reasons that some projects become "favorites" over time. My second time guest-starring on *Bewitched* in the episode titled "Junior Executive" checked all the boxes. I had worked on the first season of the series, starring in the Christmas episode "A Vision of Sugarplums," and had fallen in love with Elizabeth Montgomery. What an amazing lady she was. She radiated a fantastic positive energy; she was a wonderful actress and very easy to work with. Everyone on the set was cool and it was a pleasant environment. Elizabeth was extremely sweet to me. We talked together in between shooting scenes and she taught me how to do the "Samantha nose twitch." I was truly smitten by her beauty and her personality.

When they brought me back for Season Two, to play Darrin Stephens as a boy, that was just too good to be true. The storyline was very appealing... Endora, played by the mighty Agnes Moorehead, uses her magic to turn Darrin into a ten-year-old boy again (me). Well, having a big crush on Elizabeth and being cast as her husband with full cognitive memory of being her husband, was extremely appealing for multiple reasons, somewhat like Tom Hanks' *Big* in reverse. Also, as a regular-kid television watcher, *Bewitched* was one of my very favorite shows. I never missed an episode so when given the opportunity to play a character that I'd watched closely since the series first aired, it truly inspired the professional actor in me. I think my performance really captured the essence of Dick York's Darrin and it stands out from the bulk of my other work as a successful comedic impersonation.

I watched it quite recently and found myself really enjoying everything about that one. It's interesting how seeing an old show brings back the memories of actually making it. Memories of moments when the camera wasn't rolling, when we were rehearsing or waiting to shoot, and recalling the locations, set dressing, and props, etc.

This episode always makes for a fun trivia-type challenge: name the second actor to play Darrin Stephens. Most people will quickly say, "Dick Sargent." But they're wrong. It's Billy Mumy.

Thinking back on my *Bewitched* experiences, the magic was real for me.

PLAYING ELIZABETH MONTGOMERY'S HUSBAND WAS A DREAM COME TRUE! ONE OF MY ALL-TIME FAVORITE GIGS.

WILL ROBINSON WAS THE PERFECT CHARACTER FOR ME. HE WAS EXACTLY WHAT I HAD WANTED TO GET INTO THE TV AND BE LIKE WHEN I WAS FOUR YEARS OLD. I'M GRATEFUL FOR HIM.

84. Once a Robinson...

Having worked on so many television shows and films as a youngster, I understood a basic rule of an actor's life: projects end and you move on. It's the nature of show business. But *Lost in Space* ended after three years with absolutely no closure and that was a very hard pill for me to swallow.

When we wrapped up Season Three, we were all verbally told the series would shortly be returning for another season. There was nothing iffy about it. No, our contractual options had not officially been picked up in writing, but no one in the cast, or for that matter the main crew, was worried about it. After an eight or ten week hiatus, we'd be back on the Fox lot again, probably in different brightly-colored velour outfits designed by Paul Zastupnevich for *Lost in Space* Season Four. We all simply waved and said "See ya soon!"

But, as fate would have it, we never reconvened as a group again and Season Four didn't happen. As I've come to understand it, there were issues between Irwin and CBS regarding scripts for the new season; scripts that didn't appear when the network demanded they did. I was never privy to the whole story, but it doesn't really matter what the details were.

Lost in Space was cancelled.

I clearly remember hearing that news. I walked into our Cheviot Hills house on Forrester Drive and entered through the front door, not the side door as usual. I stepped onto the stone floor of our entryway and noticed my mother was standing in the dining room and was on the phone. I don't know why, but I immediately sensed something wasn't right. She saw me and I headed over to her and she handed me the receiver. The phone was connected to a small built-in table in the kitchen several feet away and I took it and stepped into the kitchen where I was alone. I didn't sit down. On the other end of the call was Howard Rubin, my beloved agent. "I've got some bad news for you, kiddo. CBS cancelled the show. It's over. But don't worry, we've got plenty of offers and we'll figure it all out soon." I mumbled something like, "Yeah. Okay," and hung up the phone.

Within a minute I started crying. I was fourteen and had been playing Will Robinson since I was ten. It had been my very favorite professional experience of all time and I truly loved the people I worked with. I didn't want it to be over. And if it was indeed really over, I wanted it to have a different ending. I remember saying "It's not fair!" and then sitting on our blue sofa in our den and having a short talk with my mom about how "it's the nature of the business" and "counting your blessings", blah blah blah.

I never saw Guy Williams again and to this day, that makes me sad. I didn't see Jonathan or June or Marta or Bobby either for a few years. We all exchanged Christmas and birthday cards, but that was it. Ange and I talked every day and I saw Mark somewhat regularly, but the fact that we never had a wrap party or got to tell each other how wonderful it was being a "family" together, after all the time we shared working on Stage 11 and Stage 5, going to lunches and events... it just hurt. A lot. Still does.

As the years passed, June was the only constant that never broke the tradition of sending cards and staying in touch. Slowly but surely, especially after Kevin Burns started working at Fox and passionately created projects to reunite the cast, the deep relationships we shared blossomed anew and the remaining Robinsons, Major West, Dr. Smith, and the Robot had further adventures as friends and as characters.

I've stayed close with many other folks that I came to work with on acting projects over the years to one degree or another, but nothing comes close to the *Lost in Space* family bond. It's very rare and it's very special.

WHAT A GREAT GROUP. FAMILY TO ME. DICK TUFELD, JONATHAN HARRIS, BOBBY MAY, JUNE LOCKHART, ME, MARK GODDARD, ANGELA CARTWRIGHT, KEVIN BURNS, AND MARTA KRISTEN.
WHAT ADVENTURES WE SHARED!

85. TIME

*T*ime is a bizarre river. It's easy for me to jump back into memories from over half a century ago and yet, here I am, a senior citizen with two grandchildren. Eileen and I are so blessed to have Alexa Cline Mumy as our daughter-in-law. She's an amazing woman and she and our son Seth have been a couple since middle school. Of course, there were a few teenage breakups along the way, but they never lasted long. They were meant for each other. On December 3, 2018, along came Presley Jane Mumy and on November 29, 2020, her sister Isla Lily Mumy joined the family. Those little ladies bring such joy into our lives, and like Seth and his sister Liliana, they have very different personalities. It just goes to show that regardless of sharing the same DNA and the same environment, humans come into this world with unique souls.

Eileen and I were extremely happy when Seth and Alexa and Presley ("the Peej" as I call her) moved into our house for six months when theirs was being renovated. Having Presley here morning, day, and night was a wonderful gift. We bonded in such a strong way because she was here with me constantly. The Peej learned how to walk and talk here, and her little sister Isla was conceived here. Mumy Manor, where I have lived since March of 1976, is filled with family energy. No one but us Mumys has ever lived here. It's not a particularly impressive home or location, but it's all ours and it's been very good to us.

Blessed we are indeed in many ways. Seth, Alexa, the Peej, and Isla live five minutes away from us. Liliana lives ten minutes from us. It's wonderful being so close to our children and grandchildren.

LILIANA, EILEEN, SETH, ALEXA, AND ME AT THEIR WEDDING, JULY 31, 2016.

THE BLESSING OF BEING A GRANDFATHER TO PRESLEY JANE MUMY AND ISLA LILY MUMY. THEY BOTH CALL ME "PUH." I LOVE IT.

86. Spoonful of Love

On February 29, 2020, I played a gig at the Alex Theater in Glendale to a packed house of two thousand people. It was the annual Wild Honey charity event raising money for autism. I've played several of them and they are nights of wonderful music by top-notch professional players and vocalists. Every year there is a different theme, a tribute to a band or a few specific albums by an artist. In 2020, it was a tribute to one of my all-time favorite groups, The Lovin' Spoonful. When I signed on to be a part of it, no one knew then that the surviving members of the band (John Sebastian, Steve Boone, and Joe Butler) had agreed to participate and play together for the first time in over fifty years. Rehearsals and sound check were quite amazing. John Sebastian, always a huge musical hero of mine, volunteered to play along on the majority of his songs performed by an eclectic array of talent.

He couldn't have been any nicer.

While running through my featured song, John's country rockabilly classic "Darlin' Companion," with Elliot Easton alongside me playing the late great Zal Yanovsky's lead guitar riffs, John walked over to me and asked if I'd mind if he joined us and picked along. Man, that was so thrilling! We ran through the tune, it sounded great, and when the evening performance came, it was truly exciting and fun to share the stage with John and bask in the applause next to him when the song ended. We signed hundreds of posters and albums and miscellaneous photos, and helped raise a decent amount of money for a worthy cause and made some wonderful musical memories at the same time.

PLAYING TO TWO THOUSAND PEOPLE AT THE ALEX THEATRE WITH ONE
OF MY MUSICAL IDOLS, THE GREAT JOHN SEBASTIAN WAS A REAL
HIGHLIGHT FOR ME. JOHN IS A HUGE TALENT AND A SUPER NICE MAN.

87. ADAPTING

*T*he COVID global pandemic suddenly changed everything everywhere. Within a few days of the Lovin' Spoonful tribute gig, we were in serious lockdown and that has pretty much continued ever since. I haven't played live music with any other musicians since that night, and if that turns out to be the last gig I ever play… it was a Real Good one.

I'm not really sure if it was the acceptance of knowing I'd be staying inside my house for quite a long time or if it was the fear of potential impending death, but during the pandemic, my creative output reached new levels of productiveness. Within less than two months, I had completely written and recorded a thematic album of new songs based on various American characters I envisioned and their reactions to the pandemic. It's an all-acoustic album and I sent the songs via file-sharing to Vicki and John and they added their harmonies to it and we released it as an Action Skulls album for streaming and downloads. The title is *A Different World*. We created a few videos for the album as well… without ever being in the same studio together. Action Skulls have continued to work on a number of tracks via file-sharing since, and another album's worth of material is close to completion.

I then wrote and recorded a solo album called *Good Grief.* Some of the songs had been written and recorded before COVID, but I spent a couple months writing and cutting additional songs and then getting them all cohesive and again, I made a few videos. The album, like many of my solo musical projects, was released on the GRA label.

After that, for reasons that still remain unknown to me, I began painting passionately, which is something I very rarely do. I created over two dozen paintings and released some as prints.

Angela Cartwright and I wrote a second edition, extremely expanded from the first, of our *Lost (and Found) in Space* book. It's titled *Lost (and Found) in Space 2: Blast Off into the Expanded Edition* and it's published by Next Chapter Entertainment's publishing division. For anyone who finds my thoughts on *Lost in Space* lacking in this book, I highly recommend that one.

THOSE THREE ROBINSON KIDS AGAIN IN OCTOER 2021.
ANGE, MARTA, AND I ARE FAMILY.

Another unexpected but truly inspired music project that was quickly written and recorded is *Pancake Dream*, a Barnes & Barnes album. I started out with the intention of writing and recording some ambient trance instrumentals that reflected the difficult time of the lockdown, but it very quickly changed course and shifted into an almost musical theater dramatic piece that took on a *Twilight Zone* vibe. Again, it was done by sharing files with Robert while the two of us remained ten miles apart. We even made videos for all thirteen *Pancake Dream* tracks, shooting individually, using older footage of the two of us and supplementing the clips with vintage public domain bits I found and edited in. I've described *Pancake Dream* as outsider music for insiders. The *Pancake Dream* album was released on vinyl, CD, DVD, and with cool merchandise from Demented Punk Records.

My production work on the History Channel's long-running television series *Ancient Aliens* continued throughout the lockdown, but all my work was done at home and through FaceTime, sharing concepts and viewing early rough cuts and giving notes, etc.

What began as a potential Redwood reunion to mark fifty years since the band began, ended after several months into the pandemic and morphed into a Gully album. I absolutely love it. It's an extremely unique project. Paul and I took an album's worth of never-been-released songs which we had written (or started writing and left incomplete) when we were teenagers and returned to those tunes now, polishing, adding to, re-writing, and recording them anew. Each song contains both innocence and maturity and I find it to be in some ways one of the very most enjoyable music endeavors I've ever been a part of.

Over the course of the more than half a century that I've made music with Paul, he's written several number one hit records, such as "Friends and Lovers (Both to Each Other)" and "Next Time I Fall," as well as creating and composing Broadway musicals such as *Jane Eyre*. Paul's a Tony-nominated artist, but whenever he and I create together, it's just a natural, free-flowing process that began when we were both only fourteen. Making music with Paul, both old and new, is a genuine joy and the two of us have connected strongly on making the Gully album. It's an album you've waited your entire life for but never knew it!

During this period of global woe, I also worked on several voice-over projects, a science-fiction musical comedy pilot, and on-camera and voice over work for *Space Command*, an ambitious multi-faceted project created by Marc Scott Zicree which included performances from Robert Picardo, Doug Jones and *Babylon 5* alumni Mira Furlan and Bruce Boxleitner. Speaking of *Babylon 5*, I had the opportunity to return to it alongside surviving cast members, Bruce, Claudia Christian, Pat Tallman and Peter Jurasik. Peter and I speak all the time and we share the same passion for the same music. We're both Dylan freaks. Pete's a truly wonderful, genuine, good guy. Unfortunately, so many of our fellow *B5* cast members are no longer with us and that made the top-secret *Babylon 5* project bittersweet.

NICE TO BE BACK ON SET WITH MY B5 PAL BRUCE BOXLEITNER – THIS TIME ON *SPACE COMMAND*.

All of those projects were done within twenty-two months.

And the one additional other creative project that I've worked on is… writing this book. For many years I've been asked to do it by many people. I always said that if I did, it would be something I'd do on my own, without a collaborator, because after all… no matter how we look at it, no matter how many family members or friends we have or share space with, ultimately, we all live our own lives inside our heads by ourselves.

And mine has been and remains… Real Good.

88. WORRY WART

When I was between the ages of eleven and fifteen, I read just about every comic book published every week, every Hardy Boys book, and every James Bond novel. What those stories did for me was create a sense of potential trouble popping up out of nowhere and ways to handle that trouble. I'm honestly not too certain it didn't damage my psyche somehow, though. I do tend to think about the negative potential in every situation and worry about how effectively I might handle trouble if it shows itself. "Danger, Will Robinson! Danger!" Little things, like sitting with my back to the wall, carrying a small flashlight and a Swiss army knife and some hidden cash, etc. To this day, I don't look on the dark side, but I do look at a situation and imagine "What could go wrong here?" then I ask myself, what would James Bond or Bruce Wayne or Bucky Barnes or the Hardy Boys do?

I suppose I'm a natural worrier. My grandmother, who I lived with from birth until I was eighteen, was a major worrier. When she was alone in the house, she spent most of her time looking out the window for trouble.

Trouble has found me more than several times and I can't help but feel like it's wise not to press my luck. I haven't been a perfect man by any means, and I do regret some choices I made along the way. But all those choices have led me to where I am today and I very much appreciate my "now"... although it certainly seems to be dashing along at turbo speed. As I'm writing this, it hits me: Life is a death sentence.

As Jim Morrison wrote, "no one here gets out alive."

Onward.

THOUGHTS FORM BLUEPRINTS FOR REALITY...
SNAP OUT OF IT, MUMY!

89. FAMILY MATTERS

I place huge value on friendships, and I do my very best to be a true good friend. I have never known what having a large family feels like. Although I have a step-sister, Linda was never close to me. She lived many hours and hundreds of miles away. I can pretty much count on my fingers and toes the number of times I've seen her my entire life. Linda isn't a blood relative, and she stopped using the name Mumy before I was born when she was adopted by her mother's new husband. But my father never forgot her at Christmas or for her birthdays, and when my parents died, Linda received a very nice check. I tried for several years to rekindle a relationship with her, but she avoided it. I have let that go.

ME, MY DAD, AND LINDA IN 1955 AND ME AND LINDA IN 2008,
THE LAST TIME I SAW HER.

I only ever had one living grandparent, my grandmother Lala. She and I were close, and we got along fine most of the time. Sharing a bedroom with her as a toddler was tough because she snored something fierce and sharing a bathroom with her as a teenager could be a drag because she often locked my side of the door and forgot to unlock it.

I recently discovered a few photographs of my paternal grandmother, Della Mumy, and it's astonishing how much I look like her. She passed away years before I was born, and my dad rarely spoke of his parents. Although he was quite social, owning restaurants and bars at times, he was an extremely private man. More than anything, I wish I could talk with him again and learn things about his life I long to know.

MY GRANDMOTHER DELLA MUMY. I ONLY DISCOVERED THIS PHOTOGRAPH RECENTLY. SHE HAD PASSED AWAY YEARS BEFORE I WAS BORN. THE RESEMBLANCE BLOWS MY MIND. LIKE... IT'S REALLY CRAZY!

My mother, Muriel, went through several "phases" during my young life when she and her only sibling, her sister Vail, didn't speak to each other for years at a time. It was strange. One year we'd be having family dinners and spending holidays together with my Aunt Vail and Uncle Fred and their two sons, Rick and Mark, and then we wouldn't see them for five years because my mom and my aunt had a fight over something stupid that I never really heard much detail about.

When I was sixteen, Rick and Mark had a falling out over a job and those two brothers, my only two first cousins, haven't rekindled their relationship in over fifty years. For decades I was stuck in between a rock and a hard place with them. If I spent Thanksgiving with Rick, I spent Christmas with Mark, etc. It was a frustrating drag. Seth and Liliana were very young and didn't understand why they couldn't ever see their cousins together.

ME WITH COUSINS RICK AND MARK, FAMILY CAN BE A VERY FRAGILE THING.

It was sad and it was unfortunate, but eventually I broke ties with Rick and haven't spoken to him in several years now. My relationship with Mark is fine and we speak weekly. Mark's daughter Breana and her wonderful husband Toby now have two little kids of their own, Kaius and Keaton, and thankfully, they see Seth and Alexa and Presley and Isla often and the family bond is strongly connected there.

Like me with Essie Smith, my children Seth and Liliana were blessed to have grown up with a loving nanny from the very beginning. Ana Saldana joined our family a week before Seth was born and she stayed with us until both Seth and Liliana had moved out on their own. Ana was an incredible blessing in our lives. She took loving care of all of us in multiple ways at multiple times. God bless you, Ana. Much love to you always.

ANA, SETH, AND LILIANA HUGGING IT OUT IN MUMY MANOR.

I've spent the last twenty months alone, except with those closest to me. With the exception of visiting my immediate family, I have rarely ventured beyond my property line. After a little over a year of total isolation, my "Boyz group," longtime pals Shaun Cassidy, Jay Gruska, David Jolliffe, Steve Lukather, Ben Weiss, and Fred Westheimer started meeting for lunches again every couple of months. Now, we strictly gather only in open-air outside patios, but it's been rewarding to be in the company of good old friends again, even when we're all wearing masks as we walk to and from our cars. We watch sporting events on television alone, but we text each other constantly during the games and try not to freak out at Lukather's insane over-the-top visual texts he sends us, usually disguised as something "normal" until you open it. I've also taken several long hikes and walks with Scott, perhaps my oldest "best friend," and that's family to me.

Everyone is vaccinated and very COVID cautious.

FINALLY GETTING OUT OF THE HOUSE FOR LUNCHES WITH "THE BOYS" STEVE LUKATHER, ME, FRED WESTHEIMER, SHAUN CASSIDY, BEN WEISS, DAVID JOLLIFFE, AND JAY GRUSKA. WE'VE BEEN FRIENDS A LONG TIME NOW.

My sense of "family" has always come from friends more than from blood and I do my best, even during a long lockdown, to tend to my garden of friends.

90. A Real Good Life

I get asked, "What do you like best? Acting? Music? Writing? Producing?" and I squirm when thinking about it. I'm simply compelled to be creative, and I can't stop that drive within me. It isn't competitive. It isn't about rewards, awards, or money. It simply is my nature, and as I've dived deep into my past while writing this book, I realize that I've always been this way. I'm constantly stimulated to create something new and once a project, be it an episode of a television script, song, movie, album, video, comic book story, script, painting, or a voice-over, has been pronounced completed, wrapped, printed, etc... I'm quickly on to something new. Probably because I worked so much in episodic television when I was young, one script after another, I'm programmed to do the best I can, and can the best I do, and then purge it and get on to the next thing as quickly as possible. I do realize that writing this autobiography may be a bit different, as I only have one life to reflect upon.

This undertaking has made me feel quite strange. In a way, it makes me feel like I'm dead. Which, at the moment, I am not. It should be noted that while writing this memoir, a global pandemic has taken millions of lives and changed the way humans everywhere interact. Intense political divide and senseless violence has the United States of America teetering on the brink of a civil war, while a real war has been raging in Europe, as natural disasters seem to be hammering this planet at an all-time high. It's been a challenging time, indeed. As Dr. Smith might say, "Oh, the pain... the pain."

It was truly a calling within me that rose up early and compelled me to get inside the television and become an actor at such a young age. My parents supported my energy and invested the money I made as a young performer well. Good luck came my way with the opportunities to play several memorable, iconic characters, such as Anthony Fremont, Will Robinson, and Lennier. I was blessed to have worked with, and learned from, some of the greatest talents of all time.

I have no regrets about going into show business as a child, however, I have come to understand the difficulties that accompany that as one matures in adulthood and beyond. I've often strangely felt in competition with my younger self, and I've also recognized that over the many years, some people just can't help but be disappointed that I'm not a child anymore. There's nothing, of course, that I can do about that. It can be a bit unsettling.

I've been lucky to have worked in so many different arenas of entertainment and find professional success to varying degrees in all of them. I've been even luckier to have married my wife Eileen, who has steadfastly stood by me.

There aren't many people left who can lay claim to being a part of so many eclectic and iconic projects as I have been fortunate to do. I've worked in an industry that has changed incredibly since the time I started acting. Television, film, music, comic books, production…I feel blessed to have played parts in all of those arenas. I feel blessed to have been connected to so much that continues to resonate.

It's been a good life. A real good life.

TRULY BLESSED.

"Somedays I don't know what I'm gonna do
Sometimes everything I've learned seems untrue
Nothing right now adds up too much
'Til I see your smile and feel your sweet touch
You heal my soul
You heal my soul
Deep in my heart your love keeps me whole
Darling, you heal my soul"

"You Heal My Soul" by Bill Mumy © So Boss Music 2020,
from Action Skulls' *In a Different World* album.

ACKNOWLEDGMENTS

I'd like to thank Mary and Tom McLaren for their passionate support, talent, and positive energy in the process of creating this project.

I have many good longtime friends who for the reason of volume are not mentioned in this book. You can thank me later.

To the countless artists that I have worked with in many arenas, my sincere thanks.

My gratitude to Suzie Dietz for an almost decade long run in the '90's as my manager and who suggested this project many years ago.

To all the girls I've loved before... wait... that sounds familiar.... (never mind).

In the big picture I am grateful for the who, where. and the when.

Onward.

Bill Mumy

Laurel Canyon, CA
July 15, 2022

MY PERSONAL PHOTO ALBUMS ON A SHELF IN MUMY MANOR.
I HAD A LOT OF FUN SELECTING MY FAVORITE PICS TO INCLUDE IN THIS
MEMOIR — THE IMAGE QUALITY MIGHT NOT ALWAYS BE THE BEST, BUT
THEY ARE FAVORITES FOR A REASON!

Photo Credits

Cover inset and pages 63, 78, 80, 82, 84, 89, 171, 173, 200, 201, 233, 307, 312, 360, 363, 367, 414, and 417: licensed by Synthesis Entertainment. *Lost in Space*® and its characters and designs are © Legend Pictures, LLC.

Cover photo and pages 51, 156, 163, 179, 245, 325, 375, and 393: photos by Eileen Mumy.

Page 9, 12, and 19: courtesy of Allied Artists.

Page 35: *The Wizard of Baghdad* © 1960, Twentieth Century Fox. All rights reserved.

Page 42 and 45: *Lancer* © 1968, Twentieth Century Fox Television. All rights reserved.

Page 48, 147, 148, 150, 151, 153, and 155: courtesy of Disney Image Permissions.

Page 52, 244, 381, 383, and 413: courtesy of Sony Pictures Television.

Page 64: Courtesy of Paramount Television.

Page 92, 93, and 385: *Dear Brigitte* © 1965, Twentieth Century Fox. All rights reserved.

Page 102: photo by John Cartwright, courtesy of Angela Cartwright.

Page 104, 359, and 372: photos by Angela Cartwright.

Page 114, 117, 206, 213, 220, 221, 262, 274, 330, 350, and 351: courtesy of Universal Studios Licensing LLC.

Page 128, 129, 131, 132, 135, 136, and 349: courtesy of CBS Broadcasting Inc.

Page 165, 303, 340, 353, 355, 377, 378: courtesy of Warner Bros.

Page 167, 168, 295, 296, and 300: courtesy of Stanley Kramer Productions.

Page 190: courtesy of MGM Studios. © 1992 Orion Pictures Corporation. All Rights Reserved.

Page 187, 315, and 318: Photos by Henry Diltz.

Page 209: photo by Janit Baldwin.

Page 348: courtesy of CBS Studios.

Page 423: photo by Tom McLaren.